THE NEWEST SCIENCE FICTION AND FANTASY TALENTS BRING YOU 16 BRAND-NEW WINNING STORIES!

Among them:

Alien contact with startling new twists . . .
A young witch taken by *that* old feeling . . .
Combat in the stars . . .
Murder in time . . .
A vampire in a world without blood . . .
A unique peril for space-station astronauts . . .
An eagle in love . . .
Eight-cylinder heroes . . .
and piracy and death on a sunken Earth . . .

Fast adventure, gentle laughter, slow tears, hard laughter, terror . . . and more.

A TRIUMPHANT VARIETY OF EVERY KIND OF SPECULATIVE FICTION

Beautifully Done Today by Some of The Top-Flight SF Names of Tomorrow!

WHAT THE CRITICS HAVE SAID ABOUT THE *L. RON HUBBARD Presents WRITERS OF THE FUTURE* ANTHOLOGIES

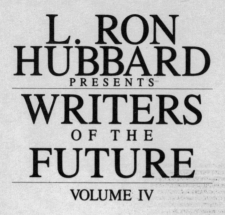

L. RON HUBBARD

PRESENTS

WRITERS

OF THE

FUTURE

VOLUME IV

L. RON HUBBARD

PRESENTS

WRITERS

OF THE

FUTURE

VOLUME IV

16 New Top-Rated Tales from his
Writers of The Future
International Talent Search

With Essays on Writing and Art by
L. RON HUBBARD
ALGIS BUDRYS
ORSON SCOTT CARD
TIM POWERS
RAMSEY CAMPBELL
FRANK KELLY FREAS

Edited by Algis Budrys
Frank Kelly Freas, Director of Illustration

Bridge Publications, Inc.

CONTENTS

FEATURES:

ACKNOWLEDGEMENTS

The judges for L. Ron Hubbard's Writers of The Future Contest serve with dedication and pleasure. They do so in order to ensure the future of speculative fiction literature. In the Contest year from which this anthology is drawn, they were:

Gregory Benford	Algis Budrys
Ramsey Campbell	Anne McCaffrey
Larry Niven	Frederik Pohl
Jerry Pournelle	Robert Silverberg
Jack Williamson	Gene Wolfe
Roger Zelazny	

Serving as instructors in the W.O.T.F. writers' workshops during 1987 were:

Orson Scott Card   Tim Powers
Ian Watson

Our cover illustration, "Moonrider", is an original commissioned painting by the "King of Illustration," as L. Ron Hubbard called him,

Frank Frazetta.

Over a thirty-year career in illustration, Mr. Frazetta has established himself uniquely as a master craftsman, inspiring millions of admirers and a host of artists who have followed his lead. He remains inimitable.

In the spirit of the Writers of The Future anthologies, his cover for this volume brilliantly evokes a scene possible only in the magic realm of speculative fiction.

The original art may be seen at the L. Ron Hubbard Gallery, 7051 Hollywood Boulevard, Hollywood, California.

C. L. Moore
1911 - 1987

Catherine Moore was a master of science fiction and fantasy; a pioneer in the field. She was also a founding member of the W.O.T.F. judges' panel, serving with a pride and dedication that continued her years of assistance to new and aspiring writers.

Introduction
by
Algis Budrys

Welcome to the fourth volume in what is the best-selling speculative fiction anthology series of all time. That means it has surpassed many classic volumes of science fiction and fantasy stories, some in print for over 40 years. Why has the *L. Ron Hubbard Presents WRITERS OF THE FUTURE* series done so well over one-tenth that time? Because hundreds of thousands of readers like what they read in these volumes, and communicate their enthusiasm to their friends.

The literary praise these books have received has been equally outstanding. So they not only please readers, which is the most important thing, but they also meet the high standards of reviewers and critics, which is an endorsement that these stories—and their authors—represent a significant, lasting . . . and continuing . . . contribution to speculative fiction (''SF'') and its future.

There is no phenomenon like it elsewhere in literature. It results from the talent-nurturing program founded in 1983 by L. Ron Hubbard, designed as his legacy to the future of the arts related to speculative fiction. The first expression of that legacy came with the appearance of his Writers of The Future Contest, from which the stories in this volume spring. The earlier three volumes published the foremost stories from 1984, 1985 and 1986, respectively.

When L. Ron Hubbard founded the Contest, he was joined by a roster of the leading SF writers, who agreed to lend their services as judges. Over the years since then, some have departed this life, sadly, as Mr. Hubbard himself did in 1986, but others have come forward to serve in deciding the prize winners, and in contributing essays of their advice for publication in these volumes.

The essence of the Contest is that every three months our judges determine the stories that win their authors outright cash grants. The First Place story earns $1000; Second and Third Place receive $750 and $500 respectively. Then, once a year, a blue-ribbon panel reading the four quarterly First Prize winners selects the story for the L. Ron Hubbard Gold Award grand prize. This is symbolized by an impressive trophy, and with it comes an additional cash award of $4000. (Complete Contest rules are given on page 426 of this book.)

The anthology series is not part of the Contest structure. When the first Contest year brought many new stories to light, Bridge Publications approached the authors with a separate offer to create a book of this work. That first book was a resounding success, and so there has been a new one every year since then. This results in additional income for the writers, apart from their Contest prizes.

With this volume, the W.O.T.F. anthology series has now introduced 59 new writers over a four-year span. Of the authors published in the first three volumes, a significant number have gone on to place other stories, some of them many times, in leading periodicals both in the SF field and outside it. A growing number have begun to have noteworthy novels brought out by other major publishers and several have been nominated repeatedly for the top "best-of-the-year" awards or otherwise recognized as significant new creative forces. But the role of W.O.T.F. in assisting worthy new talent has extended farther than that, and will continue to do so. One aspect of this is the continual growth of interest in W.O.T.F. around the world. Among the 16 authors published in this book alone are one from Canada, one from the United Kingdom, and one from Zimbabwe. Each Contest quarter sees entries from many nations, and a steady rise in volume and quality.

With the Contest and anthologies established as a prime source of new talent, L. Ron Hubbard foresaw the need to provide W.O.T.F. writers with the opportunity to enhance their skills so as to be able to continue their successes. So, the Contest now also conducts invitational workshops for its winners and the finalists published in these anthologies. The workshops were designed using expert "how-to" texts originally written by Mr. Hubbard for the best writers' magazines, and learning-methods developed by him. They are conducted to help these new talents sustain extended careers in literature. For more detail on how this is done, please see the report in this book by Orson Scott Card, twice an instructor for us.

Many attendees have gone back to their home communities and sparked workshops of their own for other new writers. In addition, private sponsors, including a number of colleges and universities, have begun using these W.O.T.F. workshop methods and test materials in their own classes.

A rapidly growing number of teaching institutions are also now adopting the W.O.T.F. anthologies as texts. This too is an expanding feature of the program, and part of its contribution to the growth of quality in SF today and tomorrow.

L. Ron Hubbard's Writers of The Future Contest represents a breathtakingly good thing in the field. In an essay in Volume II of this series, Contest judge Frank Herbert explained it succinctly: "The more good writers there are,

the more good readers there will be. We'll all benefit—
writers and readers alike!''

There have been talent-support programs in SF before,
just as there are many "literary competitions" and grant-
awarding bodies outside it. But the creative thrust represented by W.O.T.F. is the first continuously sustained,
broadly successful program of its kind, and without question the most productive of results.

The most important thing about L. Ron Hubbard's
design for the program is that it reflects a profound grasp of
how creativity works; that it must be supported, but left
unfettered. The program does two things, only. It encour-
ages talent with measured, practical rewards on which it
places no strings, and it does not attempt to impose any "editorial policy" either on the stories it names as outstanding
or on the future work of their authors.

As your reading of these anthologies will show, the
widest possible spectrum of kinds of speculative fiction is
represented. The only criterion the Contest judges apply is
that the story be a good story on its own self-evident terms.

These anthologies and the W.O.T.F. writing workshops
are all related to the Contest in the sense that they all involve
Contest entrants, but they are not directly linked into the
Contest structure, which asks only that its entrants be in com-
pliance with the rules. Neither workshop attendance nor the
sale of limited publication rights are mandatory (though, certainly, considering the effectiveness of the workshops, and
the rates offered by the book publisher, I would call them
highly advisable). In this way, the program offers rewards of
many kinds, but imposes no strictures; creativity is encouraged and nurtured, but not channelled. It can fairly be said
that the purpose of the program is to discover the future of
the SF art, wherever the diverse orientations of its participating new talents might take it.

To me the impressive thing is not so much that L. Ron

Hubbard chose this way to impart a lasting, fruitful legacy to the field in which he had done so much significant work. It is that he did it so well.

This year the anthology adds a major feature. The words of the Golden Age of the 1930s and 1940s have been preserved in books available in a great many places, and form part of the background against which readers can appreciate and judge the ways in which novice writers shape their art. The illustrations, however, while available to young artists diligently researching in special collections, are not easily found by today's SF reader.

Frank Kelly Freas, serving as our Director of Illustration, has gathered a group of truly legendary SF artists, and blended with them the most prominent and promising of newer graphic talents. Something almost totally unique in modern days has resulted.

In the great days when modern science fiction and fantasy first emerged in the pages of pulp magazines, and traditionally thereafter, author and illustrator were frequently in effect a team, bringing the reader a compounded pleasure in seeing the characters brought to life.

What has been done in this volume is to re-evoke that experience. Never before within one single "issue" of an SF periodical have so many giants come together to show how illustration is done, to display what makes them great, and to confer their own blessing on the future of the fledgling writers whose stories they have accepted in professional partnership. We are honored. And we are entertained, in the very best sense of that word as it is meant in a literature built on skillfully giving pleasure and satisfaction to its readers.

And now it's time to list for you the persons who caused this latest volume:

Jane Mailander, 1st Place, 1st Quarter
Mary A. Turzillo, 2nd Place, 1st Quarter
P. H. MacEwen, 3rd Place, 1st Quarter

Nancy Farmer, 1st Place, 2nd Quarter
Rayson Lorrey, 2nd Place, 2nd Quarter
Mark D. Haw, 3rd Place, 2nd Quarter

Paul Edwards, 1st Place, 3rd Quarter
R. Garcia y Robertson, 2nd Place, 3rd Quarter
Richard Urdiales, 3rd Place, 3rd Quarter

Michael Green, 1st Place, 4th Quarter
Flonet Biltgen, 2nd Place, 4th Quarter
Larry England, 3rd Place, 4th Quarter

Finalists:
Jo Beverley
Astrid Julian
Dennis E. Minor
John Moore

To them belongs what they will make of their future.

Introducing
"Tomorrow's Miracles"
by
L. Ron Hubbard

About the Author

L. Ron Hubbard (1911-1986) was a man with an immense range of interests and activities. From boyhood, he engaged life with uncommon vigor, and at the same time embraced every aspect of human history and knowledge. He believed the world was meant to explore with body and mind, and he was just as apt to launch an expedition into the jungles as he was to reach remarkable conclusions from many different combinations of data.

In the 1930's, after adventures such as sailing into little-understood waters, barnstorming as an aviator, venturing into pathless and sometimes hostile remote corners of the world, he turned to adventure-fiction writing as as career. After establishing an awesome reputation for productivity and scope, in 1938 he found the literature in which he would do best, and which he loved best—fantasy and science fiction, which together are now called "speculative fiction." For the fabled Unknown and Astounding Science Fiction magazines of the day, he wrote the stories that would bring him an enthusiastic following, would produce such classics as "Fear," Final Blackout, Slaves of Sleep and the Ole Doc Methuselah series, and give birth to the legend of a charismatic, vastly ebullient individual who casually took center stage wherever *the stalwarts of the "Golden Age of SF" gathered in the course of creating the modern foundations of the field.*

But under the public manner that suited him, he was anything but casual. In 1938, as he prepared to enter what was then a new field, he wrote in his journal:

"I began to wonder about the validity of this inner circle of 'science-fiction'. Was it science at all? Or was it something else, even greater? Are we children of science or, to be blunt, philosophers?"

Inquiry of this sort, proposed by a tireless genius, was to lead him farther than any existing map or text could show. In the 1980s, explorations well advanced, one stage brought to a conclusion, he returned to SF writing, as effervescent as ever in his epic novel Battlefield Earth. *Shortly thereafter, he completed a landmark work—the* Mission Earth *dekalogy, a ten-volume novel of more than a million-and-a-half words.*

Hardly like anything ever seen in literature before, even from L. Ron Hubbard, Mission Earth *is a broadly satirical, panoramic assemblage of vivid characters and dramatic situations. It uses the SF medium to boldly comment on almost every aspect of the human situation.*

Truly a magnum opus *from a remarkable source, this work was being readied for publication when L. Ron Hubbard left this life in January, 1986. With respect to SF, he could be content in the knowledge that he had had his say in a grand manner—all ten* Mission Earth *volumes have been New York* Times *best-sellers—and that he had left the legacy of his Writers of The Future program to evoke a new Golden Age.*

He had long been ready for history. At about the same time that he made his journal entry in 1938, he expanded that brief statement about science and philosophy in an essay that was found among his papers and has not been previously released except in a commemorative publication. Written before successful nuclear fission and fusion, and Moon landings . . . written, in fact, while Einstein's fledgling Theory of Relativity was still being called into question in the world of physics . . . it is a thought-provoking fundamental statement on philosophy, science, and science fiction.

How many men have ever paus-
ed in the summer night to look up at the stars
and give a thought, not to astronomy, but to
the men who first slashed the Gordian knot of planetary
motion? Of course all educated men have, at one time or
another, scraped the surface of the source of such facts. But
today we speak grandly of galaxies and consider astronomy
an exact science and bow down before facts.

There probably does not exist a professor in the world
who has not, unwittingly or otherwise, held the ignorance
of the ancients to ridicule; and there is no field where this
is more apparent than astronomy.

Some of the facts are these:

Early Hebrews and Chaldeans, among others, believed
in a flat earth, a sky supported by mountains and which
upheld a sea, which in turn, leaked through and caused
rain. The flat plain was supported by nothing in particular.
Of course we all know this, but there is a worthwhile point
to make.

The Hindus believed that the earth was a hemisphere,
supported by four large elephants. "This seems to have been
entirely satisfactory until someone asked what was holding
the elephants up. After some discussion, the wise men of
India agreed that the four elephants were standing on a large
mud turtle. Again the people seem to have been satisfied
until some inquisitive person raised the question as to what
was holding the mud turtle up. I imagine the philosophers
had grown tired of answering questions by this time for they
are said to have replied that there was mud under the mud

turtle and mud all the rest of the way."[1]

Twelve pillars, according to the Veda of India, supported the earth, leaving plenty of room for the sun and the moon to dive under and come up on the other side.

If you wish, you can find a multitude of such beliefs, all common enough. But there are two facts concerning these and their presentation which are most erroneous. By examining the above quote one sees that terms have been confused. Men who ask questions and then figure out answers are, indeed, philosophers. The masses take anything which seems to have a certain academic reverence attached and cling to it desperately. The other error is considering that these beliefs were foolish and that scientists, laboring in their laboratories or observatories are wholly responsible for the ideas which permeate the world of thought.

It is not that we here wish to maintain these facts about the state of the earth. On the contrary. But they are not presented for ridicule because they are the ideas which some philosopher developed painfully with the scant data he had at hand and who had to aid him no means of communication, travel, instruments or even mathematics. They are, what we chose to call, hypotheses possessing sufficient truth to be accepted. Today, thanks to Copernicus and all the rest, we know about gravity. Thanks to Newton we have mathematics. Thanks to a lens grinder we have a telescope.

It was stated in an early Sanskrit treatise that the world was round. Thales, Homer, Aristotle, Pythagoras, Ptolemy and others conceived various evidences which demonstrated that the earth was a sphere. In 250 B.C. Eratosthanes computed the earth's circumference, missing it only by one hundred miles (and he had no mechanical aids or "higher" mathematics.)

[1]Arthur M. Harding, *Astronomy*. (Garden City Publishing,New York) 1935. page 4.

Of course these gentlemen made errors in their hypotheses. Ptolemy, 140 B.C., conceived of seven crystalline spheres to account for planetary motion. To counter this, long before (in the sixth century, B.C.) Pythagoras taught that the earth went around the sun but erred in supposing the sun to be the center of the universe. Aristarchus, in the third century, B.C., and Capella in the fifth century, A.D., also taught that the earth revolved itself and around the sun. Copernicus, in the sixteenth century, gave the world the system which is now used.

Now the point we wish to make is this: Down through the ages men have conceived various hypotheses with regard to astronomy. Concurrently, instruments were invented and other discoveries made and into the hands of investigators was placed a complete idea plus the means of examining it. There has been considerable lag, naturally, between widespread belief and philosophic location of new truths. We are fond of thinking in terms of tomorrow. But the future is written with the pen of the present in the ink of the past. We are fond of believing that that which we now possess is infallible and not subject to any great change. And, when we begin to localize certain fields for investigation, science feeds wholly upon the statements of predecessors. Should a man put forth a new theory (there hasn't been one since the nineteenth century) then he is no longer a scientist but a philosopher.

Let us remember our Voltaire and his admonition to define our terms. What is science? What is philosophy? Further, by knowing, what can we hope to gain by it? Will we benefit enough to talk about it? The answer to the last two is definitely yes.

To quote Spencer, "Knowledge of the lowest kind is un-unified knowledge; philosophy is completely-unified knowledge."[1]

[1] *First Principles*

Philosophy is *not* the muttering of epigrams nor is the true philosopher merely one who can quote at random from various works.

Consider an explorer, casting away, all too often, his greatest securities, even his life, to stride forward into the outer dark, throwing up his star shells to view what lies in the unknown. He lacks a vocabulary suitable to record his findings because the words have yet to be invented. He lacks instruments to measure what he thinks he sees because no instruments for such are yet in existence. He stumbles and trips, pushing ever outward on his lonely track, farther and farther from the milestoned roads where statements are safe and conversants many. He is so far out that those in their safe, warm homes of "proved thought" cannot recognize the distance he has traversed when he first covers it.

His is the task of stabbing deeper into the Unknown and the dangers he runs are those of ridicule. He knows, in his heart of hearts, what his fate will most likely be. He may come back with some great idea only to find that men laugh. He may point a road which will be a thoroughfare within a century but men, having but little vision, see only a tangle of undergrowth and blackness beyond and push but timidly where the first to go pushed forward with such courage.

In all the ages of history, thinking men have been crucified either by institutions or the masses. But those very ideas which at first seemed so mad and impossible are those which science now uses to polish up its reputation.

Inevitably, the philosopher, the true searcher, is decried. But then, it is perfectly natural. His breadth of view is so great and penetrating that he can unify all of the knowledge groups, taking his findings to discover a lower common denominator.

It is quite natural that he should do this, just as it is that his work should usually be spurned by his own generation.

Un-unified knowledge is that possessed by every animal

or drudge. "A cake of soap cleans a shirt." "A cake of soap cleans a floor." "A cake of soap cleans the face."

Partially-unified knowledge on the subject would be: "A cake of soap cleans" and "let us see how many things a cake of soap will clean."

Completely-unified knowledge on the subject would be: "Any agent which holds foreign matter in solution will clean."

The argument here is quite plain. Partially-unified knowledge has become a group of men all anxious to assemble data on the science of soap. The completely-unified knowledge opens up a new vista, the possibility of discovering some medium which will clean anything.

And if you think this is facetious, know that there is no medium which will clean everything and anything equally well. It would be essentially destructive to a million volumes of hard won data on soap. The philosopher has come up against a resistant force. He reduced the matter to simplicity and indicated that it was necessary to search for a new cleaner, not a new method. Put into practice immediately and meeting with success, the idea would destroy, for instance, the business of hundreds of soap factories and would, of course, throw umpteen thousand soap chemists out of excellent jobs.

There is nothing being used today except those ideas given to the world by philosophers. For instance, Spinoza is responsible for most of modern psychology. Plato wrote about psychoanalysis in his "Republic" (in addition to most of our ideas on the political side of the ledger as well). Aniximander (610-540 B.C.) outlined our theory of evolution and Empedocles (445 B.C.) developed it as far as we have gone, originating natural selection. Democritus said, "In reality there are only atoms and the void," and went on to outline the theories of planetary evolution much as they are used today. The Ionian Greeks developed the major portion of

our physics. Kant handed out the finishing touches, with
Schopenhauer (a strange combination, this) on our psychology, Spencer on evolution; Newton put natural laws into
equations and invented mathematics to work them. Spinoza
went so far into the realm of the outer dark that no one has
caught up to him yet, though the trails are being followed
slowly and inexorably to the destinations he indicated. But
science in each case contemporarily taught and used out-
worn systems and considered that it had reached an outer
frontier when, in reality, science was always hundreds of
years behind the philosophic frontier!

In short, science has the unhealthy tendency to isolate
and expand that isolation, where philosophy tends to reach
higher or more general laws. Give a scientist a theory (wit-
ness cytology) and he immediately sets out and collects gra-
vitically all the facts pertinent to that one thing. To the
scientist is owed the particulars. The scientist inherits the theories and instruments already conceived and smooths out
the rough spots. The philosopher is challenged because he
does not do this, but, as we have remarked, he has no instruments, no tables, no aid of any kind which has reached as
far as he has gone forward.

In this manner, science tends to group and then com-
plicate any subject. It is to science that the masses owe their
benefits. It is to the philosopher that science owes all its fuel.
The citizen, seeing not very far, praises where praise is
really due but not wholly due to the point where a scientist
can laugh at philosophic ideas, the very things which gave
him the material with which to work.

That science does attempt to propagandize its importance to the extent of origination is attested by the commonly
heard statement that ''Now everything is all invented and if
one would desire fame he must specialize.'' That word specialize is a red flag to any philosopher because it automatically indicates the localizing of knowledge into hideous

complexities which, he knows very well, will be destroyed just as all other complicated structures were ripped down when the truth was isolated. Now it is indicative of the essential nature of science that it wars ceaselessly within itself in favor of this or that hypothesis as countering another hypothesis. It can be said with truth that the battles of philosophy are fought by science against science. Science comes along with measuring sticks of the already known, takes sides and begins to fire, without once inventing any substitute or new hypothesis of its own and ridiculing any which may be offered. So stubborn is science that it hangs to its achieved tomes like a bulldog. Ptolemy's weird theory of crystalline spheres was taught concurrently with the revised Copernican System in one of the oldest American universities for many years.

This is no diatribe against science, it is a defense of new theories, new ideas, new concepts and the men who made them. The laughter leveled at the heads of innovators is amusing only if it be remembered that the ideas now in use were once equally ridiculed by science. And one has only to glance back with the perspective of years to see that science has embraced many things much more weird—such as a hemisphere on four elephants on a mud turtle on mud, mud, mud. Doubtless, in this instance, there were a hundred libraries filled with tracts to the effect that the mud turtle had green eyes as against the opinion of another that his eyes were purple. Basing this on horizon stars and examining them as reflection, scientists of that day were likely very learned within their sphere of findings.

But there is such a thing as a cumulation of knowledge. By this most men envision being swamped by facts and books. Libraries crammed to the roof, laboratories humming, men shouting in lecture rooms, men writing vast discourses on electrons and positrons . . . But there is no need for alarm. Ten times as much data has been stacked away in the basement where it molds forgotten, the product of but fifty years ago but now disproved through the scientific acceptance of higher generalizations. Each time a higher generalization is reached, all men shout, "This is the ULTIMATE! Man can go no farther!" But they forget that in quiet places men are looking all about them, not at one special object but at all objects and so it comes as a shock when a perfectly simple truth which was right under everybody's nose all the time, was brought to light.

Just as God's connection with man and the Creator of the Universe (Prime Mover Unmoved or whatever God might really be) is pushed back step by step infinitely, so is all knowledge simplified.

Two hundred years ago (although it had probably been outlined already) science would have blinked at the idea of splitting an atom. Science dealt in atoms and molecules in that day and nothing smaller. Today every schoolboy knows that an atom can be split and remade into several things. A hundred years from now men will look back at this atom splitting and shake their heads over such stupidity as thinking that an electron was the smallest division.

But how do we get to the point where we can look back? The answer is somewhere in our midst. Just who will advance the theory and method for releasing atomic energy is not important. That the possibility of doing so has been often cited and that various means are constantly being proposed is the course which will lead to such a thing. And do not for one hypnotized moment suppose that the method will be born in any flashing, sparking laboratory endowed with millions. On the contrary, it will first be proposed by a thinker. The laboratory may later claim all the credit but that is of no matter, it seems, as long as men can then begin to write all about the mathematics of disintegration with which they will fill ten thousand libraries.

If this cannot be believed, if it cannot be accepted that

all truths are simple truths and need only be pointed out, recall that the splitting of the atom was a simple truth. Then, if it be a matter of concern that the only discoveries left will be complex and that specialization is paramount, remember that the discovery of the disintegration of the atom will scrap all the fine tomes (which fill ten thousand libraries) on the subject of internal combustion engines and propelling forces in general as well as all extant hull, wheel, and wing designs. The only thing of these fine flights which will remain is the essential truth from which they were born.

Knowledge is not a swamping sea of facts but a long line of simple truths, each one more simple than the last. If one would discover the next in line, let him not in any specialized field but rather in a cross between two fields or more. And as a man cannot be specialized in half a dozen fields it remains that his investigations would have to be wholly independent of any rubber-stamped outlook. The atom disintegrator may come as a cross between botany and physics. Who would dream of such a thing? But already the newest source of energy is the leaf of a tree. Would a physicist, interested only in physics, have discovered that? It is doubtful. He would have to be more concerned with the entire world around him than he would be with his immediate laboratory bench. Strangely enough, the men who have isolated the greatest truths have not been what is generally known as "an educated man." Widely read, yes. Intelligent, certainly. But above all, anxious to push into anything and everything where the devil would fear to tread.

This thirst for adventure into the abstract is the motivating force of all youth. Later, weighed down with admonitions that one must specialize, youth succumbs to the lure of security and forgets about those things he wanted to plan, in the scramble to read all everybody ever said on the subject of Trimming Frogs' Toenails.

To be very specific, today the scientist mocks wild ideas

about interplanetary travel, saying, "Welllll, yess, it might be done . . . maybe. But . . . ." With all respect to him he is perfectly right. He has a certain job of his own to do. He will probably be dead long before man first sets foot on the moon. But that the dream, any wildest dream, can be accomplished needs only the verification of the source of most of our mechanical marvels of today. Submarine? Locomotive? Airplane? Stratosphere and over-weather? Typewriter? Traffic signals? Look at what you may and where you may, you will uncover "science-fiction" or a man interested in it.

The philosophers of the great general ideas are, of course, in a class by themselves. But as far as the advanced applications of various methods and hybrid sciences, as far as the forecast of our civilization, and, indeed, our very architecture of tomorrow, one has only to search the files.

Men have been writing "science-fiction" since the Phonoecians, perhaps. At least the first story followed soon after writing itself. Once where the "pseudo" "science" sent a man west on an iron horse to fight Indians (which didn't happen really, until many, many years had flown), it now sends men into the outer galaxies.

Among the scientists of today are many outlaws, not quite philosophers, but still intrigued by the ideas which can be turned up.

Looking back into the past's dim depths one can see a great many "foolish" ideas brought to fruition. Looking ahead into the future, one can see. . . . .

?

River of Stone
by
Michael Green

About the Author

Michael Green is a librarian and lives in a quiet New England town with his wife and their three children, Justin, Jasper, and Tasaday. He appears in Vol. I of this series with a beautiful long story, "Measuring the Light." A finalist in that first Contest year, it was plainly a work by an uncommon talent, combining a genuine gift for SF with a notable depth of understanding for human feelings and day-to-day human concerns.

When he heard that "Measuring the Light" had been selected for our first anthology, he and his wife celebrated over a bottle of champagne, and the next day he resumed his pursuit of excellence as an author. A careful and thoughtful writer, Green thereafter produced a few more Contest entries but made no particular attempt to break into volume production. Instead, he was preparing himself for the story you are about to read, the First Place winner in the Fourth quarter of this Contest year.

As a First Place story, it is thus one of the four candidates for the grand prize L. Ron Hubbard Gold Award, and, as you are about to see, a worthy contender....

On the morning of his seventh birthday, **Charlie Bernhardt was awakened by the sound of someone playing basketball in the** driveway. Staring up at the model F-14 suspended from the ceiling, he stayed perfectly still beneath his blanket and listened. *Dribble-dribble . . . crash. Dribble-dribble-dribble . . . . Crash!* The ball was smashing into the garage door on just about every shot.

The digital clock on the table showed an hour Charlie couldn't ever remember seeing before: 5:15 A.M. The world through the window was a faded blue and silver. The treetops against the sky seemed hardly alive.

Suddenly, the ball stopped bouncing.

It was all very strange. Charlie reached down and lightly touched himself through his pajamas, then slowly slid from bed and crossed the room. Who could possibly be out there anyway, so early in the morning?

With his face pressed to the screen he could see the entire driveway below, except for a narrow strip right alongside the house. There was no one in sight. For a moment, Charlie wondered if he might've somehow imagined the sound of the ball, or maybe mistaken some other sound coming from next door.

But then he saw something on the ground, just to the left of the foul line, something small, fast and bright—a red and yellow diamond the size of his fist, spinning in place like a top.

When it started to melt, forming a sparkling orange puddle on the driveway, Charlie turned away and ran into the hall. He stopped at the door to his mother's room and called her name softly—once, twice—but she didn't even open an eye. He stood looking in at her for a few seconds more. There was a man lying in bed with her, a man he didn't know. His arms were hairy and marked with many black tattoos.

Charlie rushed downstairs. The house creaked as he moved through it, as if it was still asleep. One of his mother's dresses was tossed in a heap on the living-room rug. He stepped over it and looked through the window toward the garage. The crystal top, or prism, or whatever it was, was still spinning like mad. And from the puddle—which now completely covered the foul-line—a fine golden mist was rising.

Any fear in Charlie vanished as soon as the diamond lifted off from the surface of the driveway. For an instant it floated a foot or so above the ground, whirling like a gyroscope, spraying out orange flecks of liquid, several of which struck hissing against the screen and sill. Then, with a whiffle-ball kind of a whistle, and a pulse of white light, it shot skyward, arcing over the backboard and garage. "Wow," Charlie said. "Neat."

What finally made him go outside, though, was the amazing sight of his basketball lying torn and deflated right there on the grass. He couldn't believe it. His grandfather had given it to him only yesterday, a Michael Jordan Air Attack, all red and black, so new it had almost seemed weightless. And now it looked like something a dog might chew on when he or she got bored.

Don't you ever leave this house, his mother always told him, especially since she began sleeping late with her friends, *until I'm up and around.* So he opened the kitchen door as quietly as possible, and went out into the silver-blue dawn—forgetting for the moment, or choosing not to think

Illustrated by Ron Lindahn

about, the strangeness of that spinning diamond.

The smell of cinnamon was so strong and sudden that
Charlie sneezed twice before he managed to close the door
behind him: "Ha-WHAT! Ha-WHEET!" And then, before
he could even wipe his nose against a sleeve, the thing
grabbed his leg and pulled him to the ground.

He felt a blast of heat, as if his mother had opened the
oven, and at the same time a large glob of cold fluid spurted
from the thing's mouth onto his pajamas. Charlie struggled
wildly to escape its grip on his ankle. Its face was part frog
and part bulldog, with hanging jowls and eyes the size of tennis balls. Its skin was gray and slick, and seemed to slither
in upon itself as if the flesh was somehow made of worms.

Although it wasn't much larger than he was, Charlie
realized immediately that its strength was equal to an
adult's. He screamed and hooted his mom's name, but
nothing more than a whimper came out. Sprawled on its
back on the lawn, the nightmare tugged Charlie close, hugging him tightly to its chest.

"Caw," it said. "Kal."

Earlier, while Taickmane lurks, the man inserts a new
cassette and returns swaying to his station upon the couch.
Soon the figures on the screen are going at it again. Taickmane recognizes one of the females, a young Oriental from
the conclusion of the previous film. Her hair is very long
and she likes to shout as she is taken. She is quite beautiful,
Taickmane feels. Like a mountain or a thoroughbred.

The man on the couch begins to snore. Taickmane
removes another cypselia from his kit. This will be his third
dose of the night. He shrugs and swallows the capsule. After
destroying the nest he had walked for hours through dozens
of suburban neighborhoods, following the sidewalks up one
street and down another, wandering from one section of

town to the next. It's late now and he is tired. One more 'se-lia won't do him any harm.

The old tom lying on the plum carpeting isn't fooled at all by the cloak of invisibility that Taickmane still wears. When he switches the device off, the cat simply yawns. The woman on the screen, while being handled rather roughly, stares directly out at Taickmane, the depths revealed in her eyes somehow reassuring him that he has acted correctly in regard to the nest.

Watching her and her partner, it occurs to him that the monster at the core of this galaxy might perhaps be a nest itself, a kernel of darkness beyond imagining, planted by some immeasurably more powerful version of the Sowers' Guild. He makes a note to discuss this idea with the members of his team, and then realizes that of course that is no longer possible. For they are all gathered safely aboard the ship now, waiting with the other teams to be transferred to the next target world, their work here complete, their quota of nests planted and fully prepped.

And here he sits, a deserter and saboteur. B.K. Taick-mane, destroyer of nests, protector of unwary humanity, oh my.

Of course his deactivating only one of a score or so nests worldwide will have no effect whatsoever upon the eventual outcome of this planting. The harvest, as always, will be bountiful. Even a single healthy nest, given suffi-cient time, would prove to be more than adequate for a world of this type. Taickmane knows that. Just as he knows what will inevitablly follow the harvest.

He slips back into invisibility as the man sprawled beside him on the couch abruptly awakes. "Whore," the man says to the screen. "Come outta there."

Taickmane jumps to the floor and leaves the room. He feels a need for some air. It's time to move on. When he opens the sliding door to the patio, he immediately spots the d.c. waiting for him in the shadows of the lawn. Above the trees the Moon is full. Taickmane, seeing it for the first time, is surprised by the expression on its face.

The d.c. mutters something indecipherable, something about *ship* and *your guild*. Could it have sent here simply to retrieve me? Taickmane wonders. Surely not.

He steps cautiously off the terrace and approaches nearer. The crickets hidden in the grass fall silent. "What do you want?" Taickmane asks it. "How did you find me?"

"Sowers leave a trail of slime wherever they go," the d.c. sighs. "Especially renegade Sowers."

Taickmane has occasionally heard rumors concerning deserters, but nothing much is ever said about their fate. As far as he knows no Sower has ever willfully destroyed a nest —until this evening. He has no idea what the d.c. might try to do to him. Blue telltales are beginning to flash along its brow, and its hip bellows are panting.

"Go away," he tells it, pulling the bacillium torch from his kit. "Before I melt you with this."

"Oh, say, I have a better suggestion, meat," the d.c. replies, a beam of moonlight brushing its cranial dome. "Let's you and I have ourselves a little cook—".

It's on Taickmane before he can activate the torch.

Almost.

The flare lashes out and strikes it squarely on the chest. Arms flailing, and with a dreadful screech, the d.c. falls backward, smashing a lawn chair to the ground. Sparks of many colors cascade from a split seam in its throat. Taickmane aims and sends a second wave along the length of its body, then lays the tip of the weapon against the base of the d.c.'s skull.

Stretched upon the ground, it struggles weakly, trying to rise. Hoping to minimize the suffering, Taickmane clicks the power all the way up, and he keeps it there until the thing is finally still.

He steps away and his hands begin trembling. He drops the torch and it switches itself off. He can smell the d.c.'s lubricants. A faint hum is coming from its bowels. Without taking his eyes from the corpse, Taickmane backs across the lawn. Near a pair of rustling willows he finds a child's swing set. He sits down on the end of the slide.

Later, as he stares up at the alien stars, Taickmane finds himself thinking about a world he had been required to visit years ago, during his apprenticeship, where the harvest had been particularly plentiful. The nests had blossomed and multiplied until the Spites were as thick as clouds overhead. Sickness and Vice had darkened the land, and Labor was like snow on the hills. And Loneliness—Loneliness was a river of stone.

It was called Althea, and according to many of the journeymen, it was one of the most marvelous worlds ever encountered in the ship's history—at least until the nest matured and hatched, and Plague and all the others gained the upper hand.

Taickmane watches as a bat swoops low and circles beneath the willows. Everything is quiet now. He can feel the world turning. Of all the planets he has visited, few come close to matching this one's beauty. . . .

He supposes they will send another d.c. after him, or perhaps something a bit more efficient. Chances are this fellow here was in contact with the ship right up to the end, so presumably they know its present location, and therefore his as well.

He turns off his malfunctioning invisibility cloak—which the d.c., like the cat, had easily seen through—and fishes another cypselia from his kit. Across the lawn he hears a soft hissing as the d.c. begins to dematerialize. Within an hour, there won't be a trace of it left.

After a while Taickmane walks over and retrieves the bacillium torch. He swings it against a tree until it shatters, then throws the pieces into the bushes. *No more killing,* he promises himself.

He wants to do this right.

Bob Woodward came downstairs soon after nine and found Charlie. He was lying half on the grass and half on the driveway, sound asleep. "The hell's goin' on?" Bob said, seeing the crushed basketball and the puddle of orange fluid near the foul line.

He knelt and gently shook Charlie's shoulder, repeating the boy's name until Brenda, Charlie's mother, poked her head out of the bedroom window at last and screamed.

One thing led to another, and soon the ambulance arrived. Charlie still hadn't woken up.

"Ma'am," the driver said, "we best bring him down to St. Mary's, let the doctor take a look."

"It's his birthday today," Brenda told the attendants more than once during the drive to the hospital. She sat on the floor of the ambulance and held his hand, blaming herself, cursing this life. "But it's his *birth*day."

The doctors said a lot of things, but mostly: "It's a coma, Mrs. Bernhardt. Probable cause, a severe seizure of indeterminate. . . ." And, "Well, sometimes it just happens."

Charlie's mother stopped listening to them after the second week. Charlie slept on and on. They fed him with tubes and needles. Every few days or so there'd be another test, or a scan, or something. Brenda stayed right by his side. She changed his diapers when necessary, bathed him and brushed his hair, and held him on her lap for hours. The nurses got together and bought a tape deck for his room. They hung some posters on the walls.

Charlie slept for a total of sixty-seven days. He was so tired when he woke up that he immediately fell back to sleep. "Damn you, Charles Macon Bernhardt!" his mother cried. But the doctors said it was over.

It wasn't over.

Charlie had changed. He went home happy, but the world was a darker place. He remembered nothing from the morning of his "fit" (as his mother called it). Nothing at all. And yet. . . .

Weeks went by and his body slowly regained its strength. The dizziness and constant nausea faded, and before too long he was back on Cokes and Milky Ways. And although he had already missed the first month of Second Grade, Brenda was sure that with a little hard work he would catch up in no time. As he continued to improve, she came to believe that the worst crisis of her life was now safely behind her.

But then, on the day before he was set to return to school, while snooping around in the garage, Charlie found his basketball jammed beneath the snowblower. A lonesome Bob Woodward had kicked it under there one evening, when he returned from the hospital without Brenda. There was a dusty smear of oil on it, specked with dead bugs. Charlie walked over to the window and held the ball up to the light.

Suddenly he smelled cinnamon.

"Caw," he whispered, "Kal?"

Charlie didn't go to school the next morning. When Brenda went in to wake him, she found him curled on the floor in a pool of vomit and urine, his face as frozen and blank as a mask.

The memories were coming through to him now, vague and unfocused at first—but soon they were much clearer than anything in the real world. Or so it seemed to Charlie.

Taickmane's folks, his grandparents, and their parents as well—they have all been born on the ship. His is the fourth generation to have never seen Taisha, the homeworld: to have never stood upon one of her coasts and breathed her fragrant sea air, or watched her moons rise like a string of pearls over the mountains, all crimson and gold.

As he wanders along the suburban streets, where all the houses are dark and silent, Taickmane feels overwhelmingly ashamed. Without having known a world of their own, time after time the Sowers have done their best to transform the homes of others into the most hellish nightmares imaginable. And as a member of the guild, a planter of nests, Taickmane knows that he is especially guilty. Every mission he has ever undertaken burns now like a needle in his heart. *How could he have been so blind?*

The birch trees stir in the slight breeze, but the leaves of the oaks stay perfectly still. As Taickmane walks on, the Moon slips behind the horizon. Each yard he passes is elaborately designed. In the pools of illumination falling from the streetlights, the tethered saplings, pea-gravel gardens, and sculptured shrubs are like so many interchangeable props in a series of barely distinguishable displays.

There are ghosts in this neighborhood—Taickmane can feel their presence: a young woman who killed herself to spite an unfaithful lover; three children run down by a drunk policeman; an old author who never had anything published. In the hours he has spent here, Taickmane has encountered less than a dozen spirits. It seems that, at least for now, the dead of this world sleep soundly.

As he listens to the children's gentle laughter, a feeling of loneliness comes over him. He wonders if the ship has left this system yet, and if anyone has bothered to inform his ex-wife, Wulla, what her fool of a husband has done.

Maybe it's time to stop and rest for a while, he decides. Dawn is coming on, and he is exhausted.

He follows the next driveway back into the darkness, where he finds a small maple tree bent over a patch of soft grass. He stretches out, activates the invisibility cloak, and thinks about the Oriental girl until he falls asleep. . . .

He dreams of a nest unlike any in existence. Rather than

Misery, it holds the promise of peace. However, Taickmane learns this only after he has already taken his torch to it. From somewhere just out of sight, his teammates shout the news to him.

"Taaaaaick . . . maaane," they call. "Taaaickmane. Wake uuuup."

When he does wake up, the humphrey is leaning over him, grinning. "Have a good night's sleep, dear?" it asks. "Well, rise and shine, B.K. It's time to die."

"Don't," Taickmane says. "I—"

The humphrey jerks its hands skyward. Each fist grasps a silver knife. The Sower insignia is etched on both blades. *Not me,* Taickmane swears, kicking out and rolling away. *Not! Me!*

One knife catches him on the left side, penetrating through his ribs to puncture a lung. The other goes into his right thigh—once, twice—and then sinks into his groin, where the humphrey gives it a deft twist, before stepping back to examine the damage.

Taickmane, whimpering, pulls himself a few feet along the ground, but that's all he can manage. He lies with his face pressed against the grass, still except for the wounded leg, which begins to twitch as if attempting a little dance.

He can see the humphrey standing by the garage now, fooling with the radio on its sailboard. "Hump Seven to Shepherd. Hump Seven to Shepherd," it says, trying to raise the ship. "Hump Seven to—damn you!" It slams the microphone down and turns to glare at Taickmane. Removing one of the knives from its belt, it starts to walk toward him, whistling softly. But then it hesitates and seems to reconsider.

Taickmane loses consciousness for several moments. When the pain brings him back, his secondary heart flutters to a halt. As his lung collapses with a final prolonged wheeze, he watches the humphrey bounce a ball on the driveway and against the door of the garage. Occasionally it glances up at the graying sky and curses, gesturing with the knife. *What's it waiting for?* Taickmane wonders.

Then the radio crackles. "Shepherd to Hump Seven. Shep to Seven."

The humphrey jabs the knife into the basketball, tosses it aside, and hurries to the sailboard. The ringing in Taickmane's ears prevents him from hearing any of the conversation. He fades out again, and then wakes for a second time with the humphrey looming over him.

"Goodbye," it says. Before Taickmane can react, it kisses his cheek. "They'll be beaming you up in an instant or so, though why they're bothering I don't know."

Looking pensive, it leans nearer and with the knife cuts off a lock of Taickmane's hair. Standing, it places the souvenir carefully within its breast pocket. "Got to go," the humphrey tells him. "Thanks for the fun."

On the driveway it drops a marker that starts spinning right away. Then it climbs onto the sailboard, lies down, and shoots off over the garage. It must be rendezvousing with a shuttle, Taickmane thinks.

And then, all at once, death hits him.

He can feel it latch onto every cell in his body, probing and vibrant. Cloying chunks of darkness blossom in his mind, as parts of his essence burn and whisper away. It goes on . . . and on . . . for what seems like forever.

And when the boy suddenly comes through the door, Taickmane grabs his foot and pulls him down. He does it without thinking. He does it because, in an instant of weakness, the idea of dying this way fills him with unspeakable dread. He panics. He reaches for the boy like someone who is drowning, or falling into an abyss. The boy fights back, but Taickmane holds on.

Until he realizes that it's the beam he feels, and not death.

He says something to the child, as the sky begins to

howl. He says, "I'm sorry." And then he lets go—of everything.

But it's too late.

During those few seconds that Charlie and Taickmane were wrapped together in the beam, their strongest and most recent memories were scrambled and exchanged. Taickmane discovered what it meant to be a boy of seven—a blessing he was often thankful for as he recovered from his wounds, stood trial for desertion and sabotage, and eventually served his term of imprisonment, six years in the ship's penal camp.

But Charlie—Charlie didn't fare too well. He spent those sixty-seven days asleep in the hospital, and then the next three years at home, living an extended bad dream.

Soon after he turned ten, Brenda placed him in an institution. She had no choice. She couldn't handle him any longer, even with medication. She visited him every other weekend, most often alone but sometimes with Bob Woodward or another man. He came home for Christmas, Labor Day, Thanksgiving, and the Fourth. Rain or shine, he would lie for hours at a time on the grass near the back door, so peaceful and still that it always made Brenda wonder.

Charlie never spoke, except to say, "He's sorry." His only real friend at the institution was a young Oriental girl, a teacher's aide. Whenever he got especially bad, she was usually there to help. Whenever he made something in the crafts class, he often gave it to her. And whenever the humphreys came after him, she always took care of them without any fuss.

From watching the television that ran constantly in the dayroom, Charlie knew that the nests had hatched, that Terror and Secrecy had assumed a human face, and that Jealousy was now strangling millions. But he never told anyone about Taickmane, the Sowers, or the nests.

He never told anyone about how the Sowers had planted their nests here, and on thousands of other worlds, in an effort to halt an invasion that had already swept over dozens of galaxies. He never let on that he knew all about the hundreds of Sower ships, and all the worlds each had visited and seeded over the centuries—and how futile the whole operation probably was. For the invaders had little need of any resources from the seeded planets, so they simply bypassed them, and therefore were largely unaffected by the nests.

Charlie never told anyone any of this.

And the years went by. Brenda married again, became ill with cancer, and died. Toshi, Charlie's friend, was raped and beaten one night, and soon after that she quit her job and moved away. Charlie developed bleeding ulcers from all the new medication they gave him. Malice rose on the horizon, and Loneliness was a river of stone.

But then, one winter morning, a d.c. appeared on the soccer field, and Charlie talked it into taking him somewhere entirely different.

The Mirror
by
Nancy Farmer

About the Author

Nancy Farmer, who won a Westinghouse National Science Award at 16, was once a student at the University of California at Berkeley, and has taught in South America and India. She has traveled to Sri Lanka, worked as a biologist in California, South Africa and Mozambique, and as an entomologist in Zimbabwe, where she met and married her husband, Harold, who teaches English at the University of Zimbabwe. She left work to raise their son, Daniel.

She lived two years in Australia, where Harold studied under a Commonwealth Scholarship, and there began writing fiction. (At one point in her life, she had put out a weekly newspaper for the Phoenix, Arizona, Parks Department.)

She is now back in Zimbabwe, frequently far away from telephones and newsstands. But not away from her gifts. Since winning First Place in the second quarter, she has published a children's fantasy novel, and sold another and one shorter book to College Press in Zimbabwe. We give you here the first published fiction appearance of Nancy Farmer in the Northern Hemisphere, and she gives you . . . .

"**O**h, honestly," said the girl in the pink dress. "**Put it out or I'll call the fire department.**" She tapped the young man on the nose with her fan; real Spanish lace to go with her dress. The man murmured something into her hair. He was very drunk.

"You make me so cross I could just yip," she said. "Golly, Mother will have kittens if she catches me." But she did not move. Not yet. The man fumbled with her breasts and Sally looked around. The antechamber was dark and fragrant with gardenias bought at great expense from Florida. Through the doors she saw the dancers gyrate to the nigger band they imported from Harlem. They were playing "Ain't Misbehavin'." Mother looked out, searching.

"Lounge lizard," said Sally, giving the man a little push. He was very drunk because he fell right off the seat and sat on the floor looking comically surprised. Sally pranced out, flinging her feather stole across her shoulders.

"I do not approve—" began her mother as the girl swept past and clicked towards the stairs on little French heels.

"Oh, Mother, don't be so *deadly.*"

"I'll speak to your father. This is the last disgusting party you'll have here. Hip flasks and necking and that jungle music—"

Sally went on up the stairs in a fury. Mother was still in the Victorian age. It was 1924, for Pete's sake, and all those nice young men were not going to drink tea and insist on three-year engagements. The world was moving fast and a girl who sat in the parlor protecting Her Precious Jewel, as Mother called it, was going strictly nowhere.

Sally's head hurt suddenly and she leaned against the door frame. What *was* in that rotgut Tommy had in his hip flask? Golly, it made her see double. She staggered into the dark bedroom and steadied herself against a silk curtain. There was a mirror at the far end, and in it she saw the door through which she had just come and, in the shadows, a man.

"The party's downstairs," said Sally. She would sit down a few minutes until her head cleared, and then go back to the dancing. Down below, the jazz hopped and jittered, and there was a froth of bright conversation and loud, male laughter. Too loud. Mother would be furious. The man did not move.

"I told you, the party's downstairs." The man stood uncertainly, staring at her as though she were a ghost. He was dressed oddly; not in party clothes at all. He wore a long, white coat and cheap trousers and his shoes—Sally had never seen shoes like that before. They were dark cloth with white stripes and a funny sole that certainly wasn't leather. Was he a tradesman or a *burglar?* There was a small balcony on one side and she could just make out a strip of dark sky through a gap in the curtains. Had he come in over the balcony?

She was about to scream when she looked at his face. Her eyes were used to the dim light now, and she could see his expression quite well. Sally was used to the lapdog look of her beaux. She jeered heartlessly at it. But this man's face made her feel funny, kind of shy and maidenly. *I'm just a country girl,* thought Sally with a lewd grin. The man smiled back.

He wasn't the kind of man she met at parties. Now that she studied him, she saw that his hair was dark and he had a big nose and swarthy skin. A Jew. Her father didn't have any Hebrew friends, although he traded with them. How amusing! Mother would have kittens. She smiled, invitingly.

The man stepped toward her and stopped, as though he could come no farther. And then she understood: *He was in the mirror.* And she was not. She had no reflection. She walked toward the glass with her hands outstretched, but no answering hands reached back. She seemed to be walking in a dream, and as she moved the big clock downstairs began to strike Midnight. The first stroke boomed toward her, a train bearing down a track with its whistle keening through the dark city streets and the snow. It was New Year's Eve and 1924 was changing into 1925. The train passed and its howl shuddered off among the tenements and deserted office buildings of Manhattan.

And now the clock struck again, slow, infinitely slow, and the big train rolled out of the night on tracks that seemed to stretch endlessly. The lonesome whistle rose as it approached her bedroom and slowed even more until it was directly outside her door, and then it stopped.

"You want to see the gorks?" said the big man lounging behind the desk. A little gremlin doll in rubber and fur perched on his desk blotter with arms outstretched. Love Me, said a label around its neck.

Dr. Posen did not approve of the word "gork," but he was not about to antagonize the director by saying so. "Gork" most likely came from his native Polish. It was the word for pickle, a sickly, fat, green pickle smelling of garlic, but heaven on rye bread with a little pastrami added. He supposed the catatonic patients had reminded one of his countrymen of "gorks," so lumpy and quiet in their beds. It was a contemptuous word and Dr. Posen never used it. "I want to try L Dopa on them," he said.

"Oh, yes. I heard," said the director. "Dr. Sack's

experiment. Woke them up and then put them to sleep again. Seems hardly worth it."

Dr. Posen did not agree. To lie rotting in beds for years, fed by annoyed nurses and rolled around like bags of grain, was not an existence. It was living death. Dr. Sack took these golems and wrote the name of God on their foreheads and they *awoke*. They *lived*. If the name faded after a few weeks and they fell asleep again, it was worth it. Life, even accompanied by suffering, was preferable to mindless stupor. Dr. Posen was a child of Auschwitz and he knew what happened to people who gave up. They were called *musselmen* and they had no more soul than the logs they used to stoke up the ovens.

"I plan to use megavitamin therapy as well," said Dr. Posen. "My theory is that these patients have suffered a depletion of nutrients through the years. Their brains are not capable of maintaining consciousness."

"Our patients are fed an excellent diet."

"I'm sure they are," said Dr. Posen who did not think this at all, "but there's only so much you can do with comatose patients. And they do not move. I intend to start a program of exercise as well."

"They get physical therapy," said the director. "Twice a week."

Yes, twice a week they are wheeled into the garden and left to admire the roses, thought Dr. Posen. "I realize this, but accompanied with L Dopa, it could have lasting results."

"The things you scientists do to write papers," sighed the director. "Why don't you find a nice little lab to torture rats in and leave my schedules alone?"

Dr. Posen stared politely but firmly at the big man.

"Christ!" the director said at last, "I have enough trouble keeping everything running smoothly. I suppose you have a letter of recommendation from the Department of Health?"

"Yes," said Dr. Posen.

"You people always do. Well, O.K. I can let you have one patient. She's got what you might call a Ph.D. in gorkdom. Hasn't burped in fifty years."

"Only one?" said Dr. Posen.

"One to begin with," said the director. "We'll see how you get on."

And with that Dr. Posen had to be satisfied.

The first time he saw Sally was in the rose garden. On Tuesdays and Fridays, the catatonic patients were dressed and lifted into wheelchairs. Then they were pushed, heads lolling and hands curved at grotesque angles, into the yard. They sat in a row under a trellis covered by bougainvillea where the sun would not burn their skins. Some of them made meaningless smacking noises with their lips and others rocked monotonously and made their wheelchairs squeak. All of them had the strange, slack look that came from lack of exercise. Their faces, and some of them were quite old, were almost unlined. There were no laugh lines or frowns or crow's-feet, and even the elderly had very little gray in their hair.

Sally had soft, golden curls. Her nails were trimmed and, Dr. Posen saw, polished. When Sally's mother died, she left a provision in her will that her daughter would not only receive the necessary physical care, but something to brighten her life. Therefore, every week a beautician visited the sanitorium. She cared for Sally's hands and feet, styled her hair and sprayed her with expensive perfume. Sally did not seem to notice.

Dr. Posen saw that unlike the other patients, who wore cast-off Salvation Army clothes, she was well dressed. She had a light green frock with chiffon ruffles at the neck and silver slippers on her feet. Around her neck hung an old-fashioned necklace of amethysts on a silver chain. She was seventy years old.

"Hello, Sally," said Dr. Posen. The old woman stared ahead tranquilly. "You're going to be seeing a lot of me. I'm your new doctor." A breeze stirred the bougainvilleas. A middle-aged woman down the row made gobbling noises and her hands clutched convulsively.

"She can't hear you," said the nurse.

"I know, but she will." Dr. Posen wheeled Sally away from the others and into her private room. A bunch of lilacs sat in a cut-glass vase by the bed, and the curtains, brought when Sally's mother sold their New York mansion, were heavy silk. In fact the furnishings were all from the old house and all of them dated from before 1920.

Must be worth a fortune, thought Dr. Posen. Her parents were dead, but she had a sister who came to visit every week, driven by a chauffeur and wearing Paris originals.

"Wow!" said Gladys, Dr. Posen's nurse who had just arrived. "All this foxy stuff and nobody home. I could just love those amethysts."

"Leave them alone," said Dr. Posen.

"Yassuh, boss," said Gladys, insolently. "Will you look in this closet—fur! Silk dresses! Look at those shoes! What a waste."

"Not if she wakes up."

"She schizophrenic?" said Gladys.

"No. She was struck down with sleeping sickness—*Encephalitis lethargica*—when she was twenty years old."

"I didn't know there were tsetse flies in New York."

"Not *that* sleeping sickness, Gladys. Where have you been?"

"I know all about it," said the nurse. "It was a virus that struck about the time of the great flu epidemic. Got five million people in ten years and then buggered off. Hasn't been back since."

"No, thank God. Her mother found her on the morning

of January 1, 1925, standing in front of a mirror in her bedroom. She was in a trance. She's been in one ever since."

"Sweet Jesus," said Gladys, looking at Sally with real sympathy. "But that means she's, ah, she's seventy years old. That can't be. She doesn't look a day over thirty."

Dr. Posen looked at Sally more closely. He thought of her as seventy because he knew her age, but Gladys was right. There were no lines. The skin was young because it had never sweated over a stove or been drained by pregnancy or creased with emotion. The hair was eerily soft, like a child's. The eyes that stared unseeing had been closed to experience for fifty years.

For a moment Dr. Posen felt a chill come over him. Once, long ago, he had discovered an intricate creature with a rippling border in a tide pool. All blues and yellows and pinks, it seemed so lovely that he had to see it more closely. He reached down and lifted it into the air, and it came apart in his hand and the beautiful colors broke down into slime and ran over his fingers.

Of course Sally was not an animal in a tide pool. She was, now he admitted to himself, a really beautiful woman in spite of her age. He lifted her chin gently and studied her calm, passionless face. "We'll start with the vitamins and exercise tomorrow," he said.

Every morning Dr. Posen gave Sally an injection of vitamins. Then Gladys fed her, spooning the baby food into her mouth and wiping away the drips. Sally swallowed automatically when something slid down her throat, but sometimes she choked. Gladys had to tip her forward to let the food drain out.

"It's hard to imagine someone has been doing this for fifty years," said Gladys, grunting with the effort of lifting Sally to an upright position again.

"Need some help?" said Dr. Posen from the desk where he was studying a medical journal.

"She's not heavy," said Gladys, wiping a drool of mashed potatoes from Sally's chin. "It just seems like such a hopeless activity."

"That's what we're here to find out."

"Her arms and legs look better." Gladys lifted Sally's arm critically and poked it with her fingers. The flesh sprang back into shape quickly, not as it had at first when the imprint of Gladys's fingers took several seconds to fade. She flexed Sally's hand and bent each finger separately. There was a surprising amount of resistance in the fingers, and when Gladys stopped moving them the hand resumed its clawlike position.

After breakfast, the nurse went through the first of many exercise routines during the day. She lifted Sally's legs, one after the other, and bent her feet forward and back. She massaged her skin vigorously and stretched Sally's arms high above her head. "This may not be doing *her* any good, but I'm sure getting into shape," said Gladys.

"She looks much better," said Dr. Posen. He came up to the bed. Sally lay like a wax doll on the sheets while Gladys flopped into a chair, panting with exhaustion.

Sally's body, which at first had been dumpy, had responded to Gladys's care. Her breasts had firmed up and her waist curved in delicately. It was not a voluptuous body, but that was not in fashion during the Twenties. That was part of its charm. Dr. Posen forced himself to look away.

"I have to dress her really well," said Gladys. "Her sister is coming today."

When Sally's sister saw her, she cried. "She looks so young; like a girl." She dabbed at her eyes with a handkerchief. "I remember what she was like, so full of spirit. She did all the things I was afraid to try. She's all I have left, since my husband died." She took out a comb and began arranging Sally's hair. The mottled claw of the old woman stroked the childish curls. The two women did not even look related.

"My Sally's asleep," crooned the old woman as she fussed with the Chanel dress. Sally lay on the bed like an expensive toy, her eyes staring at nothing. "Will my little princess ever wake up?" sniffed her sister, wiping her eyes.

Dr. Posen did not answer because he did not know if Sally was even asleep in a normal sense. What was she thinking? Did she know what was going on around her? Some of Dr. Sack's patients said they were aware of everything but could not react. How could anyone survive such a state and not go completely mad?

His mother had told him the legend of the Golem when he was a child. "Was the Golem happy?" he asked her. "Did he like being alive?"

She laughed. "He was neither happy or unhappy. He had no soul."

"How can anything without a soul be alive?"

She looked out at the darkening Warsaw skyline. A formation of airplanes droned in the pink afterglow of the sun. "It happens," she said.

Exactly what was it he was calling forth in Sally?

He started the L Dopa. Nothing happened. Every day he injected the drug and waited in a fever to see results. There were no results.

Perhaps it was a matter of threshold, of reaching the right level of concentration in her blood. Cautiously, he increased the dose. There was nothing.

And yet he had the feeling that something was going on. When he had first walked into the room it was like a museum setting, but now it felt, well, it felt like a young woman's bedroom. A box of talcum powder sat open on the dresser with a slight spill on one side as though someone had just dipped her finger into it. An ivory mirror lay face down on the bedside table. It was almost warm as he ran his fingers across it. A dressing gown of a mistlike material lay draped across a chair, its frills rippling in the breeze from the rose garden.

Dr. Posen carried Sally from the bed to a chair. As he lifted her, an unexpected feeling came over him. It was hard to describe. He had done this dozens of times and she was no more interesting than a rolled-up rug, but this time she felt—different. Her soft breasts pressed against his coat and her breath stirred the hair on the side of his neck. He put her down hastily and arranged pillows around her so she would not fall.

"Where are you?" he asked the woman who sat with hands folded, staring into space. And then he saw: Her hands. They no longer curved in like seal's flippers. They rested, one inside the other, on her lap. As though she were waiting politely to be asked to dance.

"Gladys!" cried Dr. Posen.

"Oh, my," said Gladys, coming up and taking Sally's hand in her own. It was relaxed. "Oh, Jesus, I never expected anything to happen. She might really wake up."

"What do you think we've been working for?"

"That's terrible. I mean, she went to sleep when she was twenty. Her parents are dead, her house is gone, all her boyfriends are old men. What kind of life can she have?"

"What kind of life does she have now?" said Dr. Posen.

"Nobody knows, do they?" said Gladys. "What happens when she wakes up and looks in the mirror? She was *twenty* when she went to sleep. Men don't *think!*" Gladys bustled around, tidying a room that was already neat. Then she threw out the faded lilacs in the cut-glass vase and went out to replace them with roses. When she came back, she buried the ivory-backed mirror in the bottom of the dresser, under some sweaters.

"I liked it better when her hands were stiff," said the beautician on her next visit. "You try manicuring a limp finger."

Dr. Posen did not bother to reply. He watched Sally's hair being shampooed. Gladys had to hold her head over the basin while the beautician applied the soap and rinse. The old woman bubbled gently as water went up her nose.

"You be careful," said Gladys.

"Done this a hundred times and she never complained yet." The beautician took out a blow drier from her kit. "She's got fantastic hair. Makes you want to do things with it. Once I fixed it in an Afro but her sister made me take it out."

The old woman blinked as the beautician put mascara on her lashes. "You see that? She never did that before."

"Don't get it in her eyes, then," said Gladys.

In one of the dresser drawers was a tray with bottles of perfume. "I pick a different one each time. Marvelous stuff." The beautician sprayed Sally with *Arpege* and then herself. "Want some?" Gladys selected *Joy* and helped herself. "Once I tried on the fur and jewels, but the matron caught me and I almost lost my job. Her sister checks up every week."

"I know," sighed Gladys. She wheeled Sally to the window and looked at her critically. The old woman's hair stood out in a fuzzy mop. Her eyebrows were darkened with pencil and a skillful application of makeup almost gave her face expression. Gladys had dressed her in the Dior and pinned a spray of silver leaves to the collar.

"She looks beautiful," said Dr. Posen, coming up behind.

Sally sat up straight and grinned at him. "The party's downstairs," she said.

* * *

She was walking toward the mirror with her hands out-stretched and the clock downstairs struck in the most amazing way. It was like what happened when the Victrola ran down. The pitch got lower and words drew out until you could hardly tell what they were. She loved doing it with Lily Pons singing the *Italian Street Song*. Lily Pons had a high, sweet voice and when she sang "lalalala" and the Victrola ran down, it sounded like a frog in a well. "Lily Pond" Sally called it, and mother laughed in spite of herself.

The sound of the clock seemed to slow down until it was hardly louder than the wind that swirled the snow outside. Every now and then the wind seemed to stop, pause and begin again.

Sally looked at the man in the mirror, and now she saw he was as old as her father. Funny she hadn't noticed it before. The wind began again and blew—it was hard to say how long, but it didn't matter. It was comfortable to just stand. She felt so relaxed and her head didn't hurt any more. "I'm drunk as a skunk," she grinned. And now the wind began again. It picked up speed until she realized it was really the clock, striking the new year.

"Somebody wound the Victrola," she giggled. The clock struck again, almost normally, and one last time. And suddenly the room was full of light. How very strange. She must have been here all night. And the man was still here, too. He looked amazed to see her.

"The party's downstairs," said Sally.

"Sweet Jesus," said a voice to her right. Sally turned and saw a colored woman in a nurse's uniform. Beside her was the *most* extraordinary creature. She had brassy red hair that was certainly not natural and it stuck up like a brush. She had a dreadful, baggy shirt and pants just like a man. Sally had heard about women like that. She was thrilled to actually see one.

"Can you hear me?" said the man in front of her.

Illustrated by Frank Kelly Freas

"You bet," said Sally. "I got ears, don't I? Golly, it's morning and I guess I passed out on the floor. O.K., officer, you got me. I ate that slice of rum cake." She spread out her hands helplessly.

"She sounds perfectly normal," said the colored woman in an awe-stricken voice.

"Dr. Sack described a case like this—a sudden awakening as though there was an on-off switch in the brain." The man reached out and took Sally's hands.

She felt suddenly shy. He wasn't like the boys who pawed her over; he was as old as her father. She pulled away. "You're a doctor, aren't you? I guess Mother thought I was sick, but all I had was a snootful. Promise you won't tell. Oh," she stood up and clasped her hands. "What booful roses! For me?" She turned bright eyes upon the doctor.

He had his arms out to steady her. "You must be careful!"

"Of you, obviously," said Sally, looking at him through lowered eyelashes. She allowed herself to be seated. "Why, this isn't my room! It has my things, but it's smaller. I know! I've been sent to a hospital."

"You've been sick," began the doctor.

"There *was* something in that hooch Tommy gave me. Well, I hope he's flatter 'n a pancake. Gee, I do feel washed out, but never say die, eh, boys?" She rolled her eyes drolly. "Another victim of Demon Rum. Say, what's the matter? Why are you all staring at me?"

"I think I have to go," said the lesbian with the brush-like red hair. She picked up a small suitcase and ducked out without another word.

"How about you two? Take off your mittens and stay a while." Sally was talking rapidly to cover her growing uneasiness. There were a great many things wrong. Through the window she could see a rose garden in bloom and she knew it was Winter. The doctor's shoes were so strange, and who ever heard of a nigger nurse?

The nurse's uniform was odd—too short and tight. There were a dozen other little things: The shape of the light switch, the bulb, the doctor's pen, the drinking mug which was not glass but some green stuff like papier-mâché. Altogether, there was something terribly wrong.

"My name is Dr. Posen," said the man. "And this is my nurse, Gladys Mason. You came down with sleeping sickness. Have you heard of it?"

"I don't know anybody who had it, but I read about it. Gosh, just like Sleeping Beauty! Do I get a swell prince to wake me up, or—" she lowered her eyelashes again, "have you already done it?"

"I suppose I have," said Dr. Posen, gravely.

"In the story, he does it with a kiss," said Sally, pertly offering her cheek. The situation had its amusing side. The doctor was a nice-looking guy, for a Jew. He was a present-able addition to her collection of scalps.

The doctor hesitated for an instant, then he leaned over and kissed her. "Princess, wake up," he said, gently.

"This calls for a party," said Sally, turning to the nurse. "Run down to the kitchen and bring us some tea and cake."

"You explain to that woman," said Gladys, "that I am not a servant." It was evening and, miles away, at the sanitorium, Sally was asleep. Dr. Posen and his nurse sat in the living room of his house and each had a glass of brandy. A tape recorder played Nina Simone. The discarded bones of Colonel Sanders' Kentucky Fried lay on a platter.

"She's in a time warp," said Dr. Posen. "In her day, the only black people she saw were servants."

"Except for the nigger band from Harlem," said Gladys. "Remember them?"

"She's a child of her time."

"Child! She's seventy years old."

"You know what I mean," said Dr. Posen. "In her mind she's only twenty."

"When I was twenty, I had manners."

"She has so much to contend with, I have to move very carefully." Dr. Posen stretched his legs. He felt wonderfully relaxed. "Just think, Gladys, it's like a window into the past. She reminds me of one of those early movie heroines, fast and brittle and yet sweet in a way women have forgotten."

"Thanks a lot."

"You're sweet in a different way, Gladys. She's a product of a world without hijackings or terrorism or Auschwitz. The way things should have been." He put his arm around her, but she did not relax.

"She didn't even ask about her parents."

"She's afraid to. Don't be hard. She's got nothing and you have everything."

"You, for instance?" Gladys slipped off her shoes and waggled her toes.

Dr. Posen leaned over and kissed her ear. "I'll get around to race relations in a few days. Forgive me?"

"Yassuh, boss," said Gladys.

"Say Rudy."

"Yassuh, Massa Rudy."

"Shore likes pleasurin' you, Miss Gladys."

Gladys snorted and reached up to turn out the lamp. Nina Simone sang "I'm just a soul whose intentions are good" in the dark, and the doctor's cat settled down next to the chicken bones.

"It's about time," pouted Sally the next morning. "I was up at dawn and wanted to take a walk, but that mean old matron wouldn't let me." She was wearing a pink dress with a dropped waistline and had applied her own makeup. Dr. Posen wondered how she did this without a mirror, but the results were extraordinary. With a few strokes she had transformed the beautician's modern style into something eerily different. Her mouth was a cupid's bow and her eyebrows narrow and rounded like the brush strokes on a doll. She had two spots of pink in the center of her cheeks. Her hair had been brushed into ringlets with one coquettishly dangling over each ear. Kill-curls, he remembered they were called. It should have been grotesque. It wasn't.

"I want you to take it easy," he said. "Gladys can tell you about the exercises, but for the moment I think you should get used to things in a sheltered setting."

"I won't be a bit bored if I have *you* to talk to," said Sally. "I'm sure you can tell me simply heaps of fascinating things. For example, those *shoes*. They look ever so comfortable. Where did you get them?"

"They're called sneakers."

Sally burst into a peal of laughter. "Excuse me—oh, dear—I'm dreadfully rude." She wiped tears of merriment from her eyes. "Have you done any sneaking lately?"

"I never thought about the word," smiled Dr. Posen. "I guess they're called that because of the rubber soles. Quiet, you see."

"You know, when I first saw you I thought you were a burglar. I was just about to scream when I looked at your face and you had the nicest expression, and I just knew you couldn't be a burglar. It's a good thing I didn't know about sneakers. I would have yelled my head off."

She hooked her finger into the doctor's lapel. "Why don't you take this off? It's so doctor-y. Makes me feel like you're going to take out my appendix." She unbuttoned the coat and dropped it on the floor. "Gosh, I bet there's been a lot of new dances since I fell asleep. I'll have to sit them out unless you teach me. I'll ask mother to loan me the

Victrola—" A shadow crossed Sally's face and Dr. Posen watched her anxiously. "—or you can borrow one," she went on. "Won't it be fun?"

Gladys came into the room and raised her eyebrows at Dr. Posen's clothes.

"Take the doctor's coat, Gladys, and hang it in the closet," said Sally. "I was a really classy dancer—Father said I could have been a hoofer on Broadway, if we hadn't been so respectable. Oh, what cunning little cufflinks! That's—let me think—the caduceus, the serpents and the staff of Hippocrates or somebody. See what a classical education does for you? Gladys, I said to hang up the doctor's coat."

Gladys calmly went on arranging the perfume bottles on the dresser. She picked up *Joy* and sprayed herself.

"That's *mine!*" cried Sally, springing forward. She staggered and almost fell.

"Sally!" said Dr. Posen as he caught her. "Sally, you can't do everything at once. You've been sick too long. Gladys, put down the perfume. Oh, hell, this is ridiculous."

"What does she mean, stealing my perfume?"

"You made her angry." The doctor eased Sally into a chair and placed a pillow behind her head. She smiled and yanked lightly on his tie.

"Is oo mad wif me? Can oo forgive a naughty dirl?"

"Oh, shit," said Gladys.

"Miss Mason is not a servant," said Dr. Posen. "She's a highly trained and respected nurse and she does not like to be ordered around. Things have changed since your time. Black people are treated with as much respect as white."

"She said a rude word," said Sally.

"She was upset. I want both of you to pay attention: Miss Mason is to be treated with respect and Sally is to be treated with the care due to her illness. Has everyone got it straight."

"Yassuh, boss," said Gladys.

"Why, of course," said Sally. "Miss Mason, would you be so kind as to retrieve the doctor's coat from the floor and place it upon one of the hangers in the closet?"

Dr. Posen quickly grabbed the lab coat and put it back on. "I'm going to give you your injection and then leave while Miss Mason takes you through the exercises."

"I can't bear needles! You'll have to hold my hand first or my little heart will stop beating."

Dr. Posen refused to look at Gladys as he held Sally's hand and she laid her golden head against his lapel.

"Want me to give your girlfriend Geritol now or later?" said Gladys.

"You can't be jealous. She's seventy," said Dr. Posen. The late afternoon sun slanted into the rose garden, turning the blooms blood-red and making a golden spray of the lawn sprinklers.

"She doesn't look it and she sure doesn't act it. When are you going to tell her her age?"

"I don't know," said Dr. Posen. "On one level I think she knows. On another . . . she's only been awake a week, and while everything seems all right . . . I don't know."

"You're talking about what happened with Dr. Sack's patients." Gladys sat on the garden bench and eased her tired feet. She had spent hours answering Sally's calls for snacks or books or to have her window open or her pillow plumped. Sally always called her Miss Mason and was scrupulously polite.

"All of his patients had an astounding return to health at first, but all of them relapsed. Some only a little, but others became worse than before the treatment. Some of them," Dr. Posen sat next to Gladys and watched the shadows turn the lawn a deep emerald. "Some of them died."

"Why?"

"He thought it might be despair." A blue jay dipped

over the garden and rose with a grasshopper in its beak. It flew to the tile roof of the sanitorium and tossed the insect down its throat. It watched the roses with an alert eye as the late sun burnished its feathers. "I thought, with megavitamins and exercise and . . . lies, I might save Sally."

"You mean, you aren't ever going to tell her the truth," said Gladys.

"Not yet. I don't know."

Suddenly a scream erupted from the rooms nearby. Dr. Posen and Gladys were on their feet at once. When they reached Sally's room, they saw her backed against the wall with the lamp over her head. Her teeth were bared like an animal's.

"Get out! Get out!" she screamed and hurled the lamp. It shattered against the wall. The old woman on the floor paid no attention as glass fragments showered over her dress.

"You're all I've got. I love you," she sobbed.

"Get that old hag out of here!" screamed Sally. Gladys helped the old woman to her feet and led her out of the room. She took her to the garden bench and smoothed her thin hair while the woman wept against her uniform.

Dr. Posen steered Sally toward the bed. "She's not my sister!" she yelled and, bursting into tears, flung herself into his arms.

Sally knew who was responsible for that revolting incident. If she was the doctor, she'd send that uppity coon back to Africa; but of course he wouldn't. She knew all about *her*. One of father's friends kept a woman in Harlem and everyone made sly jokes about it. But she *stayed* in Harlem. Sally had seen her when she visited a nightclub with Tommy. They went past the most dreadful buildings; places she wouldn't store *coal* in. Crowds of colored people stood around on the sidewalks as though they had no place else to go, and made a terrific racket. But it was exciting, too. Sally

knew she was seeing Life and she wanted to know all about
Life. She felt like getting out of Tommy's Pierce-Arrow and
simply bathing herself in the noise and laughter, but Tommy
said there were pickpockets.

When they got to the club, they heard Louis Armstrong
making those divine riffs on the trumpet. Long-legged
women were being helped out of taxis, and then Sally saw
her. She wore a white pongee dress with a lace collar and
the darlingest bitty hat clamped down over her ears. But she
was really skinny. Her eyes were sunken and although she
seemed bright and snappy, Sally could almost see her skele-
ton staring out from beneath her skin. It made her shiver,
but she supposed it was the Wages of Sin.

There was nothing skeletal about Gladys—*Miss Mason*,
Sally corrected herself. She hung around the doctor like a
love-sick cow, and he stood up for her of course. Wasn't that
just like a Jew? Half of them were Bolsheviks except where
money was concerned. But he was handsome and it was
more than amusing to make him fuss around her and watch
Gladys—*Miss Mason*—simply chew her cud with rage.

So of course she tried to get even. The *idea* of passing
off that hag as her sister! *Miss Mason* brought her in and
introduced her; *Miss Mason* sat on the garden bench and
soothed the old fraud's feelings. But the trick backfired. Dr.
Posen stayed in Sally's room for the rest of the day, and she
told him all about Society, because of course he wouldn't
know about that. And he was fascinated.

Once he leaned quite close to her and she smelled his
skin. It made her quite dizzy. She felt like an Elinor Glyn
heroine confronted by a powerful dose of "It." Some quite
unsuitable men had "It" and that, of course, was part of its
allure.

"When I talk to you, Sally," he said, "I feel like it's
still 1924. I don't mean we are pretending or I'm watching
a movie—but that *it really is 1924 in this room*. Sometimes

I no longer understand the meaning of time."

"You just kill me with that brainy talk," said Sally. She turned her head to one side so he could study her nice profile. "Anyhow, speaking of movies, I could just adore seeing Rudolf Valentino again although I think he overdoes it with the eyes. Wasn't it *riveting* the way he threw Agnes Ayres onto the bed?"

"Valentino died in 1926," said the doctor. It was the first time he mentioned a date.

"How perfectly awful!" cried Sally, genuinely shocked. "Was he sick? Did he have an accident? Oh, I think I'm going to cry—such a handsome, handsome man!"

"I think he had appendicitis."

"Oh, how dreadful! It's like losing a friend. Don't tell me things like that. I want to think he's still riding across the desert sands and fighting Bedouins and carrying Agnes Ayres across his saddle—but he still is, of course. In the movies. That's a kind of immortality, isn't it?" She was crying now, openly and uncontrollably.

"It is an immortality," said Dr. Posen. "Please, I'm sorry I said anything—"

"As long as the movies exist, Valentino will still be alive and young and he'll never, never die—"

"He'll never die."

"And in *this* room, it will always be 1924," said Sally, fiercely.

"I promise," said the doctor.

"What is that?" said Sally, pushing back the opening where Dr. Posen's cuff buttoned. It looked like numbers drawn in blue ink. "You've been keeping notes on your skin. What is it? Is it about me?" She tugged at the sleeve.

"It's something that doesn't belong in this room," he said and firmly pulled his arm away. "We're walking on the water, Sally. Both of us. As long as we look straight ahead and keep the faith, we're all right. Do you understand?"

She thought she did. Under the water were her parents and friends and the funny symptoms she sometimes had: Grimaces she couldn't control and long periods of staring where time seemed to stand still. They were waiting to drown her, but she could shut them out. She would. She wondered at the doctor's mood. He seemed as desperate as she, but perhaps it was his concern for her. Yes, that was it. He was falling in love with her, but why not? Sally had ever so many beaux, all panting for the merest glimpse of her. And even though the doctor was as old as Father, he had an adorable smile and simply bags of "It."

Miss Mason came into the room and said it was time for exercise. Sally, in her most refined voice, asked her to tidy up the dresser and please, please to use the *Joy* whenever she liked. Miss Mason shoved the bottles so hard Sally thought they would break and Dr. Posen told her to be careful. Miss Mason said a rude word.

"She's getting worse, isn't she?" said Gladys.

"Yes, but she's doing better than anyone else has on this treatment. It's been three months and although she has episodes of uncontrollable movements and mental fugues, she's perfectly rational between times. More coffee?" Dr. Posen deposited some coins in the machine. He punched Extra Cream and Extra Coffee, but it still tasted like floor sweepings. "In Sally's day they didn't have shit like this. They had real, brewed coffee in a china cup and they gave you a spoon to stir it with, not a tongue depressor."

"I wouldn't know. It's before my time," said Gladys, sipping delicately at the hot liquid.

Two nurses sat at the other end of the sanitorium staff room and eagerly discussed a gruesome murder in San Francisco. "Her head was nearly cut off by a machete," said one.

"They slashed off two of her fingers and nobody can find them," said the other, ecstatically.

"That's the sort of thing people talk about today," said Dr. Posen. "Sally thinks she's wicked talking about kept women. She's a baa-lamb compared with those ghouls."

"Baa-lamb. Is that one of her words?"

"I suppose it is. I've been around her so much, I'm beginning to sound like her."

"I'll say. You're hardly home long enough to dent the pillow," said Gladys.

A third nurse joined the group and produced a description of the bite-marks on the victim's breasts.

"Look at those brutes," said Dr. Posen. "They're the same crowd that used to line up to cheer the storm troopers. You don't realize how life has deteriorated in the last fifty years until you talk to someone like Sally. Her idea of evil is a hangover."

"There was plenty of evil in the Twenties," said Gladys, "all swept under the rug where the baa-lambs wouldn't see it. You spending so much time in that room, Rudy, you might as well pack a bag and move in." She tore off little bits of her doughnut and rolled them in her fingers.

"It's so goddamn fascinating. When I'm in there, I feel completely different. Even the air is different."

"It's that musty furniture," said Gladys.

"I believe it's 1924 in that room, and at the same time I know that somehow that world exists and all the people in it. Somewhere my mother and father are alive and young, on their honeymoon in Vienna. Don't you see? It makes up for what happened later. If that time is eternal, I can always imagine them as safe and happy. Otherwise, there's no justice anywhere. Nothing makes any sense. That's *it!*" He slammed his hand down on the table so hard Gladys's cup tipped over. The nurses looked up at him with interest.

"We can save her," said Dr. Posen. "I don't know why I didn't see it before. It's a mistake to make Sally adjust to the modern world. She's like a heart transplant patient."

"I think they forgot the second half of the operation," said Gladys.

"I'm serious. A person with a transplant has to have his immune system suppressed for the rest of his life or he will reject the new organ. He has to live in a protected environment because he can no longer resist disease. Sally has been transplanted in time." He got up and paced up and down between the table and the coffee machine.

"The present is poisonous to her." He smacked his hand against the coffee machine, making it gurgle and hiccup. "We can recreate her world, we can do it: The old novels and movies, photographs, clothes from costume shops. I found a pile of *Vanity Fairs* in a second-hand store. She can read those. I don't want anything in that room that doesn't fit into the Twenties."

"Maybe I can find you a nice old nigger from Alabama."

"Don't start. Don't you see how important this is?"

"So we protect her from the present," said Gladys as she swept the crumbs from her lap.

"That's the key," said Dr. Posen.

"We can't do it. We can control her environment, but not her body. She's *old*. She had the change of life twenty years ago. She looks thirty, but it's an illusion. Underneath, her veins and brain and bone marrow are seventy, and very soon something is going to break down."

"But she won't know it," said Dr. Posen. "She doesn't see anything that doesn't fit in—like her sister."

"That poor old woman," said Gladys. "Years and years she been coming here, just lavishing love on that bitch, and look what happened. It broke her heart."

"She's had her life. It's Sally's turn," said Dr. Posen, callously.

"Anyhow, what you got in mind is crazy. That's what crazy is, a separation from reality. What do you think the director's going to say with Theda Bara in room seventeen and Rudolf Valentino making his rounds? He's going to throw you out on your pretty ass."

"Keep your voice down."

"The hell I will. You practically sleeping with that mummy and coming home too tired to trot and humming the Sheik of Araby under your breath. You know what? You as crazy as she is." Gladys stood up so violently her chair fell over. The nurses at the other end of the room stared with delight.

"Shut up the mouth!" said Dr. Posen, forgetting his English in his excitement.

"Yaa, yaa, shuddup da mouth," jeered Gladys. "You forgot your English, gonna speak sweet Polack words into mummy's ear. Come-a to me, mine liddle gork—"

"You get out of here!" cried the doctor, white with fury. "I don't want to see you in anything but an official capacity. Get your ass out on the ward and do some work for a change." Gladys swept past the nurses, whose eyes glistened.

"Don't forget the afternoon paper," Dr. Posen told them as he left. "Mother cooks baby in microwave."

"Why, Miss Mason," said Sally as Gladys stormed in. "How very fortunate you have arrived. I simply cannot reach the last button on my dress." She laughed lightly, a trill of fairy bells. "Would you be so kind as to fasten it for me? I can't think why it's so difficult."

"Arthritis," said Gladys. She came up swiftly and fastened the button.

"What did you say?"

"Arthritis. The curse of the elderly."

"My, Miss Mason, we *are* tart this morning. Did you get up on the wrong side of Dr. Posen's bed?"

"You keep your sassy mouth shut," said Gladys. She

began making the bed, pulling the sheets so hard they almost ripped. She viciously punched the pillow.

"Mother always says the way to judge a housegirl is how she plumps the pillows. It's that little touch that marks the difference between commonness and quality. Of course I would never class *you* with a mere maid. The uniform is entirely different."

"You mother is dead," said Gladys.

"For one thing, maids wear those cute little aprons with frills, ever so feminine—"

"I *said,* your mother is dead. And so is your father and half your friends. All you have left is a sister and she's sixty-five years old.

"—not at *all* like the nurse's uniform which has a rather solid look about it, especially when the *contents* have gone to seed."

"You don't care, do you?" said Gladys. "You never did care about anything but your own rotten skin. You're a spoiled brat, a seventy-year-old spoiled brat."

"And those nurse's shoes always did seem to blend right in with thick ankles—quite unfortunate, if one has that affliction."

"You know what you are? A vampire. Vamp, you called them in your day. You know how to tell one? She got no reflection in the mirror." Gladys yanked open the bottom drawer of the dresser and pulled out the ivory-backed mirror. "You never look in this thing because you *know.* Only people with souls got reflections. Let's put it to the test." She shoved the mirror in front of Sally's face.

Sally stopped talking and stared into the mirror as though hypnotized. She smiled slightly, her cupid's bow mouth making tiny wrinkles in her dead-white skin. The fretwork of lines around her eyes had deepened since she awoke, and among the golden curls were the first feelers of white hair.

And still she smiled, tenderly and with great love, at the face that mirrored back at her. She seemed to be listening to far music, to voices that vanished on the wind, to the bustle and clatter of a city that hovered about her like a perfume and then dissipated in the heavy air of the rose garden. She was still sitting there when the doctor came two hours later.

"Where are you?" said Dr. Posen to the old woman seated tranquilly in the chair. She had aged rapidly in the last few months. She was almost visibly fading away. Her hair was completely white and her face was heavily lined. Her hands had reverted to an awkward, clawlike position. One morning, quite soon, she would no longer be there, and there wasn't a thing he could do about it. At the dresser, a new nurse dangled the amethyst necklace in front of her uniform.

"Put it back," said Dr. Posen, automatically. The ivory-backed mirror lay face down on the dresser. He put his hand on it: it was almost warm, like skin.

Somewhere a young Polish couple sat at a table in Vienna and drank coffee. The table cloth was bordered with handmade lace and a crystal chandelier sparkled overhead. It was a fine place, for one that served Jews, the best they had ever seen. They were very happy.

The man put his hand over the woman's and she smiled a secret, satisfied smile. The clop of carriage horses outside the window mixed with the more exotic sound of motorcycles. The couple stared with amazement at the little machines, which had recently been purchased by the Austrian police. Such things were as yet unknown in Warsaw.

Dr. Posen took his hand off the mirror, and the bright island of the Viennese restaurant faded. But it was there. It was safe.

Sally was walking toward the mirror with her hands out-stretched when all at once she saw that the man was not who she thought at all. For a moment she had the illusion he was dressed in a white coat, but it was the curtain beside him.

Of course, how silly, she thought. If he's in the mirror, he's really *behind* me. I really am stewed.

She turned and there, standing in the doorway, was Tommy, swaying on his feet.

"You bad boy!" she cried, "barging into my bedroom like this. Mother will simply *die* if she finds out. Oh, Tommy, close the door quick! Oh, aren't we wicked!" She stepped back and bumped against the bed. "D'you still have your hooch? I could use a snort, I'll say I could! I'm as dry as Tutankhamen."

Tommy staggered toward the bed and flopped down. Sally was beside herself with excitement. Well, this was *it*. This was the Big Adventure all the girls whispered about. Tommy wasn't exactly her idea of a matinee idol, but he was presentable and simply rolling in dough. In fact, she found him just a teeny bit repellent at the moment. He was so quiet and strange. And his hands were so gaunt. She grabbed the hipflask and took a swig. A river of fire poured through her veins.

"That sure hits the spot," she said, wiping her mouth. "Oh, Tommy, throw me across your saddle and gallop with me across the sands. Take me to your Bedouin tent and —and—just *ravish* me with kisses. Oh, honey, tell me that you love me."

Tommy roused himself to pull up Sally's skirt and reached for the elastic on her pants. Her heart was pounding painfully. She lay back on the bed and waited.

After all, how else was a girl going to find out about Life?

What a Story Is
by
Algis Budrys

About the Author

Algis Budrys serves L. Ron Hubbard's Writers of The Future Contest as Co-ordinating Judge, and is Editor of the W.O.T.F. anthology series and Director of the W.O.T.F. writing workshops.

He has been a professional speculative fiction writer and editor since 1952, and a highly respected teacher and critic in and beyond the field. He has also held a number of senior editorial positions, and posts in publishing management.

Budrys was seventeen when he began writing the first set of stories he would sell to the top SF magazines at mid-century. His novels Who?, Rogue Moon, and Michaelmas are considered classics in the field. Benchmarks: Galaxy Bookshelf, a collection of his book review essays, won the 1985 Locus award as the best non-fiction book on SF.

From 1977 through 1987, he was an instructor at the famed Clarion SF-Writing Workshop sponsored by Michigan State University. He currently writes monthly book-review columns for The Magazine of Fantasy & Science Fiction and the Chicago Sun-Times.

In addition, he has taught a great many university classes and private writing workshops since the early 1970s, observing the progress of young writers. Here are some suggestions he feels every novice writer should seriously consider. . . .

One of the most important points to remember about writing is that the manuscript is not the story. Whether you're the sort of writer who "discovers" the story while typing its pages, or the sort who knows most of the story's details before sitting down at the keyboard, remember that nothing on the paper is sacred. The manuscript is only a vehicle for making a purposeful series of events appear in the reader's mind. The latter is your objective. Everything on the hard copy should contribute toward it, nothing in the hard copy should be superfluous, nothing should confuse it. Work on the manuscript until it cleanly conveys your story, and then stop.

When sitting down to write, keep in mind that writing is not the reverse of reading. Most of the rich detail, judgemental commentary and interesting digression you enjoy in the process of reading is supplied by your own mind, drawing on its experience of life. Show the reader what is necessary for a grasp of the events, let the reader overhear only what must be said between characters, and trust the reader to supply the rest, just as you do when you read.

Tell your story cleanly. Edit away all the first-draft hesitations and coyness that were your means of getting up to speed on the manuscript. Remove every word that would allow the reader to mistakenly construct some other story. You can do whatever you like to get through the first draft; just be sure all of your story is in there somewhere. Then cut away as if you had to pay the publisher by the word.

One key point I have observed is that every story is either a short-story or a structure of interlocking short stories. Every principal character has a story of his own, intersecting the stories of the other characters. Not all of every story needs to be shown in full, nor does it need to be elaborate, but it must be there in your mind, so that all the characters are consistently motivated and their contentions with each other are coherent and significant to the reader. Therefore, a grasp of what a short-story is, is fundamental to writing skilled fiction.

When writing, I suggest you keep in mind that there are seven parts to a perfect short story.

The first is a principal character; the person the story begins with. This person should have traits—that is, visible habits that reflect various important strengths and weaknesses.

Then introduce the most important problem this particular person could have. At this stage, it is stated only generally and he may not realize the degree of all-out commitment to which it will lead him: He must slay the dragon, or he must not lose his job, or he must save the day. As the story proceeds, details will emerge. In many stories, there is an "antagonist" who resists or attacks the first character, who is called the "protagonist." The antagonist isn't the problem; the antagonist acts in such a way as to bring the problem to the protagonist's attention. The antagonist is equally motivated; he wants to win what the protagonist must win. They actually share the problem, from opposite sides. Their contending actions will be associated with greater revelations about the problem, and about their resourcefulness and dedication.

Next, put them in context; show the reader the time of day and the physical setting, but also whatever else the reader needs in order to be sure of the principal characters' names and places in the world. As you write this in, also show the reader some traits these characters don't realize are important. Don't overemphasize the latter; the reader too shouldn't quite notice them at this stage, but they must be there for the reader to recollect as the story unfolds past the beginning.

After you have shown the above things to the reader, the "beginning" of the story has been completed. You cannot, in the course of any other part of the story, violate the "rules" you have just created for the beginning. If you do, you "invalidate" your story.

As a note: The beginning of the manuscript may or may not be the same as the beginning of the story. More experienced writers learn how to tell a story wrong-end to, or to mix the elements in other ways, in order to produce the most dramatic effect. It may very well be, and sometimes is, that the reader does not see the true beginning of the story until the end of the manuscript (or printed version). It may be that you can so craftily construct your manuscript that some of the story never appears literally on the page, but causes the reader to supply the "missing" parts out of his or her own experience of life as seen in the light of the words you do write down. Nevertheless, by whatever art, all seven elements must be made to appear in the reader's mind before the story will be satisfactory. And you can certainly do perfectly well by simply arranging your manuscript events in 1, 2, 3, 4, 5, 6, 7 order, with no "gaps" or transpositions. Even the most sophisticated writers usually do it that way, and many readers much prefer it.

Remember, however, that what you show your reader during the beginning, wherever it occurs, establishes the rules—that is, the universe in which the story occurs. For instance, if in that universe the characters are not said in the beginning to have prehensile tails, they cannot suddenly sprout them later when they need to whip a gun out of the antagonist's hand. That invalidates the story.

Now, we are ready to tackle the middle. Here the protagonist makes an intelligent, believable attempt to solve the problem, based on what the protagonist thinks he knows about the situation and his own resources.

The protagonist's first attempted solution fails. The problem reveals greater complications which are logical in hindsight. But the protagonist is motivated to persist and draw further on his resources. He tries and fails again and again, and each time the problem unfolds its details in such a way as to engage his resources more and more deeply and more and more quickly. Now the character cannot help but stake everything on the solution, for to fail is to be obliterated, either literally or spiritually. The character and the problem are both growing, though the character may not realize that.

When the problem is about to become a total disaster, one last gasp achieves either victory or death. In order to win, the character must turn away from some old traits, no matter how precious, and emphasize new ones, no matter how undesirable they would have seemed in the beginning. Some last straw happens; something breaks, or something precipitates. In an action story, the villain kicks a dog the protagonist suddenly realizes is the most precious thing in the world; in a more "literary" story, the "kick" can be just exactly the right word or glance at the right instant. Suddenly, the character's own idea of the character is shattered; the traits fall into a new pattern. Simultaneously with the climactic physical action, the character displays a new view of the world, grown out of the old one.

And now we reach the end. Here this new view must be validated. If it is a true winning view—if the physical action is the equivalent of finally shooting down the Death Star, or winning the garden club award—someone or something must do the equivalent of pinning a hero's medal on the character. If, instead, the character has collapsed, someone or something must show the reader that the antagonist was the hero, like it or not. In either case, this "someone" must be a trustworthy figure, because the reader must be convinced that the preceding series of trials and errors really has come to a meaningful end.

Probably the key point to remember while writing is that validation in fact proceeds throughout the story. Every incident must ring true according to the established rules set at the beginning; every asserted event must be supported either by never allowing it to have an ambiguous interpretation or by having some authoritative figure act or speak of its reality with an air of absolute conviction. Formal detective fiction of the Agatha Christie type is particularly good at apparent validation and apparent INvalidation. In fact, that is essentially what manor-house murder stories are, leading the reader through a labyrinth of false clues. Their study will repay you with an expert grasp of how validation works. It can be used craftily. But it must be used in some sufficient way, or the reader fails to believe your fiction.

If you intend to go on with fiction writing, I hope you will save these suggestions and refer back to them from time to time as you develop your skills through practice. What we have saved you, above, is the time you might have spent discovering some of these key things. But now it's up to you to test them for yourself, and fit them to your own particular way of looking at the world. Good fiction, remember, can be defined as "A clear and accurate account of real events within the writer's mind," and you are the only person responsible for attaining to that ideal for yourself.

The Zombie Corps: Nine-Lives Charlie

by
Rayson Lorrey

About the Author

Rayson Lorrey was raised just outside Waverly, Iowa, earned a bachelor's degree from the University of Idaho, learned computer programming in Houston, Texas, and is married to Wei-Lin Jung, a Dallas chemical engineer who is now a U.S. Air Force physician stationed near Salt Lake City. They have moved there from Fayetteville, Arkansas.

Dedicated to frequent changes of terrain, they hike, camp, and read compulsively anywhere west of the Mississippi River, he reports, accompanied by Nitro, their teddy bear, Earl, a stuffed cat, and probably very few other items of baggage.

Ray Lorrey discovered the Contest by reading Vol. I. Before entering his winning story, he had sold fiction to Fantasy Book and Chess Life. He definitely plans a career in writing, since it is portable.

There will be other Zombie Corps stories; a major SF book publisher has asked to see them. But this is the first one, from the second Quarter, and we're quite pleased to have it.

Charlie and I were doin' Drop
City hard when the damn Recall went off like
a klaxon inside our skulls. We tore out of the
bishop's brothel pulling on our clothes, with Charlie swearing at the top of her lungs because she'd been smack in the
middle of it with a gifted little acolyte. She cooled off down
the street and gave me a lecherous wink. "For two blinks,
Jeth, I thought that pretty cubbie was a keeper."

"And just where would you keep him, Charlie?" I
asked.

She shrugged and her big shoulders blocked out a street
light. "There's always a spare pod somewhere."

"Yeah, the Colonel would love that."

The walks were empty except for a duster hot for one
more deal. He planted himself in our path, and I figured he
had to be dusted himself. I'm a big boy and Charlie's got
me by half a head and we were obviously hustling to be
someplace else—not looking for action.

Undaunted, the duster waved a packet of sallow powder
under Charlie's nose. "How 'bout some zombie, soldier?"

Charlie smiled—slow and wide—showing off the gold
Z inlay on one front tooth and the 9 on the other. "One-
timer," she said, "I don't do zombie, I *am* a zombie."

The duster's eyes almost rolled out of their sockets. He
backed off, jabbering "Madre de Dios" and crossing himself over and over like a wind-up toy. Suddenly he waved
his arms and yelled, "No! Not these two!" I heard feet
behind me.

I turned and took a blade low in the belly. It hit bone. Painmeds and phetamines flooded my system. My muscle-amps kicked in, and I whipped a fist into the side of the ambusher's neck, before he could pull out his knife for another stroke. His head grated on shattered vertebrae and skewed sideways on his shoulders. The soothing voice of Damage Assessment purred in my brain: "Affected vessels: clamped; blood loss: nil; organ damage: non-critical; battle capacity: ninety percent."

The dead man fell, leaving his knife. I caught the blade hand of the street pirate behind him and yanked him toward me, steering his cutter clear of my ribs. With my free hand, I punched him where his knife arm joined his body. There was a ripping sound and a pop and his shoulder dislocated. He started to scream.

No one else was waving an edge at me, so I spared a glance for Charlie. Three pirates were on her. She had two chest wounds and the front of her uniform was wet. Her knees buckled, but she ripped the blade out of the grip of the nearest attacker and gutted him, crotch to sternum. He staggered away, gathering the slippery loops of his intestines in his hands.

Another pirate moved in and sliced Charlie's face. She tackled him, pulling him underneath herself as she toppled forward. He flailed wildly while Charlie crawled up his body. Her hands found his throat, and she strangled him—taking her time, enjoying it. The one-timer hacked at her with his knife like he was chopping wood, until he slowed and quit moving. Charlie went limp on top of him.

I jerked the spike from my gut and went after the survivor from the trio who'd jumped Charlie. On my way, I cut the throat of the guy holding his shoulder and whimpering.

The last bravo just stood shaking while I killed him. That left the judas; he was on his knees, begging. I grabbed his hair and snapped his head back and laid the knife across

his neck. "Find another line of work," I said. "You ain't got
no aptitude for this one."

His eyes went crazy. "Oh God I will I will I will—"

I drove a boot into his stomach and walked back to
Charlie. She and her throttled pirate looked like lovers laid
out on a sheet of blood. I rolled her off and knelt to rifle
her pockets and strip the decorations from her uniform. I
thought about digging out her bugs for Records but decided
to let the 'plants self-destruct instead. Carving on people
always made me queasy. I patted her cheek and got up,
"Later, Charlie."

The painmeds were tapering off, and my wound ached
by the time I flagged a taxi. "Port," I said to the driver,
"And make time." She did, and when she let me off at the
main gate, I tipped her good for speeding—and for my leaking blood on the seat.

An MP jeeped me from the gate to the transport; he
glanced discreetly at the growing stain on my uniform but
didn't comment. The ship was spotlighted. Its umbilicals
had dropped off, and its cargo hatches were sealed. We were
heading out. Mercifully, the personnel elevator was still in
place, and I didn't have to pull myself up a ladder. The elevator descended, its door opened, and there was Charlie.
"You get the rest of them, Jeth?" she asked.

I nodded. "Thought I'd save you a trip."

Charlie laughed and thumped me in the chest and led
me back to Medical. From habit, we took the corridor lined
with our squad's spares. I gave my empty bodies a salute as
I passed by. "Sorry, boys," I said to the sightless faces
behind the windows. "Maybe tomorrow."

One cubiculum was open and empty. A tech was
crouched in front of it, rummaging through a tool chest.
Charlie whistled to get his attention, "That's one of my
pods you're working on, Joe. See you do a good job, huh?"

The tech glanced up and grinned, "Don't worry, Sarge.

I'm betting this box only needs a new regulator and a gasket. If I don't run into any other problems, it'll be restocked before you know it."

In Medical, the doc gave me a lecture, put me out, and mended the error of my evil ways. Hours later, the first thing I saw was Charlie's homely brown face as she rousted me out of the sack. "Up and at it, Corporal. Briefing room in ten." I was so groggy, she looked good.

Charlie was career Corps—a volunteer where most of us had been dragged in kicking. I knew she was something different the day I joined her squad. I was ignorant and squeamish, but she put an arm around my shoulder and said, "Don't you mind the dying, Jeth. It's just part of the job. It's always been part of a soldier's job . . . though in the past, it was poor form to remind the troops."

I grabbed a seat next to Charlie at the rear of the dimly lit briefing room. Colonel Moss stood up front, perusing a topo map that filled the big screen. He about-faced and tapped the podium with his pointer once. We shut up and listened.

"A nest has erupted on Tregitt," Moss said. The news was answered by scattered curses from the assembly. Somebody always has friends or family too close to the action.

Moss targeted his pointer at the map. "The nest was here in rugged country, six hundred kilometers east of the settlement of Linnaeus and the only spaceport. The hatchlings are making for the port. The settlers along their route have been relocated, but before that was accomplished, the hatchlings hit an isolated farming commune. There were heavy casualties."

The Nest Builders explored this region of the Milky Way long ago. We didn't know where they'd gone since, but we knew what they'd left behind—deadly, undetectable nests on every world we humans found attractive. Each covert might put out a hundred hatchlings or thousands.

The smart money in Research was betting the nests were *No Trespassing* signs, but others figured them for some sort of alien joy buzzer. Whatever, the nests weren't quite offputting enough to prevent us from taking up residence. And if the Nesters ever showed up...well, we'd worry about that when.

Occasionally, a nest spewed the first time a human set foot on a planet; more often, it was years later. Either way, an army of bio-constructs poured out of the ground and started killing. The nest melted down behind them, leaving uninformative slag—not that it mattered, since Research got its quota of utter bewilderment from the hatchling corpses we provided.

As far as our smart folks could tell, the Nesters never played with the same deck of cards twice; hatchling genetic material varied from world to world and nest to nest like it had been culled at random, a codon at a time, from a galactic zoo. The Nest Builders rubbed our noses in our ignorance.

To add injury to insult, they forced us to fight by their rules—the chief rule being: Battles shall be waged exclusively by human grunts versus hatchling grunts. Enforcement was by means of unfashionable thermonuclear devices that exploded in arbitrary locations on the planet's surface in answer to long-range or hi-power bombardment or to use in battle of vehicles or energy weapons or poison gas or robots or probably a hundred other things we hadn't dared venture. Through some incredible oversight, the Nesters hadn't reckoned on zombies; we weren't on their *verboten* list.

The mandate of limited war preserves most of the local scenery, so we presume the Nesters find it as difficult to locate livable worlds as we do; at least, neither side seems to want things shot to pieces. It's oddly consoling to have something in common.

"Here's what the hatchlings look like this time," Moss

Illustrated by Will Eisner

said. A series of blurred photos gave us views of the critters. Ugly things. They usually were. "The hatchling data was obtained by Tregitt defense units while they covered civilian evacuations," Moss said. "It cost them."

Planetary Regulars are one-timers. There aren't enough zombies to go around.

Moss's pointer danced about the screen. "Six muscular, retractable legs emerge from the margins of a tortoise-like shell two to three meters in diameter. Despite its ungainly appearance, a hatchling can pace a man for a short sprint; and it can keep moving, albeit at a crawl, with only one functional leg. Sense organs emerge from a sliding trapdoor affair on the shell's topside, as do the manipulators—two extendible stalks ending in complex sticky pads and one stalk with a ring of boneless fingers. Weapons are stored inside the shell. They're armed with slug-throwers, grenades, and clubs." A surprised buzz filled the room.

Moss stared us into silence. "These hatchlings are highly resistant to our standard weaponry. Slugs don't often penetrate the shell, and those that do generally don't take out a vital organ. Even then, the hatchlings won't quit until they bleed to death.

"Their shells are near proof against grenades, but land mines have had some success, as the hatchlings' legs can be vulnerable. Therefore, each squad will be issued mines. Our plan of battle also requires that every trooper be outfitted with servo-armor." Groans. The armor rated zero for comfort.

Moss smiled. "And we've got a non-standard addition to your armament."

Charlie leaned over and whispered, "Last time I saw Mossy smile, we ended up with crossbows."

A new image appeared on the screen. "This is a sword," Moss said. More groans.

"Infighting will be the order of the day," he continued.

"These hatchlings tend to avoid tight formations, so you'll be able to gang up on one at a time and lop off its legs, stalks, eyes— anything the hatchling sticks out." A trooper in the front row unsuccessfully stifled a laugh. Moss singled him out. "Yeah, Trang, if it sticks it out, you chop that off, too. And if you get the chance, we think a thrust through the trapdoor will incapacitate or kill.

"We go planetside in twenty hours. Everybody gets a minimum of three hours sword practice prior." The Colonel shut off the screen, and the room lights came up. "Let's get to work," he said.

Medical had to reëxamine my wound and certify me fit for duty, before I could officially rejoin the squad. Charlie went along in case the process needed expediting. We came across Joe in the storage corridor. He was half in and half out of Charlie's as yet empty cubiculum. Tools were scattered all over the deck.

"Hey, Joe," Charlie said. "You were supposed to have this box fixed yesterday."

Joe backed out of the pod, tossed a wrench in the direction of his kit, and wiped his hands on a rag. "I've replaced everything but the hinges on this piece of crap, Charlie, and it still ain't working right."

"Well, *make* it work right," Charlie said. "You know I get edgy when I'm under quota on spares."

Joe scratched his head. "I'll do my best, Charlie."

Medical rubber-stamped me, and I accompanied Charlie to Supply. They issued us thick-bladed short swords with unnervingly keen edges. Charlie rounded up the squad, put us in armor, and drilled us for three hours and then some. She figured a hatchling would be the very devil to kill, despite our cunning secret weapons.

After a rest period, we assembled in the drop bay for equipment checks and final orders. Two hundred squads shared the vast gallery, filling it with constant motion and noise. Yeong and L'bala, our rookies, and Marna, Rico, and I were sitting on the deck in a loose semicircle when Charlie came in. "We pulled easy duty, thanks to you neo-zombies," she said, nodding at Yeong and L'bala. "Twenty hatchlings have broken away from the main formation and are headed for a grain depot. We take them out. That's it."

I patted the hilt of my sword. A score of hatchlings. Half a dozen zombies. Routine. With fortune on our side, we'd clean 'em up before the bars closed in Linnaeus.

There were only minutes left before the drop, but that was time enough for a rookie to wind himself tight, and Yeong looked it. So Charlie plunked herself down and began to give our other new kid a hard time. "L'bala, you're pale enough to be a corpse already," she said. "You worrying about down under?"

L'bala nodded. "I *know* the system works, Sarge, but that first time still has me scared."

"Take a look around," Charlie said. "All of us, 'cept you and Yeong, have been down under *and back*." We grimaced for L'bala, so he could read the numbers on our front teeth. Charlie was the squad's only niner. There weren't many in the Corps, since niners can pension out, whether they've put in their allotted time or not. Charlie had actually been down under more than nine times, but after nine, everyone except Revival quits counting.

She jerked her thumb at Rico. "Our pasta-lover here gets bumped every third or fourth campaign, L'bala."

Rico grinned sheepishly, "I'm consistent."

"Marna," said Charlie, "went from naught to fiver her first time out. Kinda rough, but she hasn't taken a hit since —learned to be careful."

"I did," Marna said. "I learned to stay directly behind Charlie's wide ass."

Charlie snorted indignantly, and everybody but Yeong smirked.

"I can't make down under any better," Charlie said, "but you can hope to get as lucky as Jeth did his first time. He didn't feel a damn thing."

I was sitting between Marna and Rico, who began to rag me and shove me back and forth. "Charlie, you don't need to tell that one," I said.

She ignored me. "We were on Hestes pulling back from an engagement. Jeth turned around to lay down covering fire and got his head blown clean off by a three-legged hatchling." Rico and Marna cackled; Yeong and L'bala were wide-eyed. "His servo-armor got stuck in a feedback loop that swung his headless corpse from side to side, and his finger happened to be wrapped around the trigger of his Lessing; so there he stood, in the thick of the firefight, blazing away like mad. The hatchlings got an eyeful and turned tail and ran. To give chase, we had to knock ol' Jeth over . . . which was a shame, 'cause that's the best shooting he's ever done."

Marna and Rico rolled with laughter. L'bala grinned and shook his head. Yeong almost cracked a smile.

L'bala leaned forward and said, "When I first got the Board's notice saying I was zombie material, I knew this was gonna be a strange business. My kin didn't think once to offer me their sympathy. They were too busy arguing about which side of the family my zombie blood came from."

Charlie laughed. "Well, you know how most of the one-timers don't really understand what's involved."

Marna and Rico and I chorused, "Not the dog story, Charlie!"

"You all shut up," she said. "L'bala wants to hear this, don't you?"

He nodded and Charlie launched into it. "The first time I'm home on leave, I get this frantic call from my Aunt Elly, who's just run over her beloved Bowser in the driveway, and she wants me to bring him back, right? Well, all you can do is send flowers. But I said, 'Auntie, get yourself some lipstick.' 'Lipstick?' she says. 'Yeah, get some.' So she scurries around and finds a tube. 'I got it,' she says, and her voice is just dripping with sweet, hopeful expectation. 'That's good, Auntie,' I say. 'Open it up. Put some on. And go kiss your doggie good-bye.' You shoulda heard the language that respectable woman used on me."

Even Yeong chuckled a bit.

Dogs don't come back, and even if they could, they'd have to be bugged and backed up for it. A zombie's transponder needs to be running—if it goes before he does, he doesn't wake up anywhere—and the spare body in the cubiculum has to be receiving the telemetry. It doesn't hurt to be lucky either; there's always a slim chance of not coming back even when everything's done by the book. That's why rookies don't get a practice run and why we treat our wounded instead of cycling them through Revival.

Six spares are held on the ship for each zombie. You can go down under and be back on the field in fifteen minutes, courtesy of a battle sled and a new suit of flesh. Some one-timers say its not the same person—different molecules and all. But to me, it still feels like me, and Mom hasn't collected on my death benefits, so I suppose it is me.

I always look like Jeth in the mirror, too. Our spare bodies are force-grown to match our physical ages and to duplicate our musculatures and any chronic conditions. The idea is to have the spares match the current body down to the hairs in its nose. That's necessary, because if the spare's apparent age, for example, is too far off, the zombie doesn't come back. Whatever this deal is, it's no fountain of youth.

Nor do zombies live forever.

No matter how many times we come back, we'll still end up down under for good some day. It's like that hoary riddle: What happens if you spit into the wind? Answer: You will die. The only questions are when and how.

Research is racking its collective brain over the whole thing. Why is less than one person in a million zombie material? No one knows, but zombies can be sorted from one-timers with a blood test and a neural map. Why can't you multiplex the telemetry, fire up as many spares as you want, and put a dozen Corporal Jeths on the field? The answer to that is an individual's consciousness can only exist in one location at a time without violating a law or two of physics. A quantum mechanic so deduced after Research's unsuccessful attempts at duplication, during which they produced quantities of healthy brain-dead bodies—spares that were good for nothing but spare parts. The mechanic now heads his own Research-funded institute.

It's been suggested the *soul* is transferred, but zombies don't come back having talked to God, seen angels, or experienced Nirvana—unlike my Uncle Tanner who has all sorts of spiritual episodes after his heart stops and before the medics get it pumping again. As far as I'm concerned, there's nothing quite like dying a few times to dampen one's enthusiasm for all things religious.

Charlie's own theory on zombies is that they used to come back as haunts and spooks—they're just too contrary to stay properly dead.

Our laughter subsided, and we got around to a subject dear to us all. "Rico, what will you do after you're out?" asked L'bala.

"I got fond of Hestes while we were there," Rico said. "I'm going back."

"You got fond of Hestes' *women*," Marna said. Rico blushed.

"He still gets letters from four or five of them," said Charlie, "so the feelings must be mutual."

Marna was going back to redo her dissertation research; the Board had pulled her away in the middle and wasted a year of her work. I imagined sitting in the sun on a world I'd helped rid of hatchlings—a hero with a pension. Maybe I'd take up teaching again; I missed the children.

"How about you, Charlie?" asked L'bala.

"Never gave it any thought, till a few weeks ago when I heard from my grandma. She's an old time voodoo witch doctor—lifts hexes and stirs up love potions and gives out bad advice, steals the occasional chicken from her neighbor and raises goats. She raised me too, which probably accounts for a lot of things. Anyway, she wants to teach me voodoo, so I'm going back to be her apprentice and to help out with her garden and the goats."

Colonel Moss's voice echoed in the bay: "Drop in five minutes. Good hunting."

The squad armored up. After Yeong finished, he bent his head and closed his eyes.

Charlie walked over to him. "Yeong," she said.

He looked up, "Yes, Sergeant."

Charlie leaned over and planted a finger on a tiny six-pointed star on a chain around Yeong's neck. Trying to keep a straight face, she said, "If you feel a need to pray, you might ought to pray to the techs looking after your spares."

For an instant, Yeong's mouth was a thin, tense line of anger. Then Charlie's infectious grin had Yeong grinning, despite himself. "All right, Sergeant," he said. "I will mention the techs."

Charlie slapped him on the shoulder and turned to the rest of us. "Into the drop boat, you zombies! Ya wanta live forever?"

We sardined in, the bay door opened, and we fell away from the ship—six zombies tied to a roaring metal pancake. Tregitt got big fast.

The boat put us down two kilometers from the advancing, widely-spaced rank of hatchlings. The squad spread out and planted mines. The hatchlings let off some fire just to give notice. We took cover and waited for them. The first grenades exploded far behind us when the hatchlings were still a half a kilometer away. Peeking from behind a boulder, I saw the limber, snaky arm of a hatchling snap forward. A grenade whistled overhead. The hatchlings were walking catapults—none too accurate, fortunately.

We concentrated our fire on the first hatchling that came into range. It drew into its shell and hunkered down. When we let up, it moved for our positions again. As a group, the hatchlings made good time; we could only hold up one or two while the rest advanced. And leg wounds didn't bother them at all.

Two hatchlings set off mines almost simultaneously. One lost a leg but kept going. The other ended up on its back, squirming to regain its footing. I took Yeong and L'bala with me, and we proceeded to hack its legs off. It was about as challenging as carving a roast turkey—though hatchling blood and guts smelled more like bleach and grease.

As I took off its sixth leg, the thing flipped over. Minus the weight of its lower limbs, the hatchling had been able to right itself with its manipulator stalks, and I got knocked head over heels by a lick from its studded metal club. Damage Assessment checked in: "Microfractures in chest plate." Hearing that, I understood why the hatchlings carried clubs—they could hit like big leaguers. I hoisted myself up, waved my sword, came in underneath the hatchling's next blow, and sheared off its club arm. Yeong and L'bala took off the other two arms.

The hatchling was a total invalid at that point, but its trapdoor remained open, so I shoved in my sword for good measure. The door snapped shut and left me staring stupidly at a broken blade. L'bala nudged Yeong and snickered. Charlie was a couple hundred meters away, but I could see her shaking her head. Her voice came over the squad circuit, "That pigsticker's comin' outa your pay, Jeth." Then the world exploded. . . .

And I was on the ship. I rubbed a thumbnail—it was soft; I'd just been pulled from a pod. I bared my teeth at the mirror that's always kept over the recovery cot. My familiar 6 was a 7. Techs shoved me into a new suit of armor. The tips of my fingers smarted going into the gloves.

I got up. A sheathed and unbroken sword slapped my thigh. Yeong and L'bala were nearby, looking dazed. "Congratulations," I said. "We never really know if you rookies are gonna come back till you've made it once."

There was a flash of murder in their eyes. "That's a joke," I said, taking them in tow and making for the drop bay.

"Jeth," said L'bala, "what happened to us?"

"I couldn't say. I was dead—like you."

We rode a sled down to the coordinates Charlie specified. She was stationed on a rise. We parked the sled and joined her. "'Bout time you goldbricks showed up," she said. From the tone of her voice, I knew she was grinning from ear to ear.

On the plain below us, Marna and Rico were working on one end of the advancing line of hatchlings. They'd taken out at least one more while we'd been gone. It was legless and its trapdoor oozed blood from the stumps of severed stalks. The remaining hatchlings were clearly more intent on advancing than fighting.

"While you were upstairs," Charlie said, "I talked over your demise with Command. We got things figured out, thanks to your getting blown to smithereens."

"What?" said L'bala, who wobbled shakily. Yeong held his shoulder and steadied him.

"Yeah," said Charlie nonchalantly. "There wasn't

enough left of the three of you to fill a dispatch pouch.''

"Lucky, boys," I said. "Didn't feel a thing, did you?"
They shook their heads numbly.

Charlie filled us in. "We've been suckered. The main
hatchling column sent skirmishers toward the refugee
camps, and most of our squads are tied up defending
civilians. These hatchlings," Charlie pointed down the rise,
"have a different mission. They've turned from the grain
depot toward the primary hydrostation—drinking water,
irrigation, and power for two-thirds of the settlers. If even
one of them gets through, the station is lost, because unlike
their brothers in the main columns, these hatchlings are
walking bombs; and they go off prematurely—with a time
delay of about five seconds—if you stick them in the gut,
like Jeth did. By the way, you three almost took a hatchling
with you. It was fifty meters from the blast and got its legs
mangled. My ears are still ringing though, so I'll thank you
to drop the practice."

Charlie got a distracted look, meaning Command was
on her line. She broke off abruptly and got on the squad
comm, "Marna, Rico. Fall back. Move. Move!"

Rico and Marna quit the hatchling they were working
on. It didn't pursue and instead resumed a course for the
hydrostation. The pair joined us on the rise. Charlie was
back on the line with Command. By the time she signed off,
her face was grim. "Command is taking a break for an hour
or so," she said, "while they try to put out the fires on the
ship."

My stomach rolled over.

"A reconnaissance drone lost guidance entering the
drop bay," Charlie said. "It plowed through two bulkheads
and caved in a storage corridor. The bay is out of service
till the fires are under control. Our reanimates can't get off
the ship, so the squads on the ground are getting more

short-handed all the time; and the hatchlings have abandoned their advance on the port in favor of a concerted attack on the refugee camps.''

Rico and Marna started to ask questions, but Charlie waved them to silence. ''Wait. It gets worse. The corridor the drone trashed was ours. Telemetry is still running, but our spares are smoked meat. We're one-timers for the duration. And our orders stand: prevent the hatchlings from reaching the hydrostation.''

I'd never felt my skin crawl till that moment, when I learned the things shooting at me could kill me—kill me dead forever.

''I've only got one idea,'' Charlie said, ''and it's just a delaying tactic.'' She put a local topo map on our suit displays. ''The hatchlings are entering this valley; the station is at the far end. We'll plant all our remaining mines here.'' Charlie indicated the valley's midpoint. ''The hatchlings are marching single file in a loose column. We're going to delay them, pile up the column, and make them fight. Then we hope the drop bay gets operational, and the cavalry shows up in time.''

Charlie looked us over. Her scheme as much as guaranteed casualties. Our lack of enthusiasm must have been obvious. ''I'm open to suggestions,'' she said. But no one had a better idea.

''Then before we get going, I want to be sure you all understand the rules of game have changed. If anybody wants out, just say so. I'll damage your armor and certify it not battle worthy. Nobody will question that—including me.''

Charlie's sense of fairness compelled her to give us an escape route. I studied the faces in the squad. Volunteer and conscript alike seemed embarrassed by the offer. We'd all gripe about the Corps till doomsday, but when you got down to it, we were special. The Corps needed us, there was no substitute; and right now the men and women and children of Tregitt needed us. If the hatchlings blew the hydrostation, the crops would die and famine would come calling.

After some awkward shuffling, Yeong stepped forward. "Sergeant," he said, "you wouldn't mind if I took a moment to pray *now,* would you?"

"Not one damn bit," Charlie said. "Give us all a mention while you're at it."

We loped along the ridge top, scrambled down a steep slope, and took positions on the valley floor well ahead of the hatchlings, who were slowing—paying the price for the weight of their shells. Yet even limited to that stately rate of progress, they'd be fast enough to get the job done on the station.

"Dig in," Charlie said. We did—with rare vigor. A few boulders provided additional cover. I still felt naked.

Marna and Rico fell back and laid mines as fast as they could. Before us, the lead hatchling came into view around a bend in the valley. It was followed closely by two others. A piece of luck—they were already bunching up.

We traded fire. Slugs whined from shells and armor; we could have shot peas at each other to equal effect. Another hatchling came around the bend and started to pitch grenades, overthrowing our position as usual. I turned my head to follow a particularly wild toss. The grenade hit a rock, bounced crazily, and headed for the mine field. "Rico, Marna! Down!" I was too late. The blast laid them both out.

Charlie roared into the comm line. "Marna! Rico! Answer me!"

Rico raised his head, "I'm still here, Sarge." He got to his feet, took a step, fell to his hands and knees, and crawled on all fours to Marna's side. She was face down. He rolled her over. . . .

And Marna tried to sit up. I stopped holding my breath.

"I'm fine, Charlie," she said.

"No, she isn't," said Rico. "She's taken a piece of shrapnel through her leg armor."

Marna pushed him away. "Damage Assessment says I'm functional."

"I expect that's a damn lie," Charlie said, "but I can't afford to argue it now. Get the rest of the mines set and take cover." Rico and Marna helped each other up and got back to work.

Charlie watched them limp around. "We've gotta buy some time," she said. "Let's try to cripple the leader and the one following."

L'bala drew his blade. "What I wouldn't give for a three-day pass," he said. Yeong nodded vigorously.

Charlie smiled for the first time since she'd told us about the drone. "You sons are gonna make some kind of fine zombies."

The four of us charged the lead hatchling. It didn't act terribly concerned. Slugs rattled on our armor like hail, but the firing stopped all at once. The hatchlings had realized the uselessness of small arms. They brought out their clubs.

We surrounded the leader. It continued to plod onward, but the stalk holding the club stood straight up. The hatchling was prepared to swing at the first attacker that moved in. We lunged together on Charlie's signal. The hatchling's club came down on Yeong, glancing off his helmet. Charlie and L'bala hacked at two adjacent legs. I took off the club-wielding stalk and picked Yeong up. He was dazed but ready for more.

We backed off. The legs Charlie and L'bala had chopped into were hanging by strips of flesh. The hatchling's pace was markedly slower.

We repeated our performance on the next hatchling in line. It must have noted who'd given the signal for the first attack. As soon as we charged, it went for Charlie. The hatchling slapped her to the ground and got in another shot while she was down, before we could hew off its club stalk.

"Yeong, L'bala, get Charlie away." They carried her, and I moved in on the disarmed hatchling. Gripping my sword with both hands, I sheared off one leg and a chunk from another. I withdrew when two more hatchlings came to join the fun.

I caught up with Yeong, L'bala, and Charlie at the perimeter of the mine field. The armor at Charlie's hip was dented and her helmet was cracked, but she was moving on her own again. "Let's be careful here," she said. "We ought to save the mines for the hatchlings." Marna and Rico guided us through.

There wasn't much else to do but wait while the hatchling column crowded in behind its wounded leaders. If reinforcements were going to show, we needed them soon. "Jeth," Charlie said. "Try to raise Command. Maybe my line is out." She tapped her helmet where the hatchling had clubbed her.

I didn't get a response either. "Colonel Moss must not be much at fighting fires, Charlie. Command's not back yet."

Charlie slammed her fist against a boulder, raising a cloud of dust. A second later, mines went off underneath the lead hatchling and the one behind it. The blasts ruined their remaining legs, and they fell heavily to the ground. The trailing hatchlings milled around them, trying to decide how to negotiate the mine field. We had the packed-in mass we wanted, but we didn't have any way to take advantage of it, and the hatchlings' confusion wouldn't last long.

Charlie faced me. Blood was spattered on the inside of her faceplate. She commed me on our personal line. "Give me your sword, Jeth, and get everybody under cover."

It took me a moment to get it. "That's suicide, Charlie."

"You think I'd try it if it was? Five seconds. No problem. Those two hatchlings are sitting ducks." She stuck out an open hand. "Your sword. That's an order, Jeth."

"I'll go too, Charlie."

"No. I'm a damn sight faster than you, and if this doesn't work . . . then I'll need you to come up with something else."

She took the sword from my hand, winked, and sprinted for the hatchlings. I shouted, "Cover!" into the comm and slipped behind a boulder. But I couldn't take my eyes off Charlie.

She was in among the hatchlings before they realized it. They didn't know what to make of an attacking force of one, who brandished a pair of swords and whooped like a madwoman. L'bala and Yeong, the dumb rookies, poked their heads up to see what all the commotion was, and they starting cheering Charlie on. I outyelled them.

Charlie leaped astride the former lead hatchling. Minus legs and club, it offered no resistance. She rammed a sword home through its open trapdoor. *Five.* The remaining hatchlings woke up and started swinging furiously at her. *Four.* Sparks flew where their clubs landed, but Charlie was a dancing ghost and they couldn't touch her. She plunged the second sword into the second fallen hatchling. *Three.* Get out of there, Charlie. She was a pumping blur. *Two . . . one.* The shock wave threw me to the ground.

I got back up unsteadily and my faceplate de-opaqued. Stunned hatchlings were scattered everywhere. Only a few moved. One had its shell split open. Glistening lumps of meat spilled out. "Yeong, L'bala, Rico," I said. "Swords. Butcher 'em." Even Marna hobbled into action.

I found Charlie meters away. She was on her back, and blood was leaking through the gaps in her broken armor. Somehow, she was still alive.

I removed her faceplate. "Hello, Jeth," she said.

"How'd I do?"

"You got 'em, Charlie."

"Good, good. Maybe I saved you a trip. I kinda remember owing you one." Her eyes closed. "Turn off my Damage Assessment, Jeth. I don't need it anymore."

I thumbed the override on her armor and took off my gloves and pulled one of Charlie's off as gently as I could. She didn't move at all, until her eyelids fluttered open again. "It's quiet now. Thanks, Jeth."

I held onto her blood-sticky hand while she died—and for a long time afterward.

A battle sled touched down behind me. It figured that the reinforcements would show late. I didn't bother to turn around, so I was still kneeling over her body when the motherless cur snuck up behind me and said, "Jeth, honey, I didn't know you cared."

I couldn't move. She peered over my shoulder and said, "I do look a mess, don't I?"

"Ch—Charlie?"

"'Fraid so," she said. "And I'm gonna have to buy ol' Joe the best bottle of rotgut he ever tasted. That incompetent tech never did get my vacant pod working, so to bring me up to quota, they had to put one of my spares in an auxiliary storage corridor. Then with all the excitement of fighting fires, Command neglected to tell me I had a spare left."

Colonel Moss himself pinned the medal on her. Charlie hocked it to a priest in Drop City, just before she pensioned out to go live with her grandma.

I inherited the sergeant's stripes. L'bala and Yeong made Corporal within a paycheck of each other. Rico went off to live the good life on Hestes, and Marna became Doctor Marna.

I'm getting out now and *Sergeant* Yeong is taking over the squad. Me? I'm gonna look up Charlie and learn me some voodoo.

High Fast Fish

by
John Moore

About the Author

John Moore had been entering the Contest regularly, often coming close to the top in any given Quarter. In fact, we recommend to any magazine editor another story of his, "Fuel Fire," which might well have been included here if it were not that he subsequently sent in "High Fast Fish."

He is nearing his degree in chemical engineering, has traveled extensively in Europe, Africa and the Far East, and once rode a motorcycle from Philadelphia to San Francisco by way of Key West. Perhaps not the most direct route, but in keeping with his sense that exposure to diverse cultures and places is a valuable, not to say enjoyable, thing.

We don't see enough stories set in the near-future of the space program; apparently this is a mode more normally tackled by established talents like Jerry Pournelle. What Moore has brought us is a splendid example of looking at that mode and seeing an opportunity to describe a hitherto-overlooked possibility. He makes it work with realistic conviction. How much of an actual possibility there is in what he depicts is something that rests, perhaps, nearer to zero than to the infinite on the scale of probability. Still . . . .

The narrow round corridor
opened up into a large cylindrical room, dimly lit with red emergency lights. Isaacson
stretched his lanky figure through the hatch, towing the
vacuum cleaner behind him, and switched on the fluorescent lights. The chamber glowed warmly. Now he could see
the wire mesh, fine but strong, that isolated four-fifths of
the room, and beyond that, the quiet, slow moving mass of
bodies, drifting gently in the humid air. As usual he looked
at once for his favorite, but was unable to pick it out from
what seemed like a solid mass of gray. "Got to get new con-
tacts," he muttered.

The vacuum cleaner floated to a stop against the fence
as Isaacson used a pair of needle nose pliers to bend back
the wires on the makeshift door. He snapped a paper filter
mask over his mouth and nose, then pulled the vacuum in
with him. "Here, Kitty, here, Kitty." He ran the vacuum
over the mesh, cleaning away the debris and droppings,
while reaching into his jacket with his free hand. "I know
what you want, Kitty." His hand came out holding a soggy,
fist-sized bread ball wrapped in a Baggie.

There was a churning within the mass. The school disintegrated as individual bodies separated and darted to and
fro within the wire cage. A vast gray shape made its way to
the far end of the cage, turned and faced the elderly scientist. Slime glistened on the smooth, damp skin. The powerful body undulated. Barbels wavered around the heavy
mouth.

"C'mon, Kitty." Isaacson waved the breadball. Cold, lidless eyes focused on him. "Come and get it." The jaws opened and closed. Then it charged.

The speed of the attack caught Isaacson by surprise. "Hey!" The massive body slammed into him at thirty miles an hour, smashing him against the fence. Before he could react his arm was sucked into the hungry mouth, clean up to the shoulder. "Let go! Leggo, dammit!" he screamed in shock, pounding on the head with the vacuum cleaner nozzle. "What's wrong with you!" The animal swung its head, battering Isaacson against the mesh. Then it twisted in the air and let go. He spun away, coming to rest, unconscious, against the ceiling.

A few minutes later it found the hole in the mesh and swam out into the station corridors.

Hammond pulled himself into the medical unit, swearing under his breath. Only three days since he had arrived as station chief and there had been an accident. Nothing, he knew, attracted the unfavorable attention of Earthside management than a flaw in their precious safety record. Dr. Provost met him as he came in. "Can I see him?"

"You can see him but you can't talk to him. He's unconscious."

"Damn. What happened?" He followed Provost into her office. The Velcro made ripping sounds across the carpet.

"Damned if we know. Left arm, broken and lacerated. Mangled might be a better word. Multiple bruises to head and upper body. Concussion, certainly."

"What happened? He get caught in some machinery?"

"Koch said there was nothing around him except some fish and a vacuum cleaner." Another man was sitting in her office, one leg hooked around a sitting bar. "John Koch,"

Provost said by way of introduction. "Project Manager." He rose and Hammond floated over and shook hands.

"Some of the boys noticed a few fish loose in the corridors down in module C," Koch began. "The biotechnology module. I assigned a couple guys to round 'em up and bring 'em back to the pen. Then they called back and said poor old Max was in a bad way. I met the medtech team there. The cage was open and Max was unconscious. Nothing in the cage except some fish and a little dustbuster. Too small for him to get his arm in the vacuum cleaner."

"What's this about fish?"

"Isaacson was raising catfish in C5 bay."

"What for?"

"To eat," said Provost. "They're great. Believe me, after a few months of living on freeze-dried and processed food, fresh fish is like a gift from Heaven."

"I didn't know we had that much unallocated water mass around."

Koch grinned. "Don't need it. It's gravity that causes the gills to collapse, you see. In free fall and a high humidity, they just swim through the air, pretty as you please."

"Interesting."

"This is just a test batch. What Max designed, if we can get the funding, is a hydroponic plant-fish polyculture, with the vegetables fixing the ammonia and using the nitrates produced by the fish."

"O.K.," said Hammond. "This is going to sound like a stupid question. . . ."

"No," said Provost. "These are small. They're only this big." She held her hands apart. "Isaacson culls them before they get too big for the microwaves."

"We're not talking sharks here," said Koch. "They're only catfish."

Gigi Nguyen was splicing an electrical cable when the

fish passed through her peripheral vision. She ignored it,
continuing to wrap heat-shrink insulation around the wire
and then warming it with a blow dryer from her tool belt.
Again, she caught a motion from the corner of her eye. She
looked up to see the fish staring at her from twelve feet away.

The sight froze her blood. The fish was monstrous, easily twice as long as she was tall, with eyes as big as her fists.
Gigi opened her mouth but no scream came out. She backed
up against the corridor wall, holding the blow dryer in front
of her like a six gun. Her left hand slid along the wall until
it found the door to a cubicle. The fish watched each move,
lateral fins waving gently, the ugly mouth slowly opening
and closing. "Go away," Gigi whispered. "Shoo. Go
away." She snapped the latch and opened the door a crack.
"Sit!" she said and pulled open the door.

The fish charged. Gigi jumped through the door and
worked the handle. The fish hit the door frame with a
resounding thud, bending the soft aluminum. The fish got
partway into the cube. The door slammed closed on its
head. "Ow, ow, ow!" Gigi yelled, bracing her feet on the
wall and pulling the door with both hands. The fish gave a
convulsive wiggle and slipped in farther. She let go one
hand, grabbed a screwdriver from her belt and stabbed the
fish in the eye. "Back off!"

The fish slid backward. Gigi shut the door but it no
longer latched. The fish swam twenty feet down the corridor, then turned around and charged the door. The metal
bent inward under the impact. Inside Gigi hit the emergency
button on her wrist comm. Then she screamed.

"Whoa, Gigi, calm down! Stop yelling. Speak English, damn it." Koch was on the phone. "Did you see where
it went? O.K., well, just sit tight. We're right on top of the
situation."

"She's sealing herself in with hot melt glue," he

explained. "Luckily she found a room with metal walls. Most of C is fabric and polystyrene. I've ordered everyone else out of the module."

"All right," said Hammond. "This station was set up to have artificial gravity, right?"

"Well, yes. We haven't scheduled any yet."

"How long to spin her up? To say, a quarter gee."

"About three hours."

"That's it, then. We'll generate some centrifugal force, its gills will collapse and we'll strangle the son of a bitch."

"Whoa!" Koch straightened up so fast his shoes unhooked and he bumped his head on the ceiling. "Mr. Hammond, you can't do that. The electrophoretic separation tanks, the crystal growing units. There's three million dollars worth of experiments that will be ruined if we lose zero gee."

"This thing attacks people," said Provost indignantly. "You can't take money into consideration."

"Damn it, no, he's right," said Hammond. "A lot of equipment will have to be bolted down or secured before we can spin up. We'll just cause more accidents otherwise."

"Why don't you just pump the air out of module C?"

"We'll lose our lab animals that way. Some of those experiments are in the fifth generation. Can we hit it with a laser?"

"We have a helium argon laser that's portable, but it's only forty watts. The carbon dioxide lasers are both permanently fixed to the welding robots."

The wall phone beeped. Koch said, "I called a comm link with Aquaculture Magazine. It's a trade journal for commercial catfish farmers."

"Good thinking. O.K., I'll take it. Wait a minute. Fish are cold-blooded, right? Call up Physical Plant and have them lower the temperature of the station as far as it will go. That might slow it down. Lower the humidity, too."

"I'll get right on it," said Koch. He went to another phone. Hammond flicked on the wall speaker. The man on the other end identified himself as Bud Calhoun, contributing editor.

"So the question is," Hammond said after telling him the story, "What kind of trouble are we in? Is this a mutation or does zero gravity have anything to do with it?"

"A fish in water isn't too much worried by gravity anyway, Mr. Hammond. I'd say that the availability of oxygen would more likely determine the growth rate. In water, they get maybe, oh, eight milligrams per liter. You're giving them more like twenty percent. And with more oxygen they'll be more active, too. Intoxicated."

"Great," said Hammond. "We've got a high fish."

"Now, the blue cat gets big. They took one out of the Mississsppi that went two-hundred fifty pounds."

"Good God! Two-fifty!"

"And I heard of one that came out of the Mekong River weighed over four hundred. What have you been feeding them?"

"Koch! What was Isaacson feeding the fish?"

"SCP, I guess."

"Single cell protein," Hammond said.

"That'll do it. Now a yellow cat, they don't generally go as big. Maybe six feet long, a hundred pounds. But with an oversupply of oxygen and food, who knows? And it's a predator. Very fast, vigorous, very aggressive."

"Just great. What can it do to a human?"

"Well," drawled Calhoun. "I don't rightly know. But a few years back I was out duck hunting. Saw a cat drag down a full-grown Labrador retriever."

"Good lord," said Hammond.

The big catfish nosed into an open laboratory empty of humans. Banks of machines lined two walls, flashing red and green LEDs. A third wall was lined with cages. Pink, frightened eyes peered from within.

The fish hit the first cage hard. The flimsy wire cover popped immediately from its holding bracket and two white rabbits skittered out. One dove beneath a table and froze, whiskers trembling. The other, unable to cope with free fall, fluttered in the air, legs working furiously. The big cat swung around and casually snapped it down whole. It turned back to the cage, where a third rabbit was huddled back against the wall. The head darted in and emerged with a pair of furry legs protruding from its mouth. A flick of the head and a swallow. The legs disappeared.

Overhead, a video monitor watched as the cat started on the next cage.

"They found it," said Koch. "The immuno-assay lab. It's feeding."

"On what?"

"Laboratory rabbits."

"God damn it. Do you know what it costs to ship those rabbits up here?"

"I know."

Provost came back. "O.K., you can talk to him now. But don't get him upset. I mean it." She led the way back to the infirmary.

Isaacson was loosely strapped to a padded table, his left arm in a cast. He managed a weak smile. "Well, I guess I screwed that up good."

"Yes," Hammond said with feeling.

"They shipped me the wrong fingerlings. These were meant for stocking lakes and rivers. You know, sport fishing. Not for farming. I was in a hurry, I took them anyway. I figured, what's the difference? Long as they taste good." He coughed. "I think I broke a rib. It hurts to breathe."

Illustrated by H. R. van Dongen

"That's just bruises," Provost said. "Why did you let it get so big, Max?"

Isaacson hesitated. "An ongoing study. Rates of growth, metabolism, that sort of thing."

"Never mind," said Hammond. He had a sudden wave of sympathy for the old man. His wife dead, children grown and far away. He had seen it before, scientists making pets out of their lab animals. "Just tell us how to stop it. Can we lure it into an airlock?"

"Use an electric field." Isaacson coughed again. "Fish are sensitive to electric fields. They'll line up facing the positive pole. Then they approach it and are stunned."

Koch looked doubtful. "We have some arc welders. But the amperage isn't all that high."

"I've got a better idea," said Hammond. "Aren't we getting a four meter rail gun in module C?"

"Yes. But it hasn't been delivered yet."

"No. But the generator has."

A homopolar generator contains a heavy, rapidly spinning flywheel. When the wheel is suddenly stopped with a magnetic field, its kinetic energy is converted to a short, but powerful, burst of electricity. It can also be slowed down in steps to supply a series of smaller bursts. Hammond plugged a remote controller into the generator's parallel port and called to Koch on a wrist comm. "Try it out."

A series of numbers ran across the the generator's LCD readouts. "O.K. from this end," Koch reported.

"Good," said Hammond. He blew on his hands. "There's not enough cable to reach all the way back to Isaacson's cage, so I'm going to hook this up to Airlock Six. It's got the strongest walls of anything in this module." He picked up a pair of ceramic and platinum electrodes, each four feet long, and looped a coil of cable over his shoulder.

He was wearing swim flippers for greater speed and he bent over to tighten them.

"He's still in the lab," came Koch's voice. "I think he's slowed down. Maybe because he's fed, or maybe the cold."

Hammond peeked cautiously around the corner. It was clear. He swam to the airlock door frame and began fastening the electrodes to the frame with insulating tape. "All green," reported Koch.

"For God's sake, don't run any juice through them till I'm out of here."

"Mr. Hammond, he just swam out of the lab. We've lost sight of him."

Hammond looked down the corridor. "I don't see him." He worked the tape furiously. When he looked up again the fish was coming right at him.

"Oh, my God!" The fish was big, ten feet if it was an inch, and it was coming fast, blindingly fast, mouth open, showing a slanting row of serrated teeth. Hammond backed into the airlock and stabbed furiously at the close button. With agonizing slowness the door began to slide and Hammond knew it was too late, the fish was going to get him, it was almost on him. "Koch," he yelled. "Hit the. . . ." There was a CRACK and a blinding flash and Hammond was slammed up against the outer door. Three-hundred sixty mass pounds of piscine flesh hit the wall beside him. He pushed off the wall, kicking hard, and was out the door before he realized the fish wasn't following him. It floated in a gentle turn and he saw the burned-out eye sockets. It was dead.

"You hit the button just in time," Hammond said.

Koch grinned. "Soon as the mother got out of sight, I was waiting for you to give the word. I was afraid my hands would slip on the keyboard, they were sweating so much."

"I sent Isaacson down on the morning shuttle," said

Provost. She was mournful. "There goes our fresh fish. As soon as Earthside management hears about this they'll cancel the whole project."

"Isaacson's gone?" said Hammond. She nodded. "Did anyone check to make sure that he only raised one big one?"

Koch looked blank. Provost shrugged. Hammond decided to stay close to the phone.

A Winter's Night
by
P. H. MacEwen

About the Author

P. H. MacEwen has been a marine biologist, a computer operator at an aerospace company, and the crew manager for an inventory service, each for extended periods of time. She has also been a dishwasher, waitress, bookstore clerk, nursing assistant, proofreader and temporary office-worker. She is 34, and has been working since she was 16. She has also held several of these jobs simultaneously.

She discovered science fiction at 13, and calls it her first and continuing love . . . "a fever I have yet to recover from." Her particular interest is in what she terms "parabiology"— the logical development of alien ecologies, and the stranger outgrowths of biomedical technology.

Recently, she quit her job, took a 10,000-mile drive around the U.S., and then concentrated on writing. She now regularly sells natural history pieces to children's magazines and is planning a series of SF novels.

And here is a story of parabiology. . . .

EXCERPT FROM ELLISTON'S JOURNAL:

I found them in early March of the third year; a man, a woman, an eight-year-old girl and a baby. After all my searching, I could scarcely believe it: *four* of them, alive and intact!

They were living in a potato cellar, of all things, in southern Idaho, and the only reason I spotted them at all was the heat of their still. I had a little Army issue Polaroid camera and a few tons of infrared film I had commandeered for making an aerial survey.

I don't quite know why I even bothered with Idaho. I knew full well that between bomb-triggered volcanic eruptions and the enemy's tailored bacteria, that slate had been wiped clean the first two weeks of the war. I was simply being thorough. Or perhaps eternity was beginning to press on me. By then I had not seen a living human being for more than a year and a half, not since the last military enclave sputtered out of existence deep in the bowels of Wyoming.

At any rate, I did take the pictures and put together any number of aerial montages. I was using infrared film because it produces a much clearer picture of crater topography—important in the extreme since the snow masks everything—and because it covers so much more ground than my own senses can. Also, I must admit, it's far more pleasant to look at red and yellow and green blots than any more of that damned everlasting muddy snow.

This particular plate was of a section near the Snake River and I nearly missed it even then, trying to sort out Shoshone Falls. The bright red squiggle was very like those left by some of the smaller cluster-type warheads, and being so near the Air Force base at Mountain Home at first I thought it nothing more than a hot spot left by some stray bomb or other. It wasn't.

It was a chimney.

I dropped everything.

EXCERPT FROM BILLY JO'S LETTERS:
Dear Frannie,

God, I wish you'd come see me, sis.

I HATE this place! I hate it so much I want to scream every time I open my eyes in the morning. I want to scream till my throat explodes, so I can please God finally DIE.

I can not STAND the smell of musty potatas. I can't face another goddamn stinking day of it! But it don't do no good to bitch about it round here.

All I ever get from Julio is that sideways cow-eyed look. Sometimes, I swear, I'd like to kill him. Him and that stupid little slut both. Maybe he thinks I don't understand what he's up to, the filthy little greaser. I understand, all right. Maybe I am just a crazy broad, like he says. Maybe I ain't never done nothing more than wait tables down to the truck stop, but I ain't THAT stupid. He's just waiting, that's all. A couple more years and she'll be plenty big enough for a little shit like him. And once she's grown enough to bleed, he won't need me for nothing no more.

Well, I got news for him. Billy Jo Hardesty ain't sitting still for none of that shit, no sir. I'm going to fix that little whore but good! This time tomorro, I'm only gonna need three potatas in the pot.

EXCERPT FROM JULIO MARQUEZ'S CALENDAR:

Today is the eight of March. I think, anyhow. My watch, it keep good time up til last Novembre and I have been very careful with this calendar. The only days I am not sure of, the blizzards have wipe out the sun, or I drink maybe too much potato juice and I forget to keep track.

In two more days, it is Megan's birthday, if I have not messed it up too bad. I have been thinking very hard what would make a good present, but what she need the most I don't can give. That woman, Billy Jo, she give nobody any peace and she is hardest on the niña. I think, if I could do it, I would give little Megan a vacation from her. Maybe, yes—maybe I can take her on a little trip somewhere.

The woman, she can stay alone with the baby for a few days. He is stronger now and the still is working pretty good. Anyway, we need so many things, rope especial, and nails, and meat.

Yes, I must study the maps and think of a good place. The sky has been quiet most of this week and I think every day is a tiny bit warmer. Quien sabé? Maybe one day soon, the snow will begin to melt. The stars will come back. If we find a church again, how I will pray for that day!

ELLISTON'S JOURNAL:

Even with the map I had made, the place was not easy to find again. Gliding overhead, I had to circle several times before I located anything.

To the naked eye, there was nothing more than a round black hole in the gray expanse of snow. No smoke at all and hardly even an odor, just a queer whiff of schnapps on the silent air. I landed on the river ice a mile away and approached with extreme care.

EXCERPT FROM MEGAN SHEEHAN'S DIARY:

I think I saw a bird today! I was sitting in the blind, just

to be outside for a while, and this little gray shadow came
floating over the drift. I jumped right off my seat, it moved
so fast and smooth, like a rat smelling blood. Then I thought
of looking up, and sure enough, there was a big black bird
with these long curved wings sailing across the sky. It was
too far off for me to see what kind it was, but it was shaped
kind of like an eagle. And I don't think seagulls are black.

I slid down the ladder and told Billy Jo, but she just said
I was crazy, or lying, or going snowblind again. She slapped
me and picked up a big stick, so I went outside again.

Jeez, but I hope it comes back!

JULIO'S CALENDAR:

I have looked at the map for half an hour now, and I
think I have decided. Going in a straight line, we are only
fourteen miles from Twin Falls.

It is across the Snake River, and the canyon of course,
which is why I have been thinking of it for all this time.
With the bridge gone, it will be a hard climb, down and up
again, and the river to cross at the bottom, but the river is
froze solid now. Jerome is most as close, and I can get there
crossing only one little creek. But almost all Jerome was
burned down by people trying to stop the plagues, the same
people that blow up the bridges. There is not much left.
Even before, it was a very small town anyhow.

I wish I can remember if anything happened to Twin
Falls. I think I heard something strange about it once on the
radio. I don't can remember. Maybe that was Idaho Falls.

ELLISTON'S JOURNAL:

Perhaps I should have been less careful. I crept up on
my quarry as silently as a falling snowflake, taking advantage of every shadow and crevice and hollow in the dingy
snow, and as a result I nearly lost one of them before I'd had
time to get a decent look at their situation.

The cellar itself was buried below some sixty-five feet of snow, and they had tunneled out of it like Eskimos from an igloo, no doubt at the cost of considerable effort.

They had arranged a clever canopy over the entrance to the tunnel, a duck-blind affair which was nearly invisible, and I might have missed it entirely if not for the noise the two females made. As I approached, I heard a heart-chilling screech, not unlike the scream of a stooping eagle, and the girl tumbled out into the snow with a mad scarecrow flurry of stick-thin arms and legs. The woman plunged after, still shrieking, and I glimpsed a naked blade in her hand.

"Whore!" she cried, her every step crashing through the thin crust of ice. She sank in nearly to her waist, floundering, flapping her arms about furiously.

The child had better luck. She had a snowshoe partly strapped to one foot, a makeshift thing strung together from rags and an old tennis racket. That carried her a good ten feet before flying off as she fell. Thereafter, the girl attacked the snow like a swimmer, using a modified butterfly stroke to pull herself over and through the frozen surface.

Another voice rose in the distance, a man's voice, although I could not see its source from the hollow where I crouched. It sliced through the bitter cold, its tone outraged and its terms obscenely Spanish.

When the woman heard it, the voice affected her like a rowel applied to a stallion's flank. She jerked her head back, eyes white-rimmed and wild, then bared her teeth and hissed like a cornered lynx.

She threw the knife.

JULIO'S CALENDAR, MARCH 9:

That crazy gringa! I swear to God, one day I will kill her the bitch! I come back from the other cellar this morning, where I been fixing the sled harness, and I find her chasing Megan!

What the hell she have against a little thing like that, I just don't know. It's not enough we got the cold biting our bones every day and every night, or that our little boy got no fingers on his hand and no hair on his head. The whole world is dying, but no! SHE got to murder this lonely little girl and make our misery con toto. SHE got to kill the only human being left in the world can make me laugh.

Ai chingada!

If not for my son, for my poor little niño, who would starve to death without his mother's teat, I would wring her neck right now!

ELLISTON'S JOURNAL:

The knife nearly missed.

It struck the girl along the top of her left shoulder and glanced off the nylon of her parka, its heavy blade grazing her neck and jaw in passing. Blood spattered the snow, sheathing the air with its rich, heady aroma. I nearly fainted.

I don't believe she ever cried out, though. It was the woman's voice that revived me. That and the fact that she had finally come within reach.

She threw herself on top of the girl, shoving her deep in the snow, then snatched up the knife from where it had landed and raised it for the killing stroke. I cast my cloak overhand, and the blade sliced through the cloth, snagging in the heavy seamwork at the hem. When I snapped the cloak backward, the knife was torn from her hand, but also from the cloak and flung over the top of the next drift to disappear from view.

I might have done more, but the man appeared an instant later, slogging across the snow on an even clumsier pair of jury-rigged snowshoes.

I was afforded only the briefest glimpse of him before he tackled the woman. What I remember now is a distinct impression of St. George racing to the rescue, but a St.

George who had rather merged with than conquered his dragon. His face consisted largely of bristling mustachios, gray-streaked beard and furious brown eyes, with twin trails of white vapor curling away from his nostrils and mouth.

He seized the woman by her hair and clothes and pulled her bodily from the child, cursing her in two languages at once as he used a fist to knock her down again.

He did not waste time on her thereafter, but turned immediately to the injured girl, whom he coddled against his shoulder once she was extracted from the icy depths. I held myself motionless, letting the gray cloak and the grayer shadows conceal me as he passed. A moment later, the woman rose also and followed him in tears.

Only when they were both gone did I dare to move again. Trembling, I flung myself down and gnawed at the bloodied snow.

Damn him, Frannie! Damn him straight to HELL!

I almost had her, and he stopped me, the slimey bastard. And he hit me. He socked me so hard my jaw joint popped and now I can't hardly open my mouth without it hurts like hell and my eye's as black as the ace of spades. I look like I'm turnin nigger.

He says he's going to Twin Falls tomorro, but he don't fool me none. He's taking that slut somewheres so's he can baby her and get his hands in her pants without me watching.

He don't fool me at all. When they come back, I'm gonna be ready. I'll be waiting. I'll get her anyhow.

JULIO'S CALENDAR:

Today is the ten day of March. A week more and it will be Saint Patrick's day. And tomorrow, it is Megan's birthday. We are leaving in a few minutes. Maybe in town, I can find her a toy or a little necklace, something to bring back the smile.

The cut on her face is not so bad, no scar I don't think, but she got shook up pretty good. A little time somewhere away, that will make her feeling better.

And I tell Billy Jo, if she ever touch the girl again, I will cut off her damned nose. I tell her like I mean it. I do.

MEGAN'S DIARY:

I wish we had some dogs. I member I saw a movie once. They had a sled kind of like ours and they had a whole army of dogs to pull it. Big fuzzy dogs. I think they called them huskys or malamoots or something like that.

We've been walking all day, and I get awful tired of pulling this thing. Julio says it doesn't matter, we need the exersize, but I think it would be a lot nicer with some dogs, specialy if one of them was a puppy.

ELLISTON'S JOURNAL:

The man and the child left early the next morning. From what I could overhear, it was a scavenging expedition and they planned to be gone the best part of a week, leaving the woman alone to care for the infant.

I watched them go, then spent the day out of sight, deep in the ruins of a neighboring farm house. Its roof had collapsed long since but there were all manner of small tunnels in and around the place. They had looted it thoroughly and were then in the process of mining it for firewood.

I lay long hours in the dark, melding with the frozen shadows, my back to a piece of splintered paneling, my mind in a ferment. Miraculously, my daydreams had taken solid shape but this sudden conversion of hope to reality was not a comfortable thing, no indeed. Instead of lifting my heart, it left me sick with uncertainty.

Nevertheless, that night, while the woman slept, I rose and slipped in through the largest of the labyrinthine hand-carved passages that lay so neatly hidden beneath the snow.

They led to all sorts of nooks and crannies, rather like an overgrown prairie dog town. The central structure, as I've said, was an old-fashioned potato cellar, built perhaps fifty years ago of reinforced concrete and steel. It was bermed with several feet of earth and sod on all sides, which explained how these people had survived both the earthquakes and the everlasting cold. The design united near-perfect insulation values with structural strength sufficient to withstand the insane snow load. It was quite large, too, measuring some eighty yards in length and twenty-five in width.

One end had been roughly partitioned with tin sheets, and insulated further with wads of sheeps' wool. The combined odor of potatoes, of mold, of damp wool and unwashed humanity was nothing less than overwhelming, despite the temperature.

The stench was so strong that I did not at first pick out the richer tang of blood in the close, gripping air. Menstrual blood. When I did, it struck me with the force of a sledgehammer, turning my knees to water.

I sank to the earthen floor, shuddering, my hands clenched in furious knots, moaning with unbearable hunger. The woman must have heard me. Her voice threaded through the dark with a question I dared not answer.

I fled, up and out again to plunge my body deep into the clean immensities of sky and air, gasping like a fish, burning.

JULIO'S CALENDAR:

Today is Megan's birthday, the eleven of March. We have camped half a mile from the canyon last night, so I can show her first thing today, and so we have a whole day to get down this damn cliff.

The snow is not so bad here. The wind sweeps it clean. And there is part of a road left. The climb, it will be pretty

Illustrated by Paul Lehr

bad anyway. The canyon is still aroun a thousand feet deep, even with all the snow piled up in the bottom.

I think Megan never seen it before.

She stand a long time at the edge of the clift, staring down. The bridge, it is still there, all the bigger pieces. They are painted white with ice and they shine in the light, so bright it made me cry. Megan cried too. All the things we have lost. There is no counting.

Dear Frannie,

Something funny happened last night. I was in bed, kinda half asleep, and I heard somebody crying in the dark. It wasn't Tommy. I checked him right off, and he was sleepin like a little buzz saw. I mean, sometimes that baby out and out snores.

Then I thought it was maybe Julio coming back early, so I called his name, his and the slut's. Nobody answered, but just the same, I felt like someone was listening. And I could've swore that I heard foot steps after, somebody running.

I was scared then, but I didn't dare get up. I was right by the heater and they could have seen me right off if I moved, so I didn't. Anyhow, after that once, I didn't hear nothing more, just the still creaking and the fire kinda hissing and popping. After a long while, I went back to sleep.

Got up this morning and looked all over, but there ain't no footprints don't belong. I guess maybe it was just the wind singing.

I wish Julio'd get his ass home.

MEGAN'S DIARY:

This must be the deepest canyon in the world. I tried to look right up the wall but I fell over backwards. Julio laffed and laffed when he caught me. It must go forever.

We are resting now because Julio is so tired. We had an

awful time getting across the river. The snow is hollow
some places. You can fall right through. He did once, and
he almost pulled me and the sled in after. He cut his leg on
the ice too, all the way up to his knee. I think it hurts a lot,
the way he walks.

I wonder if there are any people left in Twin Falls. Julio
says he doesn't think so. He says almost everybody got sick
there from the germs the Russians sprayed. The ones that
didn't probly starved to death or froze. But he didn't and
I didn't and Billy Jo didn't, so maybe some other people
didn't too.

I mean, I can't see any people or dogs or smoke or
nothing, but it doesn't FEEL dead here.

JULIO'S CALENDAR:

Today is the twelve of March. We have reach the top of
the road and got out of the canyon, but we have a long ways
to go yet. I remember all the big stores was three, four miles
from the river. Maybe we don't even find them. Everything
here looks the same as the other side of the river. All gray
lumps of snow, maybe not so high, but nothing anywhere
alive.

We find a big dead tree at the edge of the canyon, so
at least we have some firewood. I cut a walker stick from
it too. My leg is very sore today.

ELLISTON'S JOURNAL:

For two full days, I did nothing more. Panic blazed
through my every thought, like an aurora borealis trapped
inside my mind. I was paralyzed with doubt. I did not dare
return to that damnable cellar, yet neither could I stay away.

And always the awareness, the memory of her was with
me, honing my hunger, until at last I grew convinced that
I could actually hear her breathing, ten miles away. The

night was flogged by a dull pulsing roar, the remembered echo of her heartbeat penetrating air and earth together. I knew that I would be undone the moment I scented her again.

I also knew that all my plans meant nothing unless I could learn to control my own bestial urgency.

Perhaps, I thought at last, there is a way. Like the shark, I am an olfactory hunter, and perhaps, again like the shark, it could be deflected with the right counter-agent. I thought of garlic first, but of course that would never do. While it would indeed protect the woman, it would also blind me and that I could ill afford. Something similar, perhaps.

A faint memory teased at me, something unpleasant I had smelt recently, somewhere else in the dark, and then I had it. The farmhouse. Deep in its bowels, in what was left of an old-fashioned kitchen, I had seen the crushed remains of a three-tiered spice rack. I'd ignored it at the time, repelled by the exudations of so many spices, all mixed at random when the little jars were smashed. Now, I could hardly still my hands long enough to excavate the shards.

Cinnamon and cloves were there, in cold frozen lumps, and onion salt and sage, and other things whose names I neither knew nor could discover. There was also more than a hint of garlic, but I found I could ignore that at the cost of inflamed eyes and throat. Small enough price if the ghastly stuff could fulfill my need. I bundled it into a shred of someone's red-check apron and then thrust that inside a torn mackintosh which I wrapped tightly round my neck.

Then, muffling my face against it, thrusting my nose deep in the make-do sachet, I turned once more to the tunnels and felt my way along them, using trembling hands and memory to retrace my path. I crept down, ever down, back into the sea of temptation.

And nearly collapsed with relief when I discovered that I could smell nothing through that awful olio of spice. I paused long minutes, testing myself, but it was true. My nose was dead, overwhelmed, and so was my feverish appetite.

I began to explore.

The main chamber, as I've mentioned, was partitioned into tiny rooms. The rest was given over to potatoes and a large crudely constructed metal contraption which huddled right next to those "walls." It was a distillation rig and someone had been hard at work, converting peelings into semi-potable vodka.

This in turn was being burned in portable kerosene heaters that ringed the living quarters and rendered them merely sub-arctic in atmosphere. It was a fairly intelligent arrangement, given the inadequate ventilation and the general lack of fuel. The heat generated by a small amount of wood or coal could thus be multiplied, and produced disinfectant as well.

But from a safety point of view, it was deplorable. I had visions of spilled hootch and stray sparks and conflagrations in the night.

Moreover, it became obvious that these people were subsisting on nothing BUT potatoes.

I examined both woman and child as they slept and found indisputable signs of malnutrition. Not as bad as I had feared, but bad enough. The infant also displayed malformations of the left hand, though whether this was the result of his mother's exposure to radiation or due to some less fearful cause, I could not tell. Palpation revealed that the woman had three smallish lumps in the lower hemisphere of her right breast, though of course, because of the spice, I was unable to test her for the tell-tale sickly sweet odor of cancer. In any case, the lumps may be nothing more than cysts.

On that point, only time would tell, I decided.

MEGAN'S DIARY:

We're rich! Julio and me, we found the biggest pile of stuff you ever saw. There's everything here! All you have to do is dig.

We found a shoe store and a bakery and minute market too. And then we found a real grocery store! We had beef stew for dinner last nite, and corn and all the peeches I could eat. I found some baby food for Tommy too. I wish he was here, so I could feed him his share.

Frannie!

You won't believe it. Hell, I don't know if I do! There IS someone ELSE here.

I was bedded down with the baby last nite and I woke up cause I heard somethin moving around by the still. A rat, I figgured, and I got all exsited. We ain't seen a live rat in two years at least. I got to thinkin about a mouthful of fresh meat and pretty near wet myself I got so wound up, but it wasn't.

It was a man!

I was layin real still, hoping that rat would come close enough for me to grab the little son of a bitch's tail or something, and I seen this huge shadow moving crost the floor. It come tween me and the heater, and I seen by the flames that it was a man-shape, real tall, moving quiet as a mouse.

First I was scared, so goddamn scared I couldn't move. I was froze up solid, but he didn't do nothing. He just squatted down and unwrapped the baby and he touched him all over. Feeling up his bones, you know? I thought maybe he was some kind of pervert or morphrodite or something, one of them guys likes to play with kids. Then I got to thinking maybe he was one of them canibals like I heard about down to Pocatello, and I wished to god I had me my big knife back.

But like I said, he didn't do nothing. He just looked and

touched and wrapped the baby up again, quiet as could be.
I couldn't even hear him breathing.

Then he come over beside me.

He pulled the blankets down and worked his hands
inside my clothes and he felt me all over just the same as
he done to Tommy, and even in the dark, with my eyes
closed, I could feel him staring at me. I was scared half to
death, but at the same time, I was sleeping, you know? Like
it was all, I dont know, a wierd fantacy.

But it was real, cause I could sure enough feel him
touching me, and I could feel the cold air on my skin where
I was uncovered. I could feel the warmth where he come
close. I could even smell him, like hot coffee cake.

And Frannie, oh, Frannie, he had hands like an angel.

All smooth and warm and tender on my skin, never
squeezing too hard like Julio does. When he put his hands
on my tits, it was all like a wonderful dream, and I did wet
myself, if you know what I mean. I couldn't help it. And
girl, if I could've moved. . . .

But I couldn't. I was froze and I stayed froze. And then,
just like that, he was gone.

I looked around, but there was nothing, not even a shadow. Maybe something scared him off, I don't know what.
We was all alone exsept for the baby. I layed quiet a long
time after, waiting for him to come back.

Jesus God, I pray that he will.

JULIO'S CALENDAR:

Julio says this is the sixteenth of March. I am writing
this for him because he can't stop shaking. He can't move
his leg either. It's all swole up where he cut it on the ice.

I asked him if he wants me to go get Billy Jo, but he
says no. He says I can't go anywhere near the canyon by
myself. I have to do something. Julio's awful sick, and I'm

getting scared. Maybe if I dig some more, I can find him some medisin.

Please, god, don't let nothing happen to Julio. He is my onliest friend. Amen, Megan.

ELLISTON'S JOURNAL:

I began to worry. Now that I had found them, how was I going to keep them?

A complete solution to the problem was simply not possible. There were too many factors to consider. Shelter, of course, was paramount, but so was food. There were also such amenities as clothing, weapons and tools.

And there were a myriad of dangers to avoid— radioactive hot spots, fallout, storms, and the new volcanoes. As I began to catalogue the dire possibilities, I was suddenly overwhelmed with the enormity of my task. How could I ever hope to protect this little band from *everything?* I didn't even know how to keep them from killing each other.

One thing at a time, I told myself. I would begin with the basics, food and shelter, and go on to the rest as needed. At least I didn't have to worry about protecting them from other humans. As I'd already proved, there were no others, not within two thousand miles.

There was, however, a Civil Defense shelter designed to hold a hundred people and stocked with ten years' worth of supplies for them. I had run across a news article on the counter in a doughnut shop, describing its many virtues. I can only guess the news clipping was left there by a survivor who did not succeed in reaching the place, perhaps the owner of one of the bodies I also found. For whatever reason, the shelter itself remained untouched, its approaches protected from the north by the volcano in Yellowstone, from the east by the Rocky Mountains, and from the west by the fallout plume from a reactor-testing station in the Lost River Mountains.

All I had to do was to find a way to get my protégés there.

MEGAN'S DIARY:

Today is the seventeenth of March. I think that's Saint Patrick's day. Julio keeps saying it is. He keeps grinning and asking me for some green beer. He pinched me too, because I didn't have any green clothes on. He doesn't either, but he says that doesn't count because his foot is kind of green.

Sometimes I can't figure out what he wants. He talks Spanish and calls me Margarita.

I am real worryd.

Dear Frannie,

Well, my ghost lover didn't come back yet. Neither did Julio. I am getting kind of hinky about that. You don't spose nothing happened to the little shit, do you?

Long as he's got the slut, he might leave me, but I don't think he'd let go of Tommy so easy. If he ain't back soon, I guess I'll have to go look for him. Ain't that the shits?

ELLISTON'S JOURNAL:

I dared not approach the woman again.

The very thought of her inflamed me and I could not take the chance of losing control. I went instead in search of the man. Surely there would be somewhere to leave the newspaper that would let him believe he'd found it on his own.

I flew across the river and lit in the center of what had once been Twin Falls, according to a dilapidated sign. The place was at least visible, for the most part. Some vagary of the wind had swept the snow aside and into the canyon instead of piling it up over everything. The outlines of streets were clearly visible and in many parts the drifts did not even reach the eaves of the houses.

There was no activity visible, however, and I prowled about with growing suspicion. Half an hour later, it was justified.

I found the man lying in a makeshift sickbed on top of his sled, sheltered by a canvas tarpaulin, warmed by a propane tent heater. He'd slashed up his leg somehow and the wound was badly infected. He was unconscious.

I tended him as best I could, though there was little enough I could do. The wound had already been lanced. It was heavily crusted with the draining corruption, so I dusted it with sulfa and rebandaged it. A small injection of penicillin was all I dared for fear of an allergic reaction.

There was no sign of the girl during all this. That struck me wrong. She would hardly abandon him for any length of time in his condition.

The town struck me wrong as well. A queer vibration of life prickled my skin, as if something long asleep had wakened here, yet the place was utterly silent.

Warily, I set out to track the child.

Dear Frannie,

Do you know anything about babys? Tommy's been awful fussy today, like he's got the colik or something. He threw up all over my hair too, the little bastard. Sometimes I'd like to just strangle him, anything to make him shut up.

He's sleepin now, but it took for ever to put him down.

Mom used to say the best thing for colick was caster bean oil, but I ain't got any of that around here. All I got is these goddamn potatas.

ELLISON'S JOURNAL:

The subtle air of wrongness pervaded the ruins. I found myself sniffing the air like a tomcat seeking the source of his amorous urges. There was nothing I could detect, however, only the snow and the sharp tang of cold rusted metal and a faint earthy odor, as of newly dug graves.

These two had been busy. I found excavations at half a dozen spots, slanting bores where they had drilled exploratory holes. Next to one of these, a toboggan had been loaded with all sorts of canned goods and blankets and what I think are called Moon Boots. I planted my newspaper in the largest box, then continued my search.

The widest, deepest trail led to what had been a block-size shopping center containing a grocery market, a video arcade and a small department store among others. There I smelled something more; the oily odor of grease-fed smoke.

In the depths, something flickered yellowly and the sound of careful scraping came creeping up to my ears. It stopped suddenly, with a squeaking noise and then a thump.

I entered, moving fast and silently.

MEGAN'S DIARY:

I don't think I ever want to be a nurse. It stinks, all the things you got to do, worse than Tommy's dipers even.

Julio's leg is real bad now. I hope he won't be mad at me. It got a big knot on it, a great big sore, all yellow and red, so I tooked his knife and cut the top off. All this yucky stuff come out and smeled terrible, but his leg is not so big now, maybe it will be all right.

I'm going to dig some more at the store. Maybe I can find some medisin for Julio. I don't like it much in there, it smells real funny and I feel like somebody's watching me.

ELLISTON'S JOURNAL:

The department store was surprisingly intact. Only the center of the roof had collapsed, leaving the corners somewhat sheltered. The tunnel I had chosen squirreled down along one wall near the back of the store and emerged into what was effectively a cavern in sporting goods. Except for the diagonal edge of destruction and the utter darkness, it could have been taken for a vignette of pre-war business design.

A pair of rag torches guttered from the end displays of two short tables full of fishing tackle. A row of glass cases marked off a counter area where rifles and shotguns leaned against their chains and a cheap billiard table, lightly dusted with snow, still proudly advertised its summer sale price of $299.

A familiar aroma rose from the scene: an odor compounded of damp potting soil and mold with just a hint of vinegary decomposition.

My hands clenched in spasms of panicked rage as I peered into the shadows and saw the one thing I had not thought to fear here, the one danger I had not considered. One of my own kind, his dark face ferret-thin, his cloak a sodden rag, leaned over the fallen body of the child.

Oh Frannie, I don't know what to do.

Tommy's got worse today. He stopped throwing up but now he's got the diarrea. The shit runs out of him like tap water outn a fawcet and he won't drink nothing to put any of it back. There was blood in it this morning and now he don't even have enough oomf left to cry, but I know he's hurting bad.

What am I going to do, Frannie? Tommy's all I got.

ELLISTON'S JOURNAL:

There was no time for subtlety. I rushed him headlong and butted him in the ribs. Together, we crashed through a case displaying dozens of fishing reels. The glass shattered in musical cascades and I felt a hundred broken shards prick my flesh.

He fought back fiercely but I had his arms caught up in my own and he could find no leverage to dislodge me. I squeezed with all my strength but did not move to hurt him, and at last he quieted a little.

"Kinsman," I told him, "I am your friend."

And I released him, stepping back, letting him see me.

"What do you want?" he demanded hoarsely and glanced at the girl. "Not her!" he grated. "This one is *mine!*"

"No," I answered calmly. "She is not."

At this he snarled and crouched, though whether he meant to leap at me or at her I could not say. I snatched a cue from the billiards table and cracked it like a whip against the cash register next to him. The thinner end snapped off, brittle with cold, and I was armed with a four-foot épée.

"Don't," I warned him.

"Mine," he rumbled dangerously, growling deep in his throat. His eyes glowed like a leopard's by firelight.

"I am not trying to steal her away from you," I told him, "but neither can I let you have her, friend. Please, listen but a moment. I'll tell you why."

Wary of the cue, he held his peace, but I could see the wheels turning. He was only waiting for me to drop my guard. I cracked the cue again, gun-shot hard. Another sliver flew off, leaving a perfect knife-edge tip. I jabbed it at him, to get his attention.

"*Listen!*" I ordered. "This one is not for you. Nor me, my friend. She is much too important for that."

And I told him of the other three, of the baby who might become humanity's new beginning, of my plan to rebuild the race. But when I spoke of that, he laughed.

"How many? Four?" he said. "Old one, are you mad? If you had forty, it wouldn't be enough to save the species. Surely you know enough of genetics to realize that." And he shook his head. "Humanity is already extinct, and these four pets of yours won't even last the winter."

"They can," I argued. "With our help."

At that he snorted incredulously. "You *are* insane. Do you think these cattle would take anything from *us*? They'd *rather* die!"

"What other choice do we have?" I demanded. "If we stand by now and let them die out, we'll pay a higher price than any of them. They die, but we do not! We simply go on. And if there are no more cattle to feed on, what then?

"We starve," I answered myself. "And we go on starving, to the end of days."

"Don't talk to me about starvation!" he snapped. "*I've* been trapped in this damned little hole for three years now, without so much as a mouse to feed me."

And he turned that furious glare on the unconscious girl. "By God or the devil himself, if this is the last taste I'm going to get, I'll damn well drain the cup!"

"Don't," I warned him. "You're dooming all of us to eternal hunger. Can't you see that? When these are gone, there *are* no more."

He ignored me. He reached for the child, his fangs gleaming yellow in the torchlight. His black eyes glittered as the fever took hold of him.

"*No,*" I commanded, forcing all my strength of will into one compact denial. Against his need and his anger, it was not nearly enough.

He took her arms, began lifting her body toward his own. Her head fell back, the mane of blonde hair swinging free, exposing the tender young throat.

"*Think* what you are doing!" I demanded.

And he clutched her thin little body to his chest. Delicately, he tipped her chin to one side. I could see the faint throbbing of her life, now inches from his mouth.

"*Stop,*" I said one last time.

He smiled and bent to take his due.

And I could not blame him. I knew too well his suffering, his need. I had done all I could to convince him, and I had failed.

I did not dare describe my further plans. How speak of them to this starving wretch? He could not possibly comprehend anything I said, not now, while the blood fever burned through his brain. I thought of the fantastic visions I had conjured while enduring this long winter's night, my hunger-haunted dream of a renewed human race and a rebuilt civilization, all of it this time, this time in ignorance of us, yet under our guidance, our dominion. Then, I wanted to tell him, then you'll have all you need. If you can only wait a little while longer, you'll be able to slake your thirst in perfect freedom.

How could I make him understand?

There was no way.

I lunged, and impaled him.

JULIO'S CALENDAR:

I do not know what day this is. I wake up alone, the niña is gone. Not far, I think. Her diary is here still. I read it, and I am afraid. If she has gone to Billy Jo, is bad. The woman is loco and she is too little to climb that clift alone. But if she dig in these piles of snow, is maybe worse. The snow caves in so easy.

Dios! Where is my strength?

ELLISTON'S JOURNAL:

The splintered end of the cue penetrated his shoulder but missed his heart. He screamed, wrenching the cue from my hands, and flung the child away. Then he turned, snarling, and leapt on me.

His strength was enormous, born of fear and multiplied by a terrible rage while mine was that of simple desperation. Thus evenly matched, we tore at each other, fang and claw, rolling across the broken floor. He was inches taller than I and that eventually became his advantage. First he shredded the muscles of my right shoulder and arm. Then, working bit by bit, he got his arms wrapped around my throat. He began to pull.

He could not hope to strangle me, of course, but his goal was plain enough. He meant to break my neck and then, if he could, tear my head from my shoulders.

I heard my neck bones creak, and knew I had nothing left to lose, especially time.

I groped blindly behind me for a weapon, a club, anything. And I found one. Not the cue, but the end I had broken off, a thin sliver of wood not a foot in length, yet so cold and brittle it was razor-sharp. I brought my knees up, shoving them into his groin, and when a tiny space opened between our straining bodies, I cradled the chalk-blued end of the stick in my good hand and shoved it upward.

The tip of the sliver caught him just below the breast-bone, sliding under sternum and ribs, tearing through lungs and diaphragm, finally piercing the pericardial sac and the heart itself.

Mortally wounded this time, he jerked upright, his body gone stiff and unbending as steel. He howled once, like a dying wolf, a howl that emptied all the air and all the life from him together. And at last, he fell.

JULIO'S CALENDAR:

I find her, thank God! Little Megan is ok. But she was not alone. I do not know how to say it, the name of the things I find in there with her. Brujo things, two of them. I think they fight over her, they tear each other up. When I come, they are pile together and one is rotted, but the other—Dio mio, I am sick to think of it even now.

I pick up Megan and I carry her out, but when I step around these things, the eyes of the one open. It looks at me

with eyes of fire, demon eyes. The one arm twitch and the
fingers scratch at the snow. The mouth open and I see the
wolf teeth like yellow knives.

I pick up bottles and throw at this evil thing, but it
moves, it hisses like a rattlesnake. I hold Megan close and
throw everything I find. The one bottle is the rubbing alka-
hole. I throw that down and then the torch. Fire flies in the
brujo face. The thing screams and I run.

After, the store, it burned for hours. It burns until the
snow melts so much, the water puts the fire out. I sit and
watch for hours, to be sure nothing moves in the ashes. I
hold Megan tight, and I cross myself many times. I wish to
God there is a priest to come and make this place clean again.

ELLISTON'S JOURNAL:

I understand now why Hell is always painted as a flaming pit. The burning agony of the blood fever is as nothing
next to true fire. That pain is indescribable.

I tried to cast for him but the man was too quick, too
frightened and the girl was still unconscious. The flames
raced through my clothes, feeding on the brittle remains of
my kinsman as he lay atop of me. I thrust him off and scrambled for the snow, plunging myself headfirst into the frozen
piles and drifts. That served to extinguish my clothes, but by
then the rest of the place was raging. The exit tunnel collapsed even as I started toward it but the snow did nothing
to quell the rising flames. It only trapped me down there
with them.

I turned to the other wall, behind the counter, scrab-
bling at it as the very floor caught fire. The paneling lay
over sheets of wallboard. I shattered them with blows of my
fist and tore a hole through to the other side. Then, my left
leg aflame again, I forced myself through it, into the dark
space beyond.

That space had no floor at all. It was a shaft of some

kind between the inner and outer walls. I fell, nails tearing at the smooth metal surface, and broke both legs like matchsticks when at last I struck the bottom.

Frannie,

oh Frannie, I don't know. I can't do anything, I just please, Frannie, can't you come? There's no one here. I'm all alone and Tommy, he's not

Oh damn it all

MEGAN'S DAIRY:

We are going home today. I'm glad, I don't like this place any more. I want to see Tommy. I want to sleep in my own bed. It's so awful cold out here.

Julio's leg is better, but now my head hurts. I was digging in the big store and something fell on me. Julio says I'm okay but he doesn't smile. I think he got scared too, almost as scared as me. He says I could of froze if he didn't find me. I can't ever dig by myself again.

I don't mind, I just want to go home.

JULIO'S CALENDAR:

Today is the twenty one of March. The first day of spring. We bury my son in the snow this morning. The ground is froze too hard, everywhere but the cellar. I can not put him there, so close, where I can almost touch him again. I think maybe I should burn him, so he does not become a brujo too, but there is not the wood to do this. I pray instead, and I bury my heart with the little one.

The woman says nothing now, and I do not know if that is good. She was loco before, writing all the time so many letters to her sister. The sister live in Denver, where the big bombs fall. She been dead three years, but still the woman writes, up to now. She don't write nothing since Tomás is dead.

I think maybe we are better going somewhere else.

In the bottom of the food box we bring back from Twin Falls, I find a piece of newspaper all folded up. There is a story and a picture about a place inside a cave, a lava tunnel where they have put all kind of food and medicine. This place is northwest from here, near a town called Rigby. If we follow the Snake River and take interstate, is about 150 miles. We can make that in two, three weeks with the things and the food we get in Twin Falls.

One thing I know. I don't can stay here.

ELLISTON'S JOURNAL:

Humans think we cannot be wounded, but it is not so. We can be hurt. Our limbs can be broken. Our flesh can be torn apart, or even dismembered. But we heal.

The greater the injury, of course, the longer the time and the larger the amount of energy required, yet we heal. I lay a long time in the crevice where I had fallen, letting my battered body marshal its resources. It took three weeks before I could walk, five before I could fly, and eleven to repair all of the terrible damage I had endured. I crawled out as soon as I was able and followed the man and the girl back to their cellar. By then, of course, the infant was long since dead.

For him, unnaturally, I grieved. It was his death, and not that of my kinsman, that pained me. I was cast into the blackest depths of depression and for a time I did nothing at all, only watching this forlorn trio from afar as they packed up their meager belongings. I had killed one of my own, and for what? I had saved one human only to lose another.

Still, the damage is done and I can only wait and watch while the seed I have sown takes root. Now that they have reached Rigby, they will at least have enough food to eat and

antibiotics and decent clothes. And last night I learned that
the woman is pregnant once more.

If this child lives, I will dare to hope again, to plan for
the future. Already the skies have cleared enough so that I
can no longer travel by day. The long winter's night is coming to an end. I need only patience.

But sometimes, my God, I am so hungry.

The Right Kind of Writing Workshop

by
Orson Scott Card

About the Author

Orson Scott Card has risen rapidly to a high ranking in the SF profession. His novel Ender's Game *and its sequel,* Speaker For The Dead, *mark the high point of his career to date. But his current success was preceded by a decade of producing increasingly well-received SF stories and novels. Clearly, we can expect that even greater recognition and accomplishment will follow.*

In addition to his prose writing, Scott Card is an experienced dramatist, having written, directed, produced and acted in a series of plays in his native Utah. And in addition to that, he has a growing reputation as a teacher; his interest in passing his craft on to younger artists is notable. He has taught at the Clarion SF-writing workshops and at Brigham Young University, the University of Utah, Notre Dame and other universities, and in connection with novice-writers' groups in many locales. A columnist for several prestigious magazines in the SF field, he also privately produces such publications as Short Form, *a periodical devoted to the criticism of SF short stories.*

We're very pleased that Scott Card has served as an instructor at the invitational workshops conducted for writers published in our anthologies. For the writers in Vol. III, he and Tim Powers were the instructors at Sag Harbor, Long Island, in 1987. In 1988, by the time you read this he will have repeated his valuable role, in the workshop we conducted for Vol. IV *writers, at Pepperdine University. Here's what he has to say about the W.O.T.F. workshop format . . . .*

Do you have to take a writing class to be a writer? Do you have to read books on how to write? Do you have to attend a writers' workshop?

No, no and no.

You don't *have* to do *anything* to be a writer—except write.

There aren't many professions as free as being a writer. Nobody has to give you permission to write. You are never too young or too old to be a writer. You don't have to get a diploma, you don't have to pay a fee or register with the government. The only thing you must have, besides your own mind, is something to write with—and you can get around that if you find someone to take dictation! You don't even have to get anybody's permission to *publish*. In a world full of photocopy machines and computer networks, you can send your stories out into the world for only a few bucks.

But the price of a writer's freedom is *risk*. There's no minimum wage for writers. There's no guarantee that an audience is going to like your stories. And if you hope to make a living from writing, photocopy and computer network publication can be terrific for putting out words, but they're lousy for bringing in money.

That's why publishing companies and distributors and bookstores exist—to put our works in the hands of the audience, then bring a share of the money back to the writer. Even then there's no guarantee that you'll get rich. That depends on how many people like the stories you tell—and therefore how many buy your books, or the magazines in which your fiction appears. Still, finding a publisher is pretty much the only chance you have to make a decent living as an independent writer.

Yet for every book that gets published and distributed, there must be a hundred, maybe a thousand, that don't. Publishers can only afford to publish books that will sell enough copies to make back the cost of publication. So they're looking for writers who know how to speak to a fairly large audience.

In other words, they're looking for writers who have mastered the basic skills of telling a story. Writers who have something fresh and important to say. Writers who can build on structures the audience is familiar with, but then take them to places that are new and strange, challenge them with fascinating ideas, or give them a deep understanding of marvelous characters they have never met before in literature or in life.

But where do you, a novice writer, learn how to write professional-quality stories? How do you master the skills and techniques that will make your stories effective—make them powerful, believable, and clear?

That's where writing workshops come in.

At the most minimal level, almost any writing class or workshop can be helpful: provide you with deadlines to help you discipline yourself; give you an audience that will actually read what you write and then talk about it. The sheer process of writing a lot of words and having them commented on by an audience is educational—you'll learn *something*.

That's the bare minimum, however. A workshop *can* be much more.

I first took part in a W.O.T.F. writing workshop in 1987, when I was one of the teachers at Sag Harbor, Long Island, just before the 1987 Hubbard Awards event in New York

City. I am also scheduled to teach at the one on the campus of Pepperdine University in Malibu, California. That will have happened by the time you read this, just preceding the 1988 Awards.

The participants are finalists and winners of L. Ron Hubbard's Writers of The Future Contest. The Malibu work-shoppers are the authors of the stories in this very book— you now know for yourself what good writers they are. As I approached Sag Harbor in 1987, to help teach the writers from *Vol. III,* the very fact that those folks had come out on top in the best writing contest I've ever heard of suggested to me that this was going to be an enjoyable workshop—even if it didn't actually accomplish much teaching, I thought.

The writers were as good as I expected. The workshop was even more enjoyable, on a personal level, than I had hoped. But what astonished me was how much more was accomplished in only a few days than most workshops accomplish in weeks or months or even years.

These were not my first writing workshops. I have been teacher and participant in dozens of classes and workshops over the years. Nor were the W.O.T.F. workshops the only good or effective workshops I've seen. But I can tell you that the Sag Harbor experience changed the way I teach and set a standard against which I judge all other writing classes. And if you ever teach or attend a workshop, the techniques developed for and used at the W.O.T.F. workshop are worth keeping in mind.

Why?

Because they *work*. They work for three reasons, the first of which is:

The Kind of Writing Teacher

There are two different kinds of workshops: ones with teachers, and ones without. Both kinds work basically the same way. A writer presents copies of the story to everyone in the workshop. All read the story. Then, at the next workshop meeting, all the participants take turns offering their responses to the story, both favorable and negative. The teacher, if there is one, usually speaks after all the students. Only then does the author get to respond.

The Writers of The Future workshop has many teachers, all professional writers. At Sag Harbor, Tim Powers and I taught; anthologist and novelist Marta Randall and I are scheduled to be co-teachers at Pepperdine. At the first pilot project workshop in Taos, NM, in 1986, the instructors were contest judges Frederik Pohl, Jack Williamson and Gene Wolfe. In London in late 1987, the instructor was Ian Watson. But all of the workshops have been led by a single director: Algis Budrys.

One of the leading writers—and certainly *the* leading critic—in the field of science fiction and fantasy, Budrys has the experience and knowledge to completely dominate a workshop—if he wanted to.

But he doesn't. A writers' workshop isn't a motivational seminar or a revival meeting. Writers tend to be too skeptical to accept even the most distinguished teacher as an absolute authority, and Budrys is too sensible even to *want* that kind of authority.

After all, the point of a workshop is for all the participants to learn the skills required to make their *own* stories work well. One of the most important differences between good workshops and not-so-good ones is that good ones help you get better at telling your own stories, and not-so-good ones try to force you to tell someone else's stories.

This is especially important if you want to write speculative fiction (science fiction, fantasy, horror). Many writing teachers, especially in college writing classes, have come to believe that there is only one kind of story worth writing, and only one audience worth writing to. This can result in an attempt to pressure students to write stories that they do not want to write—and to stop writing the stories that they care about and believe in.

The best writing teachers don't do this. They are open to all kinds of storytelling and all kinds of stories. They are not trying to teach you *what* to write, but rather how to write it more effectively. That is what Budrys' low-key style of teaching is meant to promote. People don't come out of the Writers of The Future workshop writing like Algis Budrys. They come out writing like themselves—only better.

If the teacher is supposed to keep such a low profile, why have a teacher at all? Certainly there are good workshops without a teacher—I attend one every year, the Sycamore Hill Writers Workshop, run by North Carolina writers John Kessel and Mark Van Name. But Sycamore Hill is a gathering of professional writers. When they tell me something about my story, I know I'm hearing the views of some of the leading writers in my field.

Gatherings of writers who have not yet been published don't have that advantage. Too often the blind are leading the blind. Without a teacher who actually knows something about how to write professional quality fiction, the participants often flounder about, multiplying their misconceptions and getting little closer to professional writing standards.

The real value in teacherless workshops will come from your examination of the other participants' fiction, as you struggle to understand what does and doesn't work in their stories. Because you already believe in, care about, and understand your own story, it's hard to see the flaws; in someone else's story, though, the very same problems can practically leap off the page.

A good teacher, however, can make the workshop many times more valuable. Look for teachers who have demonstrated that they know the craft. They have already walked part of the way down the road you want to travel. They are more likely to guide you safely around all the ruts, pits, and mudholes.

Curriculum

One of the most important differences in the W.O.T.F. workshops is the fact that there is a specific curriculum. Most workshops plunge right into reading and commenting on participants' stories, dealing with different subjects only as they come up by chance in the informal discussions. By contrast, Budrys brings up the most vital topics in an orderly way, not tied to any particular story in the workshop. Then as the participants read and criticize each other's stories—and re-examine their own—they have the most important concepts clearly in mind. There is much less confusion.

This seems so obvious—to alternate coherent lectures with free-form discussion—that I wondered why I had never thought of it myself, or even seen it in someone else's workshop. Maybe it's a sort of false modesty, as if by not lecturing we writing teachers are shyly saying, "Shucks, none of us knows much about this art. Who am I to presume to teach you?" Well, when you think about it, isn't that pretty silly? We writing teachers do know some things about writing, or we have no business teaching!

So ever since Sag Harbor, I've begun my writing classes with a series of lectures, and given periodic brief lectures throughout the rest of the workshop. The results have been pleasantly consistent. I thought I was a pretty good teacher before, but now my students are making far more progress during the course than they ever had before.

Not just any lecture will do, however. Budrys draws his lectures and methods from the writings of L. Ron Hubbard. Hubbard was not only the leading writer of popular fiction in the 1930s and 1940s, he was also one of the leading contributors to writers' magazines. His articles on how to write are forty or fifty years old now, but they are not at all out of date. In fact, I found myself a little annoyed that ideas and techniques I took years working out on my own were right there in articles published before I was born.

Budrys also uses some of Hubbard's more philosophical essays on art and literature. In this area Hubbard raised many important questions, and while I didn't always agree with Hubbard's answers, the resulting workshop discussion led all of us to think more clearly about what it is that writing is *for,* and what makes the difference between good and bad writing.

We no longer do our storytelling around a fire, with our tribe listening and laughing and crying as we speak. Now we do it alone in a room with a pen or a typewriter or a word processor. When you can't see the audience, can't feel the response they give, can't see how important your stories are in their lives, it's easy to forget that you're telling stories to and for *people*. Reading and talking about essays on the nature and purpose of our art gave us a chance to remember—or discover—that all our solitary labor is a vital part of life. A workshop that never strays from discussion of specific stories is missing a great chance to break down the loneliness of a writer's life.

Getting Outside

Perhaps the most startling technique in the W.O.T.F. workshops is the way Budrys, using teaching techniques developed by L. Ron Hubbard, gets the participants out of the meeting rooms and into the streets. The writers were sent out to search for ideas in the local library. They were sent out to observe the sights and sounds and *people* in the area. They were sent out to interview strangers and learn their stories—what had happened in their lives and how they saw the world.

Then the students came back with story ideas, written on three-by-five cards. They were assigned to work with some of the ideas, expanding and developing them—what I call *inventing* the story. They learned for themselves that the world is thick with story ideas; they also got practical experience in fleshing out an idea and structuring it into a workable story.

I had never before seen a workshop or writing class that was so effective in helping young writers in the work you do *before* you write. I have long believed that we do novices no favor by referring to what we do as "writing." That implies that the important work all takes place while the words are going down onto the paper. That is laughably far from the truth—the writing is the *easiest* part of telling a story.

I have long tried to help my students understand that the hardest work in the art of storytelling is inventing and constructing the story—most of which must be done before the words ever appear on the paper. Writers who *don't* invent and construct before they write usually end up with confusion or cliché. It's as absurd as if they were jockeys who never saw their horses until a few moments before the race, and then chose a mount by its color. You might have a pretty horse and a lovely uniform, but if you don't *know* your horse, you'll never get control, never get up to speed. The W.O.T.F. workshops give you experience in getting to know your horse before you ride—or, rather, to know your story before you write. I'm doing similar things with my own students now, and the results, again, are excellent.

The invitational workshop is one of the benefits of doing well in the W.O.T.F. contest—and a chance for talented young winners and finalists to get some professional training so they'll have a better chance to turn a Contest victory into a long, strong career. But the techniques that work so well in the workshop don't have to be limited to the contestants. If you're teaching or attending a workshop right now, there's no reason you can't adopt many of the techniques and attitudes I've mentioned here. There's no reason to settle for the "minimum" workshop, when the best is within easy reach.

There is a long tradition of writers helping writers, especially in the field of speculative fiction. We don't regard newcomers as competition—we welcome them as a new source of ideas and visions that help us all to become wiser and better storytellers. L. Ron Hubbard's Writers of The Future Contest exists because he was a vital part of that tradition, and the Workshop is a logical extension of his—and all the instructors'—desire to help young writers skip as much of the early stumbling and fumbling as possible, and quickly come to write at the peak of their ability. No workshop can bestow talent or the will to succeed or the kind of vision that leads to greatness. But if you have talent and will and vision, the workshop can help you learn how to reach your full audience.

The Troublesome Kordae Alliance and How It Was Settled

by
Flonet Biltgen

About the Author

Flonet Biltgen is a slim, tall, bright-eyed mother of two who works as a temporary secretary and is married to a computer systems entrepreneur. A few years ago, with college-age approaching for her children, she reached a decision to try writing as an additional means of income.

Flonet—her name combines Florence and Janet, her grandmothers—describes herself as walking in disguise through the world; outwardly a wife, mother and good neighbor, part-time athlete, folksinger and church volunteer, underneath she is a writer who has been warily observing humanity since earliest childhood. She began entering the Contest because it provided her with quarterly deadlines to meet, and was a steady entrant. Her win has brought an end to that, but, on the other hand, we have the pleasure of the following observations on humanity... and other sorts of creature....

Wishes may not come true, but if they do, then it pays to wish big. Therefore the name of the heir of the Duchy of Gormok was: He-Stands-Strong-Like-Oakwood-In-The-Face-Of-All-Enemies. And though he had certainly grown into a size to fit such a heroic name, everyone called him simply Oakwood. Or Woody for short.

He knew his future, and that sure knowledge gave the young swain great—one might say overbearing— confidence. And his future was this: to ever do his duty to his father and the King of the Lowlands; to maintain at all cost the alliance with the Barony of Kordae; to rule the Duchy after his father; and to provide little future dukelets in his turn. This was the whole of life that Woody had bothered to consider. Truly, what else was there?

So it was unsettling in the extreme for him to find himself on his knees in the hut of little Gulie the Powder Witch, his face a study in astonishment, his hands spread in confusion. Life had just complicated itself.

"But we planned to marry someday," he said. "And now my father has agreed for you to be my wife. . . ."

Across the small room the witch stamped her little foot. "*Second* wife!" she shouted. She whirled to her workbench, grabbed the first thing that came to hand—a pestle— and hurled it at him.

Woody warded off the missile with his forearms, dismayed. "But Gulie, my marriage to Bridda means nothing.

It's just to cement the alliance with the Barony of Kordae!''

Gulie fired the mortar after the pestle.

He ducked it. "This could assure the borderlands a future free of war. . . ."

A wooden spoon bounced off his chest.

"The King himself has heartily approved and even sent an emissary. . . ."

She threw a jar.

He batted it away, and a cloud of white powder filled the air and settled slowly toward the floor.

Ordinary people would be terrified of a powder accident in the house of a witch, but Woody was a hero. Coughing only once, he continued. "Then when I marry you, everyone will know the future Duke of Gormok has a witch for a wife." He knocked aside a heavy wooden bowl. "And no one will dare. . . ."

"Oh, *that's* my importance to you, is it?" shouted Gulie. "To frighten your enemies?"

She grabbed the broom from its place by the hearth and brought it down on his head as hard as she was able.

As every warrior knows, the danger is not the size of the enemy in the fight, but the size of the fight in the enemy. The dismayed suitor began a prudent retreat toward the door, warding off blows with both arms.

"But it all seemed so simple when Father explained it to me! Ouch! Gulie, can't you be reasonable?"

She stopped her beating, glared at him over the broom.

"Men!" she shrieked. Then bashed him once again.

The Duke's son was almost wholly out the door now. "I'll come back later, and we can talk," he said.

"Don't bother, I never want to see you again!"

She threw the broom. He made his escape.

Gulie, who up to that morning had been as certain of her future as of her fiancé, shouted to the still-open door: "I'll never be your second wife!"

She slammed the door shut. Still furious, but without a victim, she kicked the overturned jar. White powder puffed from it and settled again.

Gulie paid it no heed. It was only baking soda.

She stalked her small hut, lifting things from shelves and banging them back down again.

"Now, think, Gulie," she scolded herself. "There's always a way to get anything you want. Didn't Mother always say so?"

She thumped a jar onto the worktable.

"And what I want is Woody. I won him once, I'll do it again." She sagged a little. "But how?"

As Gulie continued around her little hut, rearranging her things with some degree of violence, the truth of her desires floated around her and crystallized. And the truth was, she did want Woody—in the long run; but for the moment, what Gulie really wanted was a fight.

And Gulie's mother had been right; people have a way of getting what they want.

There was a knock at the door.

"The witch is indisposed!" Gulie shouted.

The knock was repeated.

"The witch will have no business today!" she shouted louder.

Still, the knock repeated.

"Go away!" To emphasize her words, she seized an envelope of powder from a nearby shelf, dropped a pebble in it, and lobbed it out the window.

The powder was to make the recipient of its virtues break out in a pox the size of the pebble. Not a very evil curse but annoying, and Gulie felt a sudden urge to spread annoyance everywhere.

A mistake, she knew immediately. Evil is always repaid, even minor evils.

Still, regret does not put the milk back in the pitcher.

So, let it be. A pox on whoever was without. Gulie gave her head a curt nod.

But, there was a shout in the Old Tongue outside the window, and the envelope came flying back in.

So. There was a spells-witch outside her door, and Gulie had on hand only a few mild powders.

Still, nothing is gained by plucking half a chicken. Gulie threw open the door.

"Who comes disturbing the privacy of a witch?" she said with her best haughtiness.

Outside her door was a stern man-at-arms, looking silly in his breastplate and helmet in the hot weather. Behind him was a wonderful curtained car. Two long poles stuck out of it fore and aft. Between them, like so many draft animals, four muscular louts carried the car, two before and two behind. They looked surly from the heat and their burden.

There was a shout from the car, and Gulie's feet began to approach it, taking the rest of her with them. She muttered a curse, but only to relieve her feelings. Gulie knew no spells. She refined her estimate; the occupant of the car was not a mere witch, but someone with impressively swift magical reflexes. Powders would do no good.

Still, the water's no colder in the middle than at the edge. In with a toe, in to the neck. She raised her chin.

The curtains of the car opened and an old woman's face poked out, animated with curiosity.

The man-at-arms cleared his throat and intoned dismally, "Show respect, show respect, for Lady Light, Archwitch of Mog, emissary of the King of All the Lowlands, May His Strength Never Fail."

Gulie's eyes widened. "Ah! The King's emissary! It's you who came to arrange for the Duke's son to marry!"

The Lady in the car blinked.

"Show respect," said the man-at-arms irritably. "You've already displeased the Archwitch, and the doings of your betters are no concern of yours. Show respect.''

"And name yourself," said the Archwitch in a voice creaky and dry as Gulie's roof thatch. "I'll get to your punishment later."

Gulie made an exaggerated curtsy toward the car. "Welcome," she said. "You see before you Gulie, Arma's daughter, Powder Witch of Gormok."

"Welcome, is it? A fine welcome you have for strangers. Throwing pox, indeed. The younger generation has no manners, none at all. Fetch your mother."

"Alas, my poor powers do not include raising the dead."

"Dead? Arma's dead? How did she die?"

"An unfortunate and unforeseeable accident," said Gulie. "Two powders on the table, one to banish warts, one to give strength to the weakly ill. Mother sneezed; the powders conjoined; and she inhaled the cloud of them. And disappeared."

"Powders always were undependable," said the Archwitch. "Then, who's the Witch of Gormok?"

Gulie stood as tall as she could. "I am."

"Bah. Nonsense. You're too young." She peered at Gulie. "You *are* young. Or are you spelling your age?"

"Yes, that's it," said Gulie. "I'm six hundred and forty-six, but I spell myself to appear seventeen."

"I see. But it's not a good idea. Nobody respects a young witch. Me, I'm twenty-two. But I appear to be fifty."

"Sixty," said Gulie.

The Lady frowned. "Whelp. And you just a powder witch. You need to be taught a lesson. I came to pay my respects to the resident witch as a visitor should. And you greet me with pox. Inexcusable."

"That wasn't my fault," said Gulie. "If you want to be treated like an important person, you might announce yourself so. Your man didn't say a word to make me think it was

Illustrated by Frank Kelly Freas

anything else but somebody with hives looking for a powder. And I have problems of my own today.''

"No excuse. Besides, I haven't done anything mean in at least a week. It makes me grouchy." She took a thoughtful look. "I think I'll make you a frog."

Gulie didn't hesitate. "Good!" she said with relish. "I've always wanted to be a frog! I'll hop to the moat of the castle Mog and live in frog heaven eating the flies that rise in clouds from the King's own filth. And at night I'll sit outside your window and serenade you sweetly in thanks. Hurry with your spell, come on." She stamped one foot.

Lady Light scratched one hand with the other. "Well, that's not much of a punishment after all," she said. "Perhaps we'll make you a ghost."

The man-at-arms drew his sword with as much noise and flourish as possible.

Gulie didn't even look at him. "Even better!" she cried. "I'll make the best ghost you ever heard of. People will talk of me in fear three kingdoms away. And guess who I'll haunt?"

Lady Light stared a moment, looking stern. "Bah! I haven't time for this."

She pushed back her sleeves. "You were stupid, whelp, to incur the wrath of an archwitch like myself, who is known far and wide for the ability to summon demons."

"Demons!" said Gulie. "In exchange for a pox you didn't even catch? There's a word for such a person, and it's not 'archwitch.' Shall I say it?"

But Lady Light was ignoring her. Deep in concentration, she shakily began an invocation, made only a few hand passes, and—

A cloud of smoke-that-is-not-smoke appeared between them. Gulie stepped back. Then something materialized from the smoke.

It was incredibly ugly. It's features swam and folded so

there was no telling what it looked like because it changed
constantly. But every formation was very, very ugly.

"What is it?!" she wheezed. She tried to move farther
away from it, tripped on her own feet and sat down hard in
the dust.

Ignoring Gulie's squeals, Lady Light addressed the
thing.

"Behold, knowing thy true nature, I say thy true name:
Clumsiness."

The thing writhed and whimpered.

"By the magic of this day art thou bound forever, until
death release thee."

The thing twitched and tweeted.

Lady Light pointed to Gulie. "By this thou shalt be
bound to the world. Be it so!"

The thing made a sort-of bow in the direction of Lady
Light, and settled itself on its pig-like haunches at Gulie's
feet, gazing up at her worshipfully.

Gulie stared at it, shut her mouth. "Clumsiness?" she
said.

Lady Light was looking smug. "An affectionate thing.
Likes human company. And not malicious. It can't help its
nature any more than I can mine, and its nature will be a
permanent annoyance to you, whelp. You will remember
this day."

Gulie almost laughed. "You cursed me with *Clumsiness?*"

Lady Light's composure slipped just a bit. "I *could*
have summoned a demon. But you're too unimportant for
such a spell."

"No, no, you're right, I need a good lesson! Take this
thing away and come on with your demon!"

Lady Light's mouth puckered as though her wine had
turned to vinegar. "Don't tempt me."

"But I *am* tempting you. Do your worst! Or is this it?"

The Archwitch shook one bony finger at her. "Believe me, you will be sorry you raised my wrath! Only my good nature saves your miserable life now!" And with an angry gesture she signaled to her man. He put away his sword and ordered the car turned around.

Grunting with effort, the bearers seemed to have a great deal of trouble with the maneuver.

Now Gulie did laugh. "Please, allow me to escort you," she said, leaping—stumbling—to her feet and crowding close to the car, Clumsiness right behind her.

Both bearers at the rear dropped the shafts at the same time. The car struck the ground with a satisfying crash and a string of curses. If bearers were witches, Gormok would have been rubble. Lady Light yanked the curtain aside. It ripped.

"Begone from me, you whelp! You! Get her away!" She gestured to the man-at-arms.

He drew his sword, slicing a bit off his sleeve, stepped toward Gulie and dropped the sword. It clattered over the ground toward one of the bearers who had just picked up his end of the car again. He flinched as it struck his shoe, and lost his grip. This time the other man kept the car from falling, but it dipped and joggled, and Lady Light gave a most unladylike exclamation.

Gulie laughed, held up both hands and stepped back in surrender.

Fuming, the man-at-arms retrieved his sword and followed the car down the street and out of range.

Gulie sighed and regarded the Thing closely, thinking.

It was abominably ugly. Looking at it long made her sick to her stomach.

"This has not been my day," she muttered.

But potatoes do not pick themselves. She squared her shoulders. Walking carefully, she returned to her hut and began to sort her powders.

In only a few minutes she had upset a shelf, broken an earthen bowl, and spilled half of everything. Gritting her teeth firmly, she called Clumsiness out of the house and walked it down the hill.

Gormok nestled comfortably against the Duke's castle like so many piglets against a fat sow. Gulie's hut was in a favored position near the castle wall. So she had to cross through the town to get to the woods.

As she moved down the street, Clumsiness trailed in her wake. Birds crashed into trees. Squirrels fell off limbs, dogs bumped into walls, cats tripped. Women dropped their babies.

To this epidemic, Gulie was not immune. She had bruised both knees and stepped on the hem of her dress several times before she reached what she thought might be a safe place.

A good forty paces toward the woods from the last hut, she turned to the Thing and pointed to the ground. "By me art thou bound to the world," she said. "And I bind thee to this very spot, right here, until I come for thee."

And she turned her back and walked away.

When she'd gone a little distance, she glanced back over her shoulder. Clumsiness sat where she had bound it, gazing after her mournfully.

Back in her hut, working as quickly as she was able, Gulie concocted an Invisibility from her powders.

When she was barely finished, the Thing was back, moaning with loneliness. Obviously its need for companionship was stronger than Gulie's power to command it. Sighing, and careful not to spill too much, she cast some of her powder on it.

The Invisibility didn't exactly make Clumsiness invisible, but it suitably distorted the effort of the eye when directed toward the Thing, so it became uncomfortable to gaze right at it. When Gulie forced herself to do so, she saw only a mote of disturbance as will rise above a hot stone on a sunny day.

"That's better," Gulie said to it. "But now I must think of some way to release you back into your own world. Lady Light's curse was quite specific. 'By the magic of this day thou art bound.' So I have all day to concoct some magic to free us of one another. Ouch!" She had bitten her tongue.

She began to sort her powders, setting aside those that had possibilities of long-range power in happy combination with others.

Of course, she was frightfully clumsy through the sorting. But as she began to understand the level of care the task required she spilled less. Still, the extra concentration wore her out. She began to feel irritated. And the day was heating up.

A polite knock drew her attention to the door.

It was Woody, his handsome face drawn into a scowl.

"Gulie, we have to talk," he said. He brushed at a fly that was hovering around his head, and poked himself in the eye.

"Bridda, my bride to be, has arrived for the betrothal ceremony. I haven't mentioned you to her, so I hope you can compose yourself and greet her as a citizen of Gormok."

Gulie gasped. "You came to say that?"

Woody blinked. "Did you expect something else?"

"I expected you to apologize!"

"Apologize? Me?" said Woody. "You're the one who went crazy and threw me out of your house." He sounded hurt.

"I thought you loved me!" said Gulie, almost a whisper.

"Love is beside the point. Can't you understand a political alliance?" His left stocking fell into a puddle around his ankle.

"If alliance is all you want, let the wench marry

your brother, He-Is-Never-Lazy-But-Fights-Like-A-Bear-For-
Truth.''

"Gulie, Lazy Bear is only four years old. Anyway I'm
the heir to Gormok. It's my duty.''

"What about your duty to me?''

"You're being totally unreasonable.''

"And you are heartless! None of this is my fault!''

Woody drew himself up importantly; his spine crackled. "Remember, my father is a very mubborn stan. Uh,
stubborn man. If he hears you have turned me down, he
might be insulted. And I can't say he'll accept you at all in
that case.''

"Fine! Take your father's orders like a good boy!
Ignore the one you *say* you love! And *you* remember, I will
never be your second wife!''

Woody's eyes narrowed in anger. "You'll come to your
senses, and then we'll see!''

"Don't hold your breath!''

He turned on his heel—stumbled—and strode off
toward the castle.

Gulie was smoldering. She turned to the mote of disturbance floating behind her.

"By me art thou bound to the world,'' she said. "And
I bind thee to—*him!*'' And she pointed at Woody's retreat-
ing back.

A mote of disturbance, unremarked by anyone, drifted
up the hill after the Duke's son.

Gulie smiled wickedly and nodded. A satisfying solution. Woody would cut himself shaving. Trip on stairs. Spill
his wine. Bruise his political wife. In negotiations he would
stutter. He would drool in front of ambassadors. Fine picture.

But another picture crossed her mind, a moment so
sweet and fair it glowed like a jewel in memory—she and
Woody in each other's arms, a momentary paradise so

tender and so private that surely no one ever before had been so close and so happy.

She loved him. Simply. Completely.

Stupid, short-sighted *man!*

No, she could not leave Clumsiness with him. Besides, her binding before had been only temporary. The Thing would come back to her eventually, because it was bound by the magic of this day. And Lady Light's magic was stronger than hers.

Gulie dropped herself onto the little bench outside her door with the same kind of violence she had earlier shown her pots and pans.

If only she'd paid more attention to her mother's teaching. Foolish child that she was, she'd thought she had all the time in the world to learn the mysteries. Who could have predicted her mother would leave poor Gulie alone at such a tender age?

Then her head came up. It was a poor rock, after all, that could not be made into a hammer. If she couldn't get rid of the Thing, maybe she could find some way to make it useful.

With this new thought, Gulie went back inside to try a new attack.

But before she was organized, there was a knock at the door. Better disposed toward such interruptions since the morning, she answered it.

Outside were two women, both veiled and hooded despite the noon heat. Someone who did not want to be recognized at the witch's door.

"I don't have any love potions today. Come back tomorrow," Gulie said.

"If you please, good Lady," said the taller, and unveiled herself, casting furtive glances up and down the street. "Please give welcome in your fine home to Bridda, the Future of the Barony of Kordae, May Its Orchards Ever Bear.''

"Bridda!" exclaimed Gulie. "You!"

"Not so loud, you want the world to know?" said the shorter woman. She peeped out of her hood, dark brown eyes intense with emotion and puffy from tears. "You've gotta help me!" she said in a desperate whisper.

Intrigued, Gulie stepped back and welcomed them into her hut.

Bridda's story was told in moments. Having heard it, Gulie sat back on her stool and straightened her back. "So you think this swain of yours—Lunk, is it?"

"Lunt. Lunt, the Miller's oldest son."

"You think this Lunt will still want you after all?"

The young Baroness turned her face upward in rapture. It actually glowed. "Oh, yes, Lunt loves me, I know it as I know my own breath. I must get out of this marriage! I must get the Duke to release me! Lady, give me the powder I ask for! Make me ugly! Make me so ugly the Duke's son will beg to be released!"

"Believe me, I want to help," said Gulie, with heartfelt sincerity. "But I have it on the best information the Duke's son is not marrying you because of your beauty. Besides," she scowled, "men are perverse. You shouldn't be so sure of Lump."

"Lunt. But I am. I am sure. Oh, Lady, have you never been in love?"

"Yes," said Gulie. "Which is why I say, leave nothing important to the strength of a man's love. But be at ease. I think I have just the thing."

She found the Invisibility among her powders. She measured some onto a bit of yellowed paper which she folded into an envelope. "Take this. Dust it over yourself, and I believe the Duke and his son will think new thoughts about the marriage. But be sure you do not use it until just before you march down for the betrothal ceremony in all your finery. Understand? No, no coin. It's my gift to you, and I hope it works.''

Eyes shining with gratitude, Bridda took the envelope.

When they were rehooded and gone, Gulie laughed. "The worst storm always brings flowers, eh?"

Singing to herself, she returned to her powders, confidence renewed.

Ignorant of the set of his new bride's mind, Woody was pacing his father's armory. The young duke-to-be had always liked the drafty, high-ceilinged place, all full of graceful deadly instruments, heavy tools of mayhem, and, usually, sweaty swearing men. Since reaching the height of his portly father's belt buckle, Woody had known that in this place he would learn everything he needed to know about ruling the Duchy. And ever since, he had worked diligently at it. Now, despite his youth, no arm in all the Lowlands could match his for quickness, accuracy, and brute strength.

But, alas, Woody now confronted a problem he could not batter or hack to size. Angry, he sought direction among the familiar tools of the knight's trade.

As he paced, he muttered. And his most frequent muttering was: "I am the heir of Gormok." And then, "I have a duty." And often, "Stubborn witch!"

Behind him constantly was a peculiar mote of disturbance in the air. But he was too preoccupied to notice.

He had been pacing long enough to work up a sweat and turn his anger to frustration. He paused in his trek before a one-handed battle axe which was beautifully wrought, but too heavy even for Woody's sturdy arm, and therefore hung like an ornament beside a row of practice shields.

"Gulie, why must you be so stubborn!" he suddenly cried aloud, and struck the wall with his fist. Hard.

The axe fell; fortunately, it missed Woody's foot.

Unfortunately, it planted itself solidly in the floor so close to his foot that when Woody tried to step back from the accident, he found his foot caught under the handle. Off balance, he threw out both arms, staggered, swung around the pivot of the trapped foot, and splayed himself backwards against the wall.

And the row of practice shields. One by one, like the generations, each clanged into its neighbor and took it down. One by noisy one.

In the mighty silence that followed this demonstration, Woody stood a moment against the wall in a posture of twisted crucifixion, amazed at the damage. Then he carefully leaned down to pull the axe out of the floor—with his left hand. The middle knuckle of the right was split and bruised from hitting the wall. Grasping the haft, he gave a mighty jerk.

The axe came loose much easier than Woody had imagined. He pulled upward too hard, lost his balance backward, and then the weighty axe pulled him forward again. Somehow his feet were clumsy in the fallen shields. Afraid of falling on the axe, he tried to move it safely away; but its awkward balance defeated him. As he approached the floor, he could only throw the axe aside with both hands to keep it out from under him.

He broke his fall with his face.

The axe skidded across the floor and collided with a bundle of pugil sticks stacked neatly next to a barrel of arrows. All went down.

Woody raised himself carefully on his elbows, and looked around the ruins in astonishment.

"This has not been a good day," he said, and found that talking hurt. He reached for his face and found the left side to be insulted and tender.

Like his heart.

He sighed a mighty sigh as Truth settled on his

distracted mind with the all gentleness and irrevocability of an avalanche.

"I love her. Say what she will, I love her, and I will have her for my wife. Somehow."

But how? How to persuade a witch?

Woody smiled. It hurt. "With a witch, of course!" He bounded energetically to his feet—

—slipped and sat down hard.

Afternoon was wearing on. A discouraged Gulie wiped her delicate brow with her sleeve and gave in to the fact that she was hungry. And she was still without a powder to control Clumsiness. Rummaging in the cupboard for a stale biscuit, she wondered when Lady Light's notion of 'day' ended. The Druids said, at the last shadow. The Lunarians said, with the first ray of the moon—which was odd on days the moon rose with the sun. But anyway you count it, she must not have much time left.

How humiliating it would be to have to trek to the castle and ask to see Woody. Not just to receive Clumsiness again, but because the lout undoubtedly would think she had come to see him.

The worst part of it all was that she had spent all her energy on a cure for the curse, and hadn't thought of a single thing to do about the wedding. And the betrothal drew nearer. True, Bridda would be invisible, and Woody clumsy, but knowing Woody's father, it would not be enough. The Duke was a very stubborn man. There would be a wedding.

A tear almost escaped one eye. But she blinked it back. Stones do not bleed, and witches don't cry. She still had her pride.

A firm and sudden knocking turned Gulie's head toward the door. She had left it open because of the heat.

Silhouetted against the glare of the afternoon sun was a

sturdy man-shape. "Be you the witch?" said a strong young voice.

"I am," said Gulie. "But I'm not available today. Come back tomorrow."

"Cannot," said the young man. He glanced up and down the street, giving Gulie a look at his profile, of which the kindest thing that could be said was that it was strong. He stepped inside and closed the door behind himself.

"And I have silver," he said.

He produced a scraped-leather pouch which jingled once and disappeared again into the folds of his tunic.

"Silver is the last thing I need today. Please come back tomorrow."

The man hesitated as if her words were some foreign language. Then he stepped closer and whispered, "Need poison."

"Oh, really?" said Gulie, who was just about to the point where poisoning somebody seemed like a real good idea. "Why?"

The young man's face tightened and he seemed about to cry, which alarmed Gulie. If witches don't cry, young men built like bridge abutments certainly did not. "Cannot live without Bridda!"

Gulie's eyes widened. "Say, your name wouldn't be Lunk, would it?"

"Name be Lunt," he said. "Miller's son. From Kordae."

Gulie stood. "Wonderful. This is wonderful. There, there, don't grieve yet. We'll make things right. Yes, maybe we can make things right. I happen to know that there's going to be a snag in the wedding plans."

Lunt brightened visibly. "Be true?"

"Oh, yes. And if you are there to speak up for Bridda, who knows?"

"Cannot," he said dismally. Then he raised two fists like soup pots. "Will fight!"

Gulie patted a fist amiably. "No, that won't work. All you have to do is stand up to the Duke at the right time and demand the lady's hand. Can you do that?"

Dismay sank the youth's shoulders. "Cannot speak well. Cannot speak to the Duke. Bridda be lost. Give poison!"

Gulie sighed.

"I have just the thing for you, Lout."

"Name be Lunt."

"Whatever." She turned to her powders.

She lifted several, brushing labels, squinting at her awkward printing, finally selected two. She measured some of each onto a bit of her yellow paper and folded the paper into an envelope.

"Take this. You must swallow it just before Bridda's betrothal ceremony. You must wait until the last minute. Understand?"

Gloomy but brave, he took the little packet into his big hand. "Understand," he said letting himself out into the brilliant afternoon. "Will see Bridda once in fine dress before I die."

Gulie muttered to his departing figure. "Will not see Bridda. But will find yourself a lion of courage with a suddenly very glib tongue."

She wiped her brow. "Things may work out after all."

In the west wing of the castle—the fine wing, reserved for honored guests—Woody was explaining his problem to the King's Emissary, Lady Light, Archwitch of Mog.

The Archwitch was fascinated. Not by the story, but by the handsome young swain. There was something about him. She had spilled her tea twice since he began talking. And there was this clouding of her vision occasionally as she looked at him, almost as if something had come between them.

Lady Light gave this reaction the only interpretation she could: she was infatuated with Woody. And the more she thought about him, the stronger her infatuation grew.

"So, can you help me, Lady?" finished the delicious young man, oblivious to the fact that his fate was closing in on him.

Lady Light smiled a shark's smile. "So, you want a love-spell for your bride? Is that it?"

"No, Lady," said Woody politely, ready to explain it all again. "Bridda will be my wife for duty's sake. I don't need a spell for her."

"Then what? Tell me exactly."

"A spell to make Gulie accept Bridda."

A dagger passed through Lady Light's small heart. "Gulie?"

"Yes," said Woody, embarrassed. "The girl I love."

Lady Light narrowed her eyes. So, the powder witch is the one who's turned his head, she thought. Whelp. She who dared to suggest Lady Light could not really raise demons.

The Lady smiled again. "I can arrange it," she said. "Wait here."

Lady Light bumped against the tea table on her way out of the room, and upset a candlestick. But once in her closet she moved deftly. Among the things she had transported from Mog were several teas, potions and simples.

Lady Light selected a tea leaf from her hoard, one whose natural properties would calm the mind. A simple sleep aid. Laying it carefully on a candlestand, she incanted strenuously over it for several minutes.

Her spell intensified and distorted the natural property of the leaf. When she was through, instead of calm before sleep, tea from the leaf would instill blind obedience.

"So much for you, rude powder witch. Not only will you accept the wench, you'll be her slave. And serve you right."

She laid the leaf on a sheet of parchment.

Then the Lady took a key from a chain around her neck and opened a locked cask. From it she took a vial of powder.

Now, usually spells-witches eschewed powders as being weak and unreliable. Lady Light would have cringed if anyone found she used even one. But this particular powder was so special to her that she was never far from it.

It would make whoever it touched fall helplessly in love with her.

She had used the powder several times, each time on a handsome youth. Each time, the youth had left everything that had formerly been of importance, and spent all his time pursuing Lady Light, mad with love. Delightful.

But the ungrateful things had a way of dying just when she was getting used to them, most by their own hand. She couldn't understand why. Maybe they were of insufficient moral fiber to begin with.

Woody seemed to be a stronger sort. Certainly worth testing.

Carefully, she sprinkled a liberal amount of the dreaded powder on the leaf. Then she folded the parchment into an envelope.

Cackling with anticipation, she returned to the room where Woody waited unsuspecting.

Stepping through the door, she tangled her foot in the rug and sprawled. Only Woody's quick reflexes kept her from falling flat on her face. He tried to place her gently in her chair, missed twice, and finally managed to get her seated.

The Archwitch was not upset. She liked the strength of Woody's arms, and the incident only let her see more clearly what she had to look forward to.

Grinning, she indicated the envelope, which had fallen on the floor. "Take that," she told him. "There's a leaf inside. Boil it long in just a little water, make an infusion. You must do it yourself. Understand? It's very strong. Only a few drops in your lover's tea will do the trick."

Woody blushed to hear Gulie referred to so. The flush set off the bruise on his cheek. Lady Light grinned her shark grin.

"But, mind, the leaf is coated in a powder to protect it from spoiling. Be sure you wipe it off carefully before you brew it. Understand? Use your fingers, they're much more reliable than a brush. Understand? Brush the powder off the leaf yourself."

"I understand," said Woody, delighted. "Thank you, thank you so much, Lady."

"No thanks necessary," said the Archwitch. She enjoyed Woody's exit; he bumped the doorway in his charming enthusiasm.

One floor above, Bridda, the Future of Kordae, sobbed into the pillows of her mother's couch. She seemed to cry all the time lately. Her mother, the Widow Kordae, sat beside her, helplessly stroked her daughter's hair, and crooned the palliative of all mothers of all time:

"There, there, it'll all come right."

Bridda pulled her head away. "Don't you care for me at all? Don't you listen? I am in love! How can things come right for me and Lunt if I'm married to Oakwood of Gormok?"

The Widow, distressed, wrung her pudgy hands. "Ah, but Gormok is a strong Duchy. And the Duke is such a stubborn man. Don't forget, the King himself has suggested the alliance. Kordae is such a small barony. How can we defy the King? Kordae has always been loyal. Why, when your father was alive. . . ."

Bridda punched the pillows with her little fists. "Father could have thought of a way out of this!"

The Baroness was hurt. "Bridda, dear, I've only done my best. Of course I'm not the man your father was. Why, I'm not a man of any kind. And that's the problem, dear. Men always have the say in the world, and women must do their duty. Try to be brave."

Bridda stared. "Brave!"

The Baroness wilted at her daughter's hard gaze. "What else can we do, dear?"

Bridda leaped up off the couch. "Well, there's something I can do! And I'm going to do it! If you won't stop this marriage, I will!"

And turning with a great swish of petticoats, she stormed out of the room.

The baroness, erect on her couch, continued to wring her hands. Her maid, discreetly unaware of the storm, entered and curtsied in readiness to follow any order that might be forthcoming.

"This is my fault. She was always a spoiled little thing," said the Baroness.

"Yes, mum," said the maid obediently.

"But I spoiled her out of love," said the Baroness.

"Yes, mum."

"Love. It gets people in such trouble. Riles up the blood. I never loved the Baron, rest him, and look how peaceful our life was. How quiet. How . . . dull."

"Yes, mum."

The Baroness signed. "Bridda is my only daughter. If I could, I'd do anything to make her happy. But what can I do? Oh, my stomach! Mard, fetch me some tea, and my stomach powder."

"Yes, mum," said Mard, the maid, dropping another obedient curtsy. And she quickly headed down to the kitchen.

Outside, in the shadow of the castle wall, Lunt the

Miller's Son took out the yellow envelope of powder that Gulie had given him and thought about the death he believed it carried. He gazed mournfully at Bridda's window. Without Bridda there could be no pleasure in life. When Bridda agreed to the Duke's son, Lunt's life would be over. Sad as any lover had ever been, but less articulate, he moaned his misery to the cold stones of the castle.

Then a thing happened, a marvelous thing, so unusual as to be almost miraculous. Slowly but surely as the sun's rise, something grew and formed in Lunt's mind: he had an idea.

"We'll run away!" he cried. Once the idea entered his head, he was as helpless to turn aside from its execution as a moose in rut. Bold as only the doomed can be, he strode manfully into the castle, forgetful of the yellow envelope in his hand.

Within minutes, he was lost in the castle's irregular corridors.

Mard, the maid, was returning from the kitchen with a small tray on which she balanced a small tea pot with satisfying wisps of steam drifting from its snout, other tea things, and the pink envelope containing her mistress's stomach powder. Rounding a corner, she was surprised by Lunt standing in the middle of the hall, confused and shifting his weight from foot to foot. They gazed at one another a moment, dim recognition beginning to dawn on each.

Then Woody, energetic as always, appeared striding purposefully down the hall.

Mard glanced at him, then did a double take, recognizing Bridda's future husband, and tried to drop a respectful curtsy under the tray.

At the same moment, Lunt turned to see who approached. Recognizing his rival, he was frozen in surprise. Something told him this was an opportunity, but his mind was working much slower than Woody's energetic feet. He could only turn to watch Woody move past them.

But when he turned, he bumped Mard's tea tray. She moved with it, trying to keep the tea things from falling, and banged the edge of the tray into the wall. Lunt reached to steady the tea pot, and his large hand swept the cup and saucer onto the floor.

Mard and Lunt stared into each other's eyes across the tray, Lunt apologetic and Mard furious. Woody, used to people stepping out of his way, moved on down the hall without a glance in their direction.

"Clumsy oaf!" scolded Mard. "At least you can pick up what you dropped."

"Oh, of course." Lunt went to his knees and retrieved the cup and saucer. Fortunately, they were of chased brass and almost indestructible.

"And there's my Lady's stomach powder. Find it."

Lunt went back to the floor and came up with an envelope.

"Fine, then, and be more careful around gentlefolk!" she said.

Lunt, properly chastised, stood with his empty hands dangling and watched her climb the stairs. She was right. A castle was no place for a man like him. He decided that maybe the direct route to the lady of his intentions would be more his style. He made his way back outside.

Mard, meanwhile, fussed over the tea tray, making sure everything was in place before she presented it to the Duchess. She blew gently on the yellow envelope of stomach powder in case it had picked up any lint on its journey to the floor and back.

She paused. Yellow? Wasn't the envelope pink? Oh, well.

She knocked on the Duchess's door.

Minutes later, Lunt appeared in Bridda's window. This was no small feat, since she was housed on the third floor, and the stones of the castle wall were fairly well set, affording only fingertip holds. Besides, the wall had overgrown with blackberries that no one had been inclined to remove. Scratched, bruised, strained, but ardor undimmed, Lunt finally tossed one elbow over Bridda's windowsill.

There was a frightful wailing and weeping going on in the room. But the room was empty.

"Bridda?" said Lunt.

The wailing changed in tone. "Oh, Lunt, my darling, darling Lunt!"

Lunt pulled himself wholly onto the sill. "Bridda, where are you? I've come for you. We run away!"

"Oh, Lunt!" came a voice from nearby. "I can't go with you! I'm ruined! Ruined! Oh, that miserable witch!"

Lunt waved his hand in the direction of the voice, bumped something.

"Look at me!" said Bridda's voice. "I'm invisible!"

Lunt almost fell out the window.

Next door, the Baroness's stomach powder had worked its usual magic on her ailment. In fact, it had worked better than it ever had. In fact, thought Mard, it had made the Baroness a new woman.

"Conniving men!" said the Baroness. "What do they care for us? Nothing, that's what. Love? What's that to a man? Nothing, that's what."

She paused for another sip of tea.

"So the Duke wants an alliance, does he? And the King, another *man,* wants it, too, does he? Well, what about me? Eh? And what about Bridda? Does any *man* care what she wants?"

Alarmed, Mard curtsied. She didn't know what else to do. She had never seen the Baroness in such a state.

The Baroness set the tea cup down firmly. "Mard," she said with such strength and confidence that the astonished maid curtsied again like a knee-jerk. "Mard, go at once to the Duke. Tell him I am coming immediately to see him.''

"The Duke!'' said the distressed Mard. ''But. . . .''

"No buts,'' said the Baroness, which brought on yet another curtsy. ''Tell him I am coming. Don't ask. *Tell* him.''

"Mercy on us!'' said Mard. She performed another dip on the way to the door, which was not a curtsy but a weakness in the knees. And dutifully, she headed toward the Duke's side of the castle, to confront that stubborn man as she had been commanded.

Downstairs in the kitchen, Woody was creating a minor sensation. True to form, he was totally unaware of it. The chief cook, curious as to why the young lord was in his kitchen, and a little miffed at the same time that one of the upstairs crowd should have imposed on his bailiwick, had made a polite and pointed overture to the young duke. Was there something, sir? No, Woody had said. Oh, maybe a small pot.

So the cook had made a small pot available and then left the duke's son alone. But he wished the young master would leave; his presence seemed to be having a negative effect on the kitchen staff. Since his appearance, several bowls had overturned, a large sack of flour was dropped and split, and the soup chef had allowed the Duke's first course to boil over into the coals, which cooled the fire and would probably ruin the new bread. The chef cast one more of several cloudy looks at the Duke's son.

Woody, however, paid no attention to the stir he was causing. He had only one thing on his mind; the witch's packet of magic. He was eager to set free its secrets.

Boil in a small amount of water, the witch had said. Woody could follow orders. He set his little pot to boil at the edge of the great hearth.

Of course, there were other things cooking in the great hearth, and several of the chef's minions scurried about it tending the evening feast which was a-borning thereon. Woody was in everyone's way. Besides that, the day was very hot, and the cook fire had heated up the kitchen unbearably. Everybody was irritated.

Except Woody. Excited, he took out the witch's envelope.

Gripping the paper in both hands, he gave it a tug—

The envelope ripped suddenly in two; the powder and the leaf within it splashed in a cloud before Woody and rained down in a snowdrift.

On something.

Around Woody, noise and bustle stopped. Everyone stared. Briefly, something was covered with the powder. Something was there, something short and piglike and ugly, staring at Woody.

Woody blinked.

The thing seemed to shake itself—

Then it was gone. There was a puddle of white powder on the kitchen floor.

A cook's assistant, a young boy with a bad complexion, turned to Woody, eyes wide, and said, "Did you see...."

Then he realized he was talking to the heir of Gormok and made a quick bow from the waist.

"I'll clean it up, sir, don't worry, I'll clean it up!" And the lad fairly flew to the nearest broom.

Woody bent, and with two fingernails and a daintiness unusual for one so constructed as himself, he delicately picked up the witch's tea leaf by the very end of its stem, tapping it twice against the floor to shake off the last speck of powder. He dropped it carelessly onto the nearest table and moved to check the progress of the boil in his little pot.

The cook's assistant reappeared with a whisk broom and pan, eager to show off his ability. Untouched by human hands, Lady Light's powder was dumped on the compost heap.

Satisfied that the water was boiling almost hard enough, Woody stepped back from the heat. He turned his thoughts to how he might coerce Gulie into sharing a cup of tea with him. Thinking about Gulie was totally pleasurable, now that he had the witch's potion to make his wishes come true.

Life, Woody mused, was good.

A commotion distracted his reverie.

"Immediately! The Duke himself sent word, tea immediately! The Baroness of Kordae has made a call, and he needs tea NOW!" The chef punctuated his words with sharp blows of his pudgy hand.

Woody backed up another step as the kitchen help mobilized into a frenetic level of activity that amazed the Duke-to-be. In moments a lordly tea service was assembled and on its way to the Duke's quarters.

Thinking he might commend the chef and his staff, but some other time, Woody turned to the witch's tea leaf, excited.

The leaf was gone.

Three floors above, in the Duke's sitting room, the Duke glowered while the Baroness of Kordae continued to expound. Exhausting woman! The Duke held his tongue only because of years of training in the lordly arts—and because this exasperating lump of femininity was the key to the alliance on his northern border. But she was trying his short patience.

With a discreet knock, his chamberlain entered with the tea service. The Baroness chose not to notice and continued her speech. The Duke watched as tea was poured for himself and his guest.

"Therefore, my lord," said the Baroness, putting her two fists together and plumping them into her lap with great resolve. "Therefore, I suggest this marriage be rethought."

The Duke had not been listening. But he heard that. "Rethought?" he said, smoldering. "What is this? Rethink the alliance?'' His countenance darkened dangerously, and he turned upon his visitor the glare that had shriveled the emissaries of kings.

The Baroness was unmoved. She waved one small hand. "I realize the importance of an alliance. But that's not the discussion. I find that Bridda's happiness is more important to me than any alliance. We must rethink this marriage.''

The Duke's face reddened further. "I'll rethink it right now," he said with dangerous menace. "The alliance will be cemented immediately! The usual waiting period will be waived. Oakwood will marry Bridda tomorrow! How's that for rethinking!''

"That is not at all what I had in mind," said the Baroness. "You're not listening, sir. Please pay attention and I'll tell it again.''

The Duke choked.

The chamberlain, used to his master's moods, gracefully raised a cup and saucer.

"Tea, sir?'' he said calmly.

The familiar move distracted the Duke. He took the cup and tossed back a quick mouthful.

The chamberlain retreated to his place against the wall. He knew the Duke, knew his tempers. The tea might forestall the rage, but nothing would save the Baroness from what would come next. The duke was a stubborn man. He would have his way with the Baroness as he always did with everyone. Too bad. They were about to become in-laws; it was not a good way to begin such a relationship.

So it was a very astonished chamberlain who marched dazedly from the sitting room a short time later to announce to the page:

"Assemble the staff. There will be a wedding. The Duke is going to marry the Baroness!''

Later, in the late shadows of sunset, Gulie and Woody

were sitting on the little bench in front of her hut. It was a very little bench, and the young people were forced to sit very close together, but they didn't seem to mind. They were focused on each other rather completely.

Woody giggled like a schoolgirl as Gulie told him how grateful the runaways Bridda and Lunt had been when she showed them how to remove the Invisibility. And Gulie laughed heartily as Woody described his adventures while in the company of Clumsiness.

In fact, they were so involved with one another that a visitor might have had to break a bottle over Woody's head to get his attention.

"By the way," he said into a lull in the enchantment. "Whatever happened to Clumsiness?"

Gulie laughed, completely content. "I don't know," she said. "But if it comes back—" she laughed, and Woody laughed with her. In their present condition neither could imagine anything dire.

In the west wing of the castle, Lady Light sighed into her pillow. Hopeful that she may have finally found her deathless love, she had retired early with a sleep potion of her own concoction, to dream of her coming affair with the young Duke. A faint smile curled her bitter lips as she slept.

"Ah, Woody," she muttered.

On the headboard of her bed, Clumsiness perched, invisible. It sighed with her, throbbing with love from the top of its ugly head to the bottom of its little pig feet. It couldn't remove its ardent gaze from the object of its affection. The very thought was painful. No, never would it leave the side of this woman, to whom it was bound.

Forever.

In her sleep, deep in her dreams, Lady Light brushed at her own lips.

And scratched them.

Growlers

by
Larry England

About the Author

"I feel that being selected as one of the Writers of The Future is not only an honor, but an adventure that I will try to take as far as I can," Larry England told us. It is an honor his story earned him; the attitude he brings to it is, we think, one of the right ones. Life and art are nothing without exploration.

Old enough to have two grown sons living independently, Larry England began in the arts as a young cartoonist, and has worked extensively in that field, from doing newpaper cartoons to designing inflatable punch toys. After going to work as an artist for educational television, he became interested in video production, has since taught video graphics, and video and graphics, and now teaches video to high school students in Minnesota.

In 1982, he began attending a writing class, whose members he thanks for encouraging him and lending moral support. We thank them, too.

What follows is a realistic war story. It is paradoxical to suggest that it might make you feel better about things. But it might.

DAY EIGHTEEN

Six Growlers, recon squad, from Slime Stompers Company on patrol. In lead is Spirit Devil, just sniffing out danger, trouble and woe. Spirit Devil has re-upped three times and been in the field longer than anybody. He *knows* Slime and he *knows* how they think and what they'll try to do to us. Pee-sticks, snipes, set bombs. Spirit Devil *knows* through his nose, his pores, Ned, maybe even through his hair. We're all glad he's walking lead, 'cause he big, he mean and he ours.

Next is Baby Doll, our top dog, looks like he just a baby, maybe he was in the not-so-long ago, but here and now he's all guts and gristle. When he say hump we hump. When he say, "Drang!" we say, "How deep?" Not a Growler in our squad wouldn't walk through Hell for him and then ask for a return ticket.

I'm right behind Baby Doll, his shadow, his second-in-command, only I don't command, I'm too young, silly, and irresponsible. I watch him like a Antivillian Leaf Hopper, 'cause I know I'll keep my guts on the inside if I follow his lead. They call me Yip Yap, 'cause I like to talk and I know life is too short to take serious. The only thing I put high on my agenda is sucking air. Let's keep Graves and Registration away another day.

Behind me is Doctor Minus. He's on our side, but I do

watch him close. He been around killing too long and he went and got too good at it. When he goes out at night, the next morning Slime is minus personnel. Sometimes we're minus too. So we got to keep him pointed at the Slimes. Go get 'em, Doc.

Shank was double-timing in behind the Doctor. He's the guy that if there's a way to mess up, he'll find it. I'm amazed that he hasn't checked out already. Pa Pa doesn't put Growlers in places where they can mess up too often and keep sucking air.

Bringing up the rear is Attention Brodie. He called Attention because he believes everything headquarters puts out. He won't even get in out of the rain, which this pee-lucka of a planet has plenty of, unless headquarters issues him an order. Most Growlers know we do the work, take the chances, but we *know* what's going on. Just the opposite for headquarters. They don't do the work, don't take the chances and they don't know a drang what's going on. End of case.

A danger signal.

Spirit Devil says to Baby Doll, "Something's breaking. Don't know what; just feels funny ahead."

We all stop. Bunch up. Baby Doll says, "Keep spread out, you drang-heads. Want to make it it easy for the Slime?"

We spread out again. Baby Doll motions us down. We collapse onto the ground. He turns to Spirit Devil. "Move around. Check it out," and he turns back to us and says, "Keep alert—even though we on break."

I loosen my field pack same as everyone else, except for Doc Minus who never relaxed since he been born. "We're Slime-stomping, killer-diller, woman-thrillers," says Shank as he pulls some liberated fruit out of his pack.

"Hey, Minus," I call out. "You got any halluciblast left?"

"Suck on your Walloper!" Doctor Minus comes back.

I know he wouldn't share his drang, let alone any halluciblast, but I have a bad habit of pushing to see what might happen.

The Walloper that Minus referred to is a Pa Pa issue Z-18 Walloper, over-and-under full automatic blaster with a hot light and prolar-casing shells. Cost the taxpayers twenty-nine hundred S per and to me was well worth it. My Walloper was my companion, my good buddy.

"It can keep you alive when your friends let you down," they said back in Basic. "Keep it clean, soldier, keep it clean."

If you didn't believe that line when you started, you sure as Ned did when you finished. A Walloper could grind Slime up faster than a Whir-a-Mix on purée. I saw a few Slime, when we first hit planet, that had been caught in Walloper fire.

Slime are exactly like us, only different. For an example, I stand at nine G four and weigh in at an even three hundred and twenty N, and you could say I'm no giant and you'd be right. Just a snok under average. I make up for it with raw courage and being a wiry Prince. Now I never saw or heard of a Slime that stood over seven and a half G or weighed more than maybe two-fifty N. Right there is a good difference. Another, of course, is what their skin feels like. Just enough difference to disturb you. Yee-uck.

What happened was, we were crossing a field. I hadn't been planetside too long and here were these two Slimers strung over a wire fence. It looked as though they had been trying to crawl over when some Growler caught 'em in Walloper fire. The Walloper put punch-press holes for entrance wounds, but the exit wounds were big enough to stick your head in and look around without getting your hat wet. They were both wearing liberated Growler uniforms cut down to fit and both carried Growler weapons. I knew the only way they got their gear was off the cold dead bodies of brave

Growlers. Being X'd out with your own weapons wasn't a great thought.

I was close to the bodies, eyeballing them. I'd never seen a Slime before, let alone a dead one. Ned, I'd never seen a dead anything before. My stomach was starting to turn like a mixer full of bad soup, but my curiosity kept pulling me closer. Suddenly, Doctor Minus, who had ghost-stepped up behind me, grabbed my wrist with the speed of a heat ray. "Here, Yip Yap," he said, "Feel them. See what the enemy feels like. Touch a Slimer, baby."

Minus was as thin as death, but he was as strong as a slink cat. My palm flopped over onto the arm of a dead Slime. I could feel, even in death, the moisture on the skin. I yanked my hand away and looked at the fingers that had touched the dead arm. There on the tips were two damp Slimer stains. It was then that I finally started to throw up. If I could have done it on Minus I would have been glad to, but he was too fast. When I was bent over, losing it, I could hear him off somewhere laughing like a maniac. Until then, I'd never known that he could laugh.

I guessed I knew why they were called Slime then. The feel of them never seemed to leave me. I dreamed about them over and over. These little Slime, with damp bodies coming at me, dozens of them, all grinning, all with Growler weapons. I could see that they knew some black secret that I didn't know. They'd raise their weapons and I'd wake up. Eyes wide, mouth open, a scream locked in my throat, and then I'd hold up my hand again and I could always feel the moisture, no matter how many times I'd cleaned myself.

"Something out there, Baby," says Spirit Devil; he slides into sight. "Couldn't see anything, but I feel something." He pokes his stomach. "Right here. Thought for just a micro I saw some kind of flash. Don't know now," Spirit finishes.

Baby Doll squints into the hot sun back across from where Spirit Devil has just come. "You know H.Q. wants us to recon all the way through the swamp and see if we can still get over the causeway." Baby Doll looks into Spirit Devil's eyes with his innocent baby eyes. "We can't sit here . . . forever."

"We can always go back," I say.

Baby Doll gives me a look that would burn a heat ray. I shut up quick.

He turns back to Spirit Devil. "We go on. We pretend there's someone out there and we go as careful as a tri-legged drim." He looks, searching for a clue in Devil's face. There is only resignation there.

"We stop once we reach the swamp and we call our location in." Baby Doll turns to the rest of us. "Everybody got what I said. Move out. Move like every Slime on the planet is out there. Hump, hump, Johnny Cake." He waves us forward, we cinch up and follow his lead. Twenty paces between each Growler. All loaded up with the bolt home. All with the drang scared out of us. But all willing to follow our leader. Because Pa Pa had picked us to go and kick ass, and we were trained and paid to kick ass better than any outfit in the whole by-God Universe.

So that's what we did.

We move single file across a field of saw grass, twenty paces apart for two thousand L and move into the cool, wet, mucky, ucky swamp. Pa Pa didn't send Growlers to no vacation spots. Nobody ever seemed to need their ass kicked in a resort, and if they did we'd turn it into a rubble heap anyway.

"We hold up here. Attention, call H.Q. and report where we are," Baby Doll says. "Rest of you can relax."

Shank gets up. "While you girls are relaxing, think I'll go take a drang." He picks a sheaf of home newspapers out of his pack and moves into the dark trees.

About two minutes go by and we hear a clamor coming through the underbrush right at us. Five bolts snap home, all at the same instant. Shank runs into the clearing. Baby Doll knocks Minus's gun down. Two dull thuds as mud geysers into the air. Doctor Minus and Baby Doll glare at each other, veins standing out on their necks. Suddenly, it's over. Shank stands there with his mouth hanging open, staring at the two holes in the mud which are slowly filling with swamp water. "You almost got yourself Xed out. Announce yourself! Follow procedure! Stay alive!" yells Baby Doll, Minus forgotten.

"Great Ned . . . I, oh, yes." Shank tears his eyes away from the two muddy holes in the ground. "Action taking place across the field, sir." Shank points back the way he'd come. "Better go and take a look."

Baby Doll turns to Attention, who's finishing his call to H.Q. "Attention, bring the Vid-Lid. Let's take a look-see." He motions for us all to follow, which we do, but cocked and ready.

We reach the clearing that Shank indicated and Attention sets up the Vid-Lid. Something is taking place far across a field. The Vid-Lid will tell us what.

Attention aims it and turns it on. Snow, crackle, and the picture comes to life. There is a giant transpo-grinder/stomper, nine crew and full armament, bearing down on a lone Slime running for his life. It was a deluxe anti-personnel grinder/stomper and fired three hundred and fifty plasto-cased shells a maxi-micro. It costs the old tax-payer seven hundred and a quarter S and that dog could really move out on its land-grabbing tires.

The Slime is running and dodging like a maniac. The grinder/stomper wails off a volley and the Slimer disappears in a huge cloud of dust and smoke. Dust clears and the Slimer, he's gone. Can't be seen anywhere. Suddenly, two

Slimer, he's gone. Can't be seen anywhere. Suddenly, two Slimers pop out of the long grass *behind* the grinder/stomper, they both got Joy Juice bottles in their hands, flashing in the sun. They are just like the one I'd finished for breakfast and tossed into the bushes; maybe one of them is the same one. The Vid-Lid shows a flame dancing out of each bottle.

"AMBUSH!" yells Baby Doll. Seems weird three Slimers can ambush a seven and a quarter S grinder/stomper. "Quick, call that stomper. Warn them . . . NOW."

Attention punches coordinates for the stomper, but too late. The Vid-Lid shows the two slimes throw their Joy Juice bottles, a giant wheel goes up in black curling smoke. The undercarriage, poof, flames, gray smoke. The turret guns begin to turn toward the Slimes, but the wheel is throwing hunks of burning material, falling apart and not tracking right.

The Slime that I thought had gone down, rises up out of the weeds with his own Joy Juice bottle. He chucks it straight at the front of the stomper. Flame gushes out. A hatch opens, a figure starts to get out. It looks like a match burning. His mouth forms an "O."

The stomper's thermal tanks explode. A micro later a dry thump reaches us. The stomper continues to turn in a circle and there is another explosion, throwing pieces of stomper and men five hundred L away.

The Slimers stop once to look at their handiwork, then they turn and disappear back into the swamp.

We all just sit there dazed and helpless, watching the destruction of a stomper before our eyes.

"It's a good thing that was a top-of-the-line stomper went after that Slime. Anything less wouldn't of lasted that long," I say. Baby Doll shoots a look at me that freezes my mouth open in mid-word.

* * *

DAY TWENTY

"Fifty-nine P worth of our liberated garbage and three measly Slime ambush a marvel of engineering with a full crew," says Spirit Devil. "I can't believe it." He is laying in his bunk with his hands behind his head. Shank has a halluciblast pellet in my helmet in a half a G of water and we are breathing the fumes, my shirt tented over both of our heads. Doctor Minus is more hard core, he just zipped a pellet straight into his nose. He's sitting there with a glazed-out look on his face.

Attention is sitting on his bunk trying to clean the mud out of his boots down to the treads. "Those Slimes are slimes," he says.

Shank sticks his head out from under our tent and says, "We shall have our revenge. We're killer-dillers and Pa Pa wouldn't have sent us to this slime-infested planet if we couldn't kick ass on these backward bastards from Hell."

"The only weapons they have is our own liberated garbage," I say, taking a heavy suck on the blast. "Hell, if we guarded our garbage dumps the Slimes would be weaponless."

"Seen 'em use liberated Narcette cans as mortars," says Spirit Devil. "They use Zip-Dip cans filled with blaster paste as mines. Work really well too. Seen ten Growlers go down humping across a field because of pee-sticks. They sharpen a bunch of sticks, poke 'em into the ground, below the level of the grass. Sticks been dipped into pee-lucka or drang or both and boom, you got blood poisoning. Slimes don't lose much personnel that way, either."

A voice drifts out of Doctor Minus like a soft wind. "I kill 'em, but I love 'em. They're real Growlers. Just as much as us. War's for the Growler. Growler's can't be beat. If we got a real enemy . . . it's the leaders."

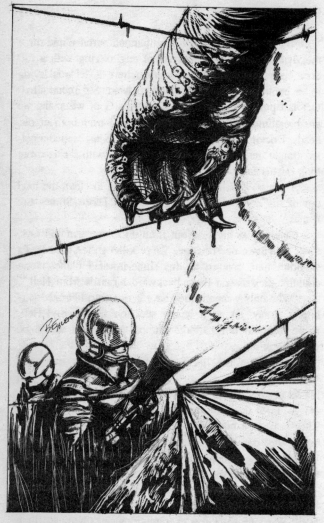

Illustrated by Bob Eggleton

DAY TWENTY-SIX

Slimes blow the causeway in about seven different spots. At the end of the causeway is a city, old and delicate, looking like something out of a fairy story. We wouldn't have a city that old. We'd have torn it down and rebuilt it, new and shiny. When a building gets old, zip, it's yanked down and a parking lot is put up. This city is on a big river; maybe one day it was a great port . . . today, it's a battlefield.

We had to push the Slime back through the great swamp, herding them toward the city. Always danger, trouble and woe follow us. Shank got into trouble because of his ass. Too bad, too sad. He decides to take a drang while we're up to our knees in the swamp. He walks off a few L into the deadly swamp, away from the protection of his friends. Suddenly with a roar a huge swamp monster rises out of the stink and muck. It has a mouth full of teeth and has to be almost twice as long as a person. Zingo, it grabs old Shank by the arm, ripping and tearing, and drags him underwater. We open up like maniacs on it, killing it dead-o, but that doesn't help the Shank. We finally find his body, got some good teeth marks in his arm, but the beast had drowned him. I always knew he wouldn't make the long haul.

I think about the long haul a lot.

The city is like a fragile flower as we penetrate its outer borders. Only about ten micros after we enter the city I turn a corner, look, and there's a Slimer, he's got a Narcette can set up. A huge fwoomp and I feel heat pass by my ear. Doctor Minus blooms into flame and he goes down burning. I look down into his crazy-with-pain eyes and he locks in on me with his eyes. Now I never believe in telepathy, but in that micro, Doctor Minus sends me a message.

Before I can think I answer his message with a burst from my Z-18 Walloper into that thin writhing chest. I know that both the enemy and us are better off without Doctor Minus. My brain tells me that, but I can't seem to take his face out of my mind. Not for very long.

My first kill on the Slimer's planet and it is one of my own squad, but I put one into the win column when I turn around and drop a steady stream of shells down the street through the building and see them eat through the Slimer. He tumbles onto the stone street. I walk over very slowly and look down. It wasn't much of a sight. It was just a kid, not quite into adulthood. Small, wearing Growler pants tied with a rope, Growler shirt tied at the waist, and a knapsack. Two canisters of blaster paste had rolled out of the knapsack. They were stencilled: SLIME STOMPER COMPANY.

Not much of a trophy. Seemed about the same age as me. But my first enemy kill.

Baby Doll comes over. "You handled yourself well."

"Sure," I say, not convinced.

"You looked like one of Pa Pa's Growlers."

I say, "And that's where I want to stay. Footloose and fancy free."

Doctor Minus's eyes told me it was all right to drop shells into him, but the Slimer's eyes held no message that I could read.

We thought we K-bombed them into oblivion, but they stole our garbage and dug in. We sent Growlers in to mop them up and they just dodged around and fought harder. Where was the winning?

If you weren't winning, were you losing?

DAY TWENTY-NINE

We spread out through the city. Blow old buildings,

incinerate others. Rubble everywhere, bodies everywhere. Slimes and Growlers. Frozen in death. Growlers are bigger, but it was difficult to tell one from the other. Somehow everyone seemed the same size when they were laying cold in the rubble.

DAY THIRTY-ONE

We continue to push through the city. Slimers hide and shoot, hide and shoot.

Spirit Devil and I are fooling around, wrestling, shoving, fooling around. Growlers sometimes fool around to keep from screaming. That's true. He calls me an ass-wipe and then he says, "I gotta get back to sniffing out Slimes," and then he grabs his Walloper and slides around a corner. I get up to cast an eye after him. We got to watch out for each other. They mean us harm here.

I see a Slime step out from a collapsed wall of wood and stone directly in front of Spirit Devil, as though he just was going to say good morning. The Slime is carrying a zip-shot made from a stomper's antenna with a rubber band firing pin. He holds it like a pencil.

I'm starting to call out.

A small pop. Spirit Devil jerks like he was slapped. Another Slimer steps out and points his zip-shot. Pop. Another jerk from Devil; he tries to bring his Walloper up, only his hands don't work so good anymore. Pop. Spirit Devil drops hard onto his knees.

I'm running forward, I hear a roar and it is me screaming. I try to get my Walloper unslung and clip in place. The Slimers bend over Devil. I look away for a second to slap the bolt home and I look back up, the Slimers are gone. I point my Walloper. Nobody, but Spirit Devil on his knees. I hear the wind. I come over to him and look down; three small spots of blood on his jacket. Like a messy kid when he's eating, but he's no more. His Walloper and shells are gone. Ready to go after Growlers.

His expression says he knows a secret he will never share with me. I want him to tell me, but he won't.

DAY THIRTY-THREE

In camp tonight we get three replacements, re-pee's. I think that maybe we have an endless supply of re-pee's. I know there is an endless supply of Slimes. We kill 'em and kill 'em, but they take us with them before they go. It is their world, why do we need it. H.Q. says we are winning. Growlers say we're not. Growlers *know*.

I don't think I will get to know any of these re-pee's. I don't want to even know their names. No.

DAY THIRTY-FOUR

There is a wall of flame in front of us. It's at least eight V high. Waves of heat pour out of it, frying the world. Our Squad of Growlers are about one hundred and fifty L from it. We couldn't get any closer without frying our ballarenos.

We have a wall of flame in front of us because we were walking down this street and came to a square. Attention was on lead. Whang. One sound. Attention goes down like a sack of laundry. Like he never existed. I see him go down and I think, it's their damn world. It's a drang-hole. Who wants it? H.Q.? The taxpayers?

But there is a sniper out there. We are stopped. Something *does* have to be done. Baby Doll points out three more

lumps of laundry out there. Fresh kills. Not stripped of clothing or weapons. Naughty Slime sniper. Four Growlers Xed
out, he has to go and I want to do it, but Baby Doll says,
"No. We'll do it the safe way." He turns to the squad and
calls out, "Pie Face, get on the horn and give them the coordinates for that row of buildings." His hand makes a sweep
indicating the buildings across the square. "I want those bastards incinerated to the ground."

"Yessir. Incendiary fire. You got it, sir."

Pie Face? I wondered who in Hell he was. I couldn't
remember seeing him before. A stranger in my squad, talking like he knew what he was doing.

The kid gives the coordinates and soon the explosions
begin to walk across the square. Pillars of destruction walking on legs of flame. Pie Face confirms when they are onto
the buildings and then they go in huge waves and blossoms
of fire.

"We aren't going to walk any more Growlers into the
path of that sniper. We'll let the taxpayers foot the bill for
fried Slime instead of Xed-out Growlers," says Baby Doll,
scanning the smoldering ruins of the buildings on our Vid-
Lid.

Baby Doll snaps the Vid-Lid closed. "Nothing could
live through that. Let's move on out." He rises and gives a
hand signal to the rest of the squad. "Nothing is ever a picnic. So be alert."

You can say that again, Baby Doll, I think, and then
say, "Pa Pa don't send no Growlers on no picnics." I slip
behind Baby Doll, keeping twenty paces between us.

The squad moves out.

Whang! Whang! Baby Doll goes down. I run like a bolt
snake, hook Baby Doll under the arms and slide into an
incendiary crater, still hot. We both roll to the bottom. I was
too fast for the Slime. Some weren't so fast. Out of my

peripheral vision I see two re-pee's crumple. The rest scramble behind debris.

I wonder if one of those that got it was Pie Face. I hope not.

A river of blood runs out of Baby Doll's chest, a sucking chest wound. Not close to a picnic. No.

I hold his head in my lap. He looks up at me with a look of a bewildered child. "How could anyone not be fried in that Hell?" he asks me through bubbling wheezes. "How?"

I rock him like a baby in my arms, making little noises to him like a mother makes. I can't answer his question. I got no answers for anybody, not even myself.

"You got to get our Growlers safe," he burbles.

"I can't," I answer; my words sound flat. Heat from the earth warms through my pants bottom. "I don't know what to do. I'm just a kid."

I hear the squad open fire. They're blowing apart everything left standing across the square.

"Great Ned, I'm scared," I say to the person I hold in my arms.

His hand reaches up and touches something wet on my face. "You're drowning me," Baby Doll says and he coughs like a maniac. Blood starts to come out his mouth. "You're two W older than me, Yip Yap. You now head of the house." He coughs worse than before, breaking my heart, and then he's just this beat-up uniform I'm holding in my arms and I want to scream real bad. I don't scream, not just then, not in front of my Growlers.

DAY FORTY

We move on out and we kill Slime and they kill us.

When Baby Doll Xed out on me I looked into his dead kid eyes and he shared a Growler secret with me. We were winning the battles, but we were losing the war.

I look around at the Slime's world. I see their prairies, their swamps and their cities. They live here. It's their world. They're fighting for their world. It makes them fight harder with less than we do. They make us pay an awful price and they're winning.

I look at their burnt, charred city and I know they'll rebuild. I look at a twisted street sign and I know it'll be replaced after we're gone. I know that the sign that reads "Bourbon Street" will stand again, because I know the Slimes are Growlers in their hearts. I know how Growlers would fight if it were our world. That was my Growler secret. We were going to lose the war because it cost too much to win. It wasn't *if* but *when*. H.Q. didn't know this yet, but the Growlers *knew*. Growlers always knew. Growlers can't be beat.

What Do I See in You?

by
Mary A. Turzillo

About the Author

Mary A. Turzillo is a college professor, long active in scholarly inquiry into SF literature, who has published books on Philip José Farmer and Anne McCaffrey. But, from the age of 16, she had occasionally been trying fiction as well. In 1985, she was a Contest finalist, and came to the 1986 W.O.T.F. workshop in Taos, NM, as someone whose entry might very well have been anthologized. This was among the criteria we used for that pilot project.

In due course, like a striking number of her other class-mates, Mary began producing quite a bit of attractive new work. "What Do I See in You?" took Second Place in the first quarter of the year, and here it is.

At various periods in her life, she has been heavily involved in theater, as a costume-designer, actress and play-wright. She is also a published poet. At the present time, the writing group she co-founded in the Cleveland area includes W.O.T.F. authors Jay Sullivan and Ken Schulze, has Paula May as a corresponding member, and also includes Astrid Jul-ian, on whom more later in this volume.

Mary has directed educational tours to Shakespeare fes-tivals in the U.S., Canada and England, walked across the Grand Canyon three times, and climbed Mt. Whitney twice. The following story, then, may well have gained from all these perspectives . . . .

On a mountain ledge on the northern continent of Aeyrrhi, a man and an eagle quietly conversed.

The eagle was not quite an eagle. Her name, in English, was Wing Before Others. She was *Aquila sapiens,* the only female of her species. Her feathers were a glossy tawny brown, shading lighter toward gold on her head and tail. Her face was not quite an eagle face; it was broader and showed intelligence quite beyond any natural raptor's. She was twice as large as the eagles she had been bred from, and had never flown in Earth gravity. Early pregnancy made her heavier still. But she had learned to fly with joy on Aeyrrhi.

Her eyes were orange-red, flaming with emotion. She was getting ready to say goodbye.

Tomorrow was goodbye for her and the man, and she wished not to make a fool of herself. She would stay here. He would go home, to Earth.

"What would happen to the chicks if I should die?" She spoke the eagle language, the artificial language the human scientists had created for her tongue.

The man, Taylor, fiddled with a silver and turquoise ring he wore, impatient. "Don't die, Wing. We all love you. You'll make our work come to nothing."

"But what if? Suppose your indigenous wildlife gangs up on me. The question isn't theoretical to me."

Taylor spoke the eagle tongue, also, but it was not made for his lips. He slurred and lisped, despite long practice with Wing. "I've told you. We put up fences so the indigenous simians and rodents can't get to the nesting areas. But, if you must know, the nest area is monitored from orbit. If the trackers up in Sky Aerie fail to sense activity immediately outside the nest for three days, they'll send help to feed the chicks.''

"Would it be you? Would you come back?"

Taylor sighed and folded his arms against the brisk mountain wind. "I can't, Wing. I'm sorry."

Wing's neck feathers fluttered slightly in the wind. To divert herself from bleak thoughts, she gazed out over the darkening valley. Her keen eyes saw a pair of edible rodents several kilometers away. A pair. How sweet to belong, not to be one of a kind. When the chicks were hatched, there would be more of her kind, thought Wing. Except that she was the first, the only, alone. And though she was genetically *Aquila sapiens,* in her mind she was half human. A sport. Different.

She would rather be one of those mountain rats, stupid, always in danger of sudden death, than a half-human heart-bound to a human who could not love her.

Taylor broke the silence again. "A beautiful planet."

She said nothing. Her grief was like a stone in her breast, but the exhilaration of flight, the lighter gravity, gave the emotion a sense of unreality. As if she could not believe Taylor would ever leave.

"Almost as if it were made for you, Wing."

"A planet made for lovers." She closed her eyes and tried once more to envision herself dancing in the sky with someone who looked like her, a powerful flyer who extended his talons to her and wheeled through the air linked to her before consummation. This was the way it was supposed to be. She could imagine everything but the act itself.

That was, and would always be, Taylor's.

"I'm sorry." He ventured nearer, stroked her hackles

with the back of his hand. She twisted her head around and looked at his hand—freckled, tanned, guarded with the ring. The ring seemed loose. The planet did not seem to agree with Taylor, and she feared for his health.

"You've lost more weight," she murmured.

"Worry about yourself. I'll be home in a few months."

"Home to Karyn."

Taylor raked his hair in exasperation. "There is nothing between me and Karyn. Never has been."

"But there will be."

"Wing, who can know the future?"

She lifted her wings delicately and settled them again. She was embarrassed to display her feelings, not that they were any secret from Taylor.

"What do I see in you?" She tried to make it a joke.

"I'm sorry. We tried to give you the right images, but we misjudged the timing. Where there should have been one of your own species, there were only humans." He hunched in his parka, a picture of remorse.

Wing fought the impulse to reach out and stroke him with her beak. She allowed him to touch her, but was too shy to return his caresses. It was the early images, yes. Selene, the first person she remembered, who had coaxed her in infancy to eat bits of chicken, had had amber eyes, just the color of Taylor's eyes.

She shut her eyes. "Humor me. Suppose you could be my lover. Would you fly with me today?"

Taylor turned away and muttered, "I can't fly."

"But suppose you could. Would you fly over those rocks there? Would you bring me sprigs of evergreens to deck my nest?"

"Stop teasing, Wing. We didn't ask for this, either of us. I've said I'm sorry. I can't do anything more." He turned to her, eyes wet with that excess moisture humans used to wheedle each other. "I'm sorry," he said in English.

"I'm sorry," she repeated, mocking him, also in English. But her mouth wasn't made for the sibilant, and she lisped. "We're not even Heloise and Abelard, are we? Or Pygmalion and Galatea."

Taylor looked puzzled. She had never told him, or anybody in the project, that she could read English, and in fact, it was slow going for her. But she had taught herself, motivated at first by the thought that it might help her to create an alphabet for Aeyrrhin, her language, which existed as yet only in computerized phonemes. Later, she had intensified her efforts, to surprise Taylor. But she hadn't told him yet.

"I don't remember reading you either of those stories. Who in the project told you about Pygmalion and Galatea?"

Wing laughed her clipped shriek of a laugh. "No one. Do we have to go down to camp now?"

Taylor began twisting his ring again. "Soon. Sunset is nearly on us."

"Don't fall. You poor wingless kid."

"Don't pity me. Humans make wings out of metal. And humans made you. If we wanted to fly, we could." He gestured broadly out over the valley, and his ring flew off and bounced down onto rocks below. "Damn!"

"Let me get it for you," Wing said, and leapt out into the air.

"Never mind!" yelled Taylor. But she was gliding out above the valley.

Wing flew upward when she launched herself, then floated in the air, beating lazily to maintain her loft. Then she drifted downward toward the ring.

She was a dozen meters above the ring when she saw it.

She also saw its inscription, engraved in the soft silver. "To Taylor, love, Karyn," it said. Just like that. And a number, part of a date.

Wing flew upward in horror.

Then, to cover her surprise, she wheeled out from the mountain face.

Could he see the ring? She doubted it. And did he suspect she could read English? Probably not. No.

She beat upward, rode the wind, and landed in a rush of feathers on a ledge above him.

"Can't get it," she said shortly. "It's under rocks. Sorry, Taylor." And her heart burned like lye in her breast.

Taylor was trying not to look upset. "It's all right. It didn't cost much."

Wing's perspective was spinning. She glanced into Taylor's eyes, covering her suspicion with jerky movements, as if she were scanning the valley.

Why had he lied?

She was afraid to speak much. Her alienness made it possible for her to conceal her emotions from most humans, but Taylor had lived with her on a daily basis ever since the scientists discovered that she had accidentally bonded to him. So he might read her thoughts where nobody else could.

"Is it where I might be able to get at it? I mean, you have wings, dear, but I have hands."

"No. Not tonight, anyway. It would be a hard climb down, and you're none too footsure on this scree anyway."

Taylor poked his fists deep into the pockets of his parka and looked downward. She was sure now he couldn't see the ring. "Maybe tomorrow I could climb up to it." He sighed. "We've got to go back to camp. I'm cold. Aren't you?"

"Not in the slightest."

He muttered something in English about avian metabolism and turned to walk down the path.

"Can I ask you a question?" Wing shifted her weight to her other foot.

"Hurry it up. I'm freezing and I don't like walking

after dark. And I don't like you flying down to camp in the dark, either."

Wing chose her words carefully. The Aeryrrhin tongue was not well designed for questions involving subjunctives, but she didn't want to switch to English. "If I should die before the chicks could fend for themselves, you say Sky Aerie would send help."

"Yes. I assure you."

She fluffed her breast feathers, trying to conceal her suspicion. "How would they feed them?"

Taylor looked puzzled. "With local game. The rodents, snakes, I suppose. Same as you'll do."

"Then they would imprint on humans, as I did?"

Taylor waved the question aside. "No, no. Of course not. We couldn't have that, because then they'd never mate with each other. Sky Aerie personnel would use robots or hand puppets that look like *Aquila sapiens.*"

"I see."

Why had they not used robots or hand puppets to feed her? Why had they permitted her to imprint on humans? Surely they could have predicted what would happen.

She didn't like to guess.

"One other question."

"In camp, Wing. Spare my freezing toes."

"I just wanted to know, what happened that there was only one of me? Why were there no male *Aquila sapiens?*"

"The virus wouldn't give rise to males. We told you all about this, Wing. Weren't you listening all that time?"

"No, no. I remember now. You humans gave me a wonderful education. Wonderful. I wish you had taught me to read English, though."

"There just wasn't time, darling. There just wasn't enough time."

He stroked her hackles, then turned and picked his way down the mountain. There was no path, of course. This was their ritual every evening. They would come up here, on a high pass, and look out over the valley. This valley was to be the seat of civilization. Here she would hatch chicks, two or three a year for perhaps twenty years. Thanks also to the virus, she would become pregnant each spring without benefit of sperm. She would teach the chicks the language and all the lore she could remember.

Taylor and she looked out over the valley each night. Then he would walk down to camp while she glided above him, fretting that he would slip and fall. She often scolded him, told him to be careful. Mountains were for eagles, she said, not for half-blind, earth-crawling little simians like him.

God, she had loved him.

She hopped to a higher rock and extended her wings, letting the wind lift her, and finally, leaning onto the air, floated away from the side of the mountain. The valley was light and shadow, deep, with colors more intense than she had ever seen. As the air bore her up, she felt as if Aeyrrhi itself was a dream pierced through with beauty and pain, a dream from which she could not awaken.

What should she do? Why had Taylor lied to her? Surely it was not to spare her feelings. She had known from the beginning that humans and eagles could not mate, that aside from the fact that she was destined to live on Aeyrrhi, mother of a race of *Aquila sapiens,* anatomy itself was against the lovers. Nor had Taylor encouraged her to think that he returned her love.

He had been her language instructor. No, he had not created the eagle language; that had been done by others in Project Aquila. It was because she had begged them to teach her to read. And after weeks of her pleading, begging, and sulking, they had produced Taylor.

That first day, he had burst into the laboratory like a

Illustrated by Val Lakey Lindahn

man bearing hundreds of little gifts. "Chirp, chirp," he had said to her. Other newcomers to the project were always intimidated by Wing. Taylor was at ease with her at once.

"Are you going to teach me to read?" she had asked.

Taylor had laughed. "They told me you had a one-track mind."

No, in the end, he never taught her to read either Aeyrrhin or English. He had spoken Aeyrrhin with her, sometimes with his own clumsy tongue, sometimes with the aid of a computer simulator which made the "correct" avian noises. As if the machine had a beak.

But he read to her. He read her love stories, human classics, stories of mythology.

Maybe it was something as simple as the color of his eyes. The same color as Selene's. And his easy humor, his way of dominating the space around him, as if he were the lab's sole proprietor and she his guest.

And one day, when he had been reading her a story (it was a story translated from Italian, something about two lovers in Hell, whose punishment was remembering their past pleasures) she had looked at him, and made a little happy sound, halfway between sighing and laughter. He had stopped reading and looked at her, questioning, gentle, smiling.

Neither said anything for a long time. Then Taylor reached over and stroked the feathers on her neck with the back of his hand.

The touch made her shudder, as if at once frozen and scalded. Few in the project dared stroke her feathers, dared touch her at all. Birds do not bask in promiscuous caresses. And Wing was aware of his eyes, tawny-gold. Eyes the color of trust.

He had taken up the story again, but something had happened. She became fascinated, invented reasons to ask him questions about the minutiae of Aeyrrhin syntax. When

those were exhausted, she quizzed him about English pho-
nology. She loved to hear him talk, yearned to dazzle him
with her own conversation. And that was why she began,
secretly, to learn to read English. To please him.

She had meant to tell him that she could read. Many
times the words were on the tip of her tongue. Look what
I can do Taylor, she thought of telling him. Now you'll have
to love me.

Oh, he would be so proud of her. She had meant to tell
him before he left Aeyrrhi.

The project personnel had all seemed so utterly surprised to learn of the accidental bonding. But they had
accepted it.

Perhaps they had not been surprised at all.

"Whom do you wish to accompany you to Aeyrrhi,
Wing?" they had asked.

"Who else but Taylor?" she had returned. Of course.

Now, on Aeyrrhi, her thoughts were chaos. The valley
spread below her, shadows of the peaks growing as the sun
set. Aeyrrhi had no moons, and its night was dark except for
stars. She beat her wings and climbed higher.

She had to know. She had to know more.

The novelty of flight had not erased the illusion that Taylor, far below her on the trail he had blazed through the
scree, was a toy or an insect. She realized that if he took
the way he always did, he would pass on the other side of
a rock-pile before he came to an opening that looked out
over the valley again.

She waited for him to pass behind the rocks.

Immediately when he did, she dove for the camp.

They (or rather he, because she was clumsy with her
talons) had erected a tent, not in the valley, but in a sheltered
area on one side of the mountain, a few kilometers from the
top. Inside was cooking equipment for him (she increasingly
depended on native wildlife, which was digestible to her,

like Earth's) a few gadgets, and his computer. He used it both to communicate with Sky Aerie, orbiting above them, and to keep notes.

It was the log that interested her.

Her talons were clumsy, and she found it irritating that Taylor had not used a voice-activated computer. But then, perhaps he wanted privacy that oral messages would not permit.

Her heart beat hard. She knew he could not make it to camp fast enough to surprise her in the tent, but if he saw she had gone in without him, there would be questions.

She was lucky in her search, though it still took too much time. The spheres on which memory was wound like a ball of yarn were hard to handle, but the third one she tried was his log, and it alluded to another eagle installed some months earlier some 500 kilometers to the east. Back on Earth, she had memorized a map of the planet, and now she recognized the place.

Pinions prickling with tension, she spooled ahead in the diary. Reading was agony; the log was in English, but she was never sure she recognized words. The computer projected letters against the wall of the tent. The thing was meant to work after dark, of course. And the spellings were odd. She had never had the benefit of Taylor's explanations for English spellings, which even after the Great Simplification were grotesque and whimsical.

She had to know the gender of that other eagle.

If it was female, why had he never told her of its existence? Why had the scientists at the lab insisted that she was their only viable product? "We were going to make more," they'd say, "but there was no time."

Hah. Here. "... he fledged after only three days ..." *He.* The other eagle was male.

Were there more of them?

Wing jammed the sphere back into its case. It didn't fit.

She fumbled, knocking the whole case over. Spheres rolled over the floor of the tent, coming to rest against Taylor's sleeping bag.

But why did she care? Why conceal her spying?

Taylor hailed her with windmilling arms. "Where have you been? What were you doing inside the tent?"

She used her wings to brake her fall onto a tree root growing from a crack in the austere rock. Taylor's eyes, she saw, were wide with concern. For her? For what she had seen in the tent?

"Stay a while with me, Taylor. The wind has died down."

He exploded. "It's getting dark. I'm freezing. You're endangering government property by trying to fly in the dark."

"Government property?"

Taylor colored, still furious. "You know very well what I mean. You're still the ward of the government until I leave this planet."

"Ward, property. Isn't there a difference?"

He bit his lip. "Thirty years ago the Supreme Court ruled that products of laboratory research carried out under the auspices of the government were government property. I'm sorry to put it that way, but it's true. I want you to stop acting like a child!"

Wing extended her neck and screamed laughter into the sky. Her hoot echoed across the valley. "A child? What am I, Taylor? A child, property, a rational being? Are my children government property, too?"

"Let's not discuss this. You're using this foolish infatuation to excuse the inexcusable."

"Taylor, how am I supposed to establish a civilization here? You've told me there is little metal on this continent.

On the whole planet. And I have these talons instead of hands. I can't even hold a pencil with them."

"That will be taken care of. Stop concerning yourself."

"Taken care of? God, Taylor. Who's going to take care of it?"

"Never mind! You could—let's say we could remove the talons. Then you could write, use tools. You'd use a glove for flying, so that you'd have the purchase necessary for landing."

"You've thought this through."

"Look, I don't want to talk about it now. No, I wasn't the one that thought of the talon removal and the flying glove. I won't lie; the project directors looked into the problem."

"Then why didn't they discuss it with me?"

Taylor was silent.

"I have other questions, too," she said, so quietly the now-soft breeze nearly muffled her voice.

"Save them for camp."

"Why did the project directors not realize that creatures bond to those who feed them? This was known about birds, wasn't it? And even humans. Wouldn't a human fed consistently by snakes grow up and bond to snakes? Taylor, they had to know it."

Taylor turned away from her and spoke through gritted teeth. "They didn't know about it. Or nobody thought of it. I don't know. It isn't my fault, and I'm damned if you're going to bludgeon me with it any more. I've humored you. I've never encouraged you to think your insane love could be reciprocal, though." He faced her, his face hard. "I'm sorry it happened, but we all have our crosses to bear."

Wing extended her wings and beat one powerful stroke. Taylor winced as dust blew in his face. "I'm not expecting you to do anything about it, Taylor."

"Thank God for small favors. Then why are you bringing this up here on the face of this goddamn mountain and not in camp?"

"*I want to know why it was done to me.*"

Taylor's whole body twisted with exasperation. "I told you—"

"Every stupid evasion you could think of. They never invented a good lie, did they?"

"You don't believe me. Sorry, old girl. I'll never convince you, but by tomorrow I'll be gone. I'm sorry our romance had to go sour at the end, but it's over. It had to be. You are the mother of a new race, and I'm just—a soldier following orders."

"A soldier following orders." The mockery stuck in Wing's craw like a bone too sharp to cast up.

Taylor observed her, mute. For a moment she saw the flicker of love and hate in his eyes. Yes, he could never desire her sexually. Of course. She knew that. But there was a more transcendent love, the love of a father for a child. Or a god for its misshapen creature.

And there was hate, too.

"What was the date of first landing on this planet?"

Taylor's mouth gaped and closed, like that of a dying salmon.

"Go ahead, lie. You're trying to figure out a plausible date so I don't figure it out. But I've already figured it out."

He breathed out, grim. "Figured out what?"

"Aeyrrhi was discovered long before the Project Aquila was even dreamed of. It seemed a perfect planet for humans, except—no metals, right? It'll be timber products here and fisheries, and cattle grazing on the savannahs. Hard, boring work, tracking the cows, scouting the best forest growth, locating the schools out at sea."

"I won't pretend I understand what you're talking about."

"So you needed a surrogate. What did humans use for scut work before the age of technology?" She lapsed into English. The eagle language lacked slang.

Taylor grimaced, false mirth. "Scut work? Darling, your vocabulary astonishes me."

"You know. Errands. Carrying stuff from one place to another. Domestic chores. Watching the cattle or the baby. Keeping the native wildlife down. Dangerous work. What you sons of bitches never want to do." Her outburst was in Aeyrrhin mixed with English.

"I don't know, Wing. Are you about to give me a history lecture?"

"You used slaves."

Taylor blanched, then rallied. "Yeah. So?"

"But slaves revolt. Human slaves, that is. You've used dogs for guards, monkeys to help quadriplegics, dolphins to carry torpedoes to enemy submarines. They didn't revolt, because they were too dumb. *Aquila sapiens*, on the other hand, is too smart."

Taylor interrupted her quickly. "Can we continue this conversation in camp? Okay, there are a few things I meant to tell you that I just haven't gotten around to. But I really need to get to camp. We both do. You have no night vision."

"But if the mother of the slave race was in love with a human, she'd teach the chicks dependence. It would be a tradition."

Taylor laughed; a genteel, affected laugh. "What nonsense, Wing! I can explain everything. Back there. In camp."

And he flashed her a nervous smile with his mobile, simian face, that face so good for expressing emotion and lying, lying, lying. She lowered her head, bowed with her whole body.

"My love. No longer my love. I lied, too."

"Lied, Wing? About what?"

"I can read English."

His frozen smile disappeared. He looked out over the valley and into the sky, as if for help. And then he grabbed his walking staff and scrambled, half falling, half running, down the mountain, away from her.

She screamed and beat her wings hard, launching away from the mountain face. She strained every muscle to climb above him, high above him. He stretched his arms out, inhaled as if to call to her. She tucked in her wings.

And dived. Talons extended, she raked his face, tearing his flesh like tender meat. He lashed out, grabbed at her breast. She wrenched out of his grasp, leaving a handful of feathers in his clawlike grip, some of her own featherdown swirling in the air. She beat upward, away from him, her throat too tight to scream.

Taylor staggered from the blow, clutching his mangled face, lost his balance and fell backward.

She flew higher and watched his body cartwheel and bounce, until it came to rest at the foot of an evergreen halfway down the mountain.

She dove to investigate. He still clutched feathers he had torn from her breast. Blood, flowing from the ragged incision made by her talons, soaked his parka dark and wet. His eye, the one she had not gouged with her talons, stared blankly.

And she labored up again into the darkening sky, high, high, trying to climb so high that she couldn't see what that speck of darkness on the grey rock really was.

There was no way to go back. There was no way to pretend it had been an accident. Taylor was dead, and she had killed him. What else could she have done? There had been no other way. She had killed a tyrant to save her children. But the guilt could not be washed off like the slick blood on her talons. The mad grief would last her whole life.

There was a way out, of course. She could dive into the

FREE

Send in this card and receive a FREE GIFT.

Send in this card and you'll receive a free MISSION EARTH POSTER while supplies last. No order required for this Special Offer! Mail your card today!

- ☐ Please send me a FREE Mission Earth Poster
- ☐ Please send me information about other fiction books by L. Ron Hubbard.

ORDERS SHIPPED WITHIN 24 HRS OF RECEIPT!

PLEASE SEND ME THE FOLLOWING:

___ MISSION EARTH hardback volumes (specify #s:_____)	$18.95	_____
___ MISSION EARTH set (10 vols)	$142.12	_____
___ MISSION EARTH Vol 1 paperback	$4.95	_____
___ MISSION EARTH Vol 2 paperback	$4.95	_____
___ Battlefield Earth paperback	$4.95	_____
___ Writers of The Future Volume I	$3.95	_____
___ Writers of The Future Volume II	$3.95	_____
___ Writers of The Future Volume III	$4.50	_____
___ Writers of The Future Vols I-III pck.	$9.95	_____
___ Buckskin Brigades	$3.95	_____

SUB-TOTAL: _____

CHECK AS APPLICABLE:
☐Check/Money Order enclosed
(Use an envelope please).
☐American Express ☐VISA ☐MasterCard

SHIPPING*: _____

TAX**: _____

TOTAL: _____

Card #: _____

Exp. Date: _____ Signature: _____

NAME: _____

ADDRESS: _____

CITY: _____ STATE: ____ ZIP: _____

Call Toll-Free 1-800-722-1733 (1-800-843-7389 in CA)

Copyright © 1988 Bridge Publications, Inc. All rights reserved. 2004881024

* Add $1.00 per book for shipping and handling. ** California residents add 6.5% sales tax.

BUSINESS REPLY MAIL

FIRST CLASS   PERMIT NO. 62688   LOS ANGELES, CA

POSTAGE WILL BE PAID BY ADDRESSEE

BRIDGE PUBLICATIONS, INC.

4751 Fountain Avenue

Los Angeles, CA 90029

rocks, die in a hammer-blow of pain, dimming consciousness, peace.

But she wouldn't.

She flew to camp. There, she slowly tapped out a mes-
sage to Sky Aerie. "WILD VIRUS HERE. LOCAL
FAUNA IMMUNE. AQUILA SAPIENS DEAD. AM
DYING. DANGER. DO NOT SEND HELP. TAYLOR."

Perhaps that would keep the lying simians in orbit.

Meantime, with her poor clumsy talons, she must begin
to build a civilization.

Diving In at
Sag Harbor
by
Tim Powers

About the Author

In two swift recent years, with his novels The Anubis
Gates *and* Dinner at Deviant's Palace, *Tim Powers
won prominence in the forefront of today's SF writers. In
effect, he was an overnight success, although he had published earlier novels and had been a professional for some
years.*

*Both books are marked by an adventurous scenario, a
zestful style, and an uncommon depth of education held discreetly in the background. A basically literary person, one
decides from reading the work, and with that forms a be-
spectacled sort of image for its author.*

*To meet Tim Powers is to see someone else; a blue-eyed
Black-Irishman, trim and quick, who tends to remind one of
a good college fencer ... which he has been. Then to hear
him speak as a convention Guest of Honor is to discover oneself in the presence of the best sort of natural comedic wit;
an anecdotal purveyor of seemingly spontaneous images and
concepts that dart unwaveringly to the truth under the side-
splitting monologue.*

*He was a person, I said to myself, who could think while
in motion. Supervising the W.O.T.F. workshops requires*

that . . . their approach, based on L. Ron Hubbard's creative principles, has the students make as much use of study, and action toward new stories, as it does discussion of their pre-existing work. And it moves swiftly.

Powers was someone I wanted as a workshop instructor. He told me he had never taught, had never been in a work-shop, didn't know how to teach. I said he did. I was right . . . .

It was early in the overcast morning of the day after Easter Sunday, and Sag Harbor was *cold*. I wasn't *in* the harbor, of course—though a giant black dog named Buster was gaily swimming through the low gray waves after a stick his owner kept throwing out into the water—but even on the shore, with a jacket on and a cup of steaming coffee in my hand, I was realizing that they make a whole different kind of *cold* on this northeastern coast. It was coming in from Greenland—Sag Harbor is an old whaling village on the tip of Long Island.

In spite of having flown in to New York from California the previous evening, my wife, Serena, and I had gotten up early to walk around the village a little. I was nervous—I had to begin to "help run a writer's workshop" in a little less than an hour. I'd never attended any sort of writers' workshop aside from college-years sessions in which people tell each other how wonderful their pretentious poetry is.

More than a year earlier, in Seattle, Algis Budrys had asked me if I would work with him, and I had agreed blithely. I always agree to anything that's to take place more than a year in the future.

Now it was only minutes away. My coffee cup was empty, and though Buster had paddled back in to shore and dropped the stick at his owner's feet—and was wagging his soaked tail eagerly, hoping to be able to jump one more time into the unthinkably frigid water—I had to go jump into this workshop business.

Serena and I walked back up the sand slope and crossed the pavement to the meeting room of the Baron's Cove Inn where we were all staying. A number of the students were already there. I certainly didn't know any of them well, and we all chatted in that cheery, vaguely on-edge way that people do with strangers at airports.

Then Algis and Orson Scott Card walked in—Scott was my fellow instructor, with Algis in charge—and things got down to order. In spite of having read all the stories the students had submitted, I felt the way I used to feel when I hadn't done my homework and Sister Clementissima would look straight at me. I had a fresh cup of coffee, but I don't think I got a chance to take a sip of it until we broke for lunch.

First, Algis provided a lecture on story structure—Scott and I would lecture on topics of our own later in the week—and then we workshopped stories. For that, we all wound up sitting in a wobbly circle, and when Algis announced which story we would workshop first, the student sitting to the right of the author said what she had thought of it: where the story worked effectively, where it had seized up, how to salvage it if indeed it could be salvaged; then the next person to the right got a chance, and so it went around the circle, with Scott and me commenting after all the students had had their says, and Algis delivering his judgement last of all. The author got to reply, after this, if he or she cared to.

If this sounds a little rough, that's because sometimes it was—everybody was at least civil, but at the same time everybody was serious and opinionated about the craft of writing, and there were to be only four days in which to cover more than a dozen stories, plus a hefty set of assignments designed to show ways to *approach* stories like a pro . . . which is a big step not all promising novices ever take on their own. I quickly caught on that I wouldn't be doing any of these people any favors if I was less than absolutely frank.

And so it was, and we all were, and, after my initial thankfulness at not having to bring a story of my own, I half began to wish I had—there were a lot of sharp, merciless scalpels being brandished, and I'd have been curious to see whether my own fiction would repel them or be gutted.

That took care of the morning. There'd be another batch tomorrow. The students' afternoon would be taken up with other tasks. Just before the lunch break Algis gave the students an assignment—I don't remember which it was; go interview chance-met citizens or research in the local library or write a scene based on some randomly-chosen object—and told them to write it up as a brief paragraph or two. The assignments were based on some pragmatic nuts-and-bolts writing articles done by L. Ron Hubbard; every student got copies, along with reading assignments every day.

It was a busy schedule for them.

Serena and I walked along the beach to the village and had scallops and crabs at one of the restaurants on the main street. I was glad I was having more free time than the students.

Back in the meeting room we continued to work on assignments and discuss them until about five, and then Algis and Scott and I took the index cards on which the students had written their assignment results and adjourned to Algis' room to write comments on them. After that most of us wandered back to town for dinner.

Back in our room at last, I managed, before we turned out the light, to read a little of the book I had brought along; but our room had a connecting door with Algis's, and I could faintly hear the keyboard of his portable word processor clicking away—he was writing himself a memo, as it turns out, on how to improve getting the students in tune with the principles behind the assignments. I'll be dropping in at Pepperdine to see what's different this year—I don't suppose it'll be any less demanding. God knows what Scott Card was doing—probably writing something of his own. I just went to bed, marvelling at the industry of all these people.

The next day went the same way, though Serena and I got up even earlier and managed to explore the beach quite a ways before having to head back. Buster was as busy as ever, bounding off into the surf and then coming out to shake a shower of cold Atlantic water over anyone near him. I said hello to his owner, hoping to get the chance to throw the stick out myself a time or two, but nine o'clock was looming over us, and I had to get to the meeting room.

Again the students were given an assignment to do after their lunch break, and as Serena and I sat over our own unhurried lunch—and saw a couple of the students at the next table scribbling furiously on cards, between bites of unconsidered food—it occurred to me that Buster wasn't by any means the only one in town being sent out into the cold waters to fetch things.

Again Scott and Algis and I spent the early evening going over the cards the students had written—they could fit a lot of words on one of them—and again I heard Algis's keyboard going as I turned off our light. This time, it was a book review column.

The day after that the students were assigned to write a short scene involving suspense and, just as I was getting to my feet and thinking about where to go for lunch today, Scott Card cheerfully said that this time the instructors, too, should do the assignment.

I stared at him in horror. This was like having asked Buster's owner if I could participate in the game, and him hauling the stick back over his shoulder and pointing at the water and saying to me, "Sure, go out for it!"

I don't remember what I had for lunch. I spent the

whole hour scribbling and crossing things out, and came puffing back to the meeting room just as the session was starting up. Scott asked to read my scene, but my writing was so scrambled that he couldn't read it; I could hardly puzzle it out myself, when the moment came to read it aloud.

And I had not done perceptibly better than most of the students—and the criticism was polite, or at least civil, and I had to admit most of it was valuable.

The next day was our last. We workshopped the last three stories mercilessly enough, but afterward we had a graduation party with a huge cake. The night before, our last night, the whole gang of us had gone exploring the docks and piers, and wound up at a 7-11 where, as I recall, Scott bought M&Ms for everybody. Several of us sat up very late in the meeting room; this was the last time we would be there, and this time there was none of the formality there had been the first time. We had argued and gossiped and joked until well past midnight. I had been impressed with how quick to learn they were, and how eager they were to do it. I was glad Scott and Algis and I had had this chance to pass on some hard-won know-how.

Tomorrow would be the Hubbard Award ceremonies, and a grand time it was, with rooms at the Vista in Manhattan and great meals and drinks—but it's the Sag Harbor days, with their non-stop focus on writing *purposefully,* that I remember best from that trip. Many of the students have sold stories since, several have written novels, and at least one has a multi-book contract with a major New York publisher.

I've had to revise my original opinion of workshops and the teachability of writing. No doubt many of these people would have published eventually, but I really don't think they'd have done it nearly as fast without the focused assignments I saw at Sag Harbor.

And they're out there somewhere today, diving into

waters colder and deeper than old Buster could ever swim in, buoyed by the confidence that the stick is worth the effort to go in after, and then go in after again. It may well be a delusion, but it's one that I share, and I'm proud to have had some part in their progresses.

The Gas Man

by
Richard Urdiales

About the Author

Of Mexican descent, Richard Urdiales is in his thirties and teaches in the Journalism and Telecommunication Department at the University of Wyoming. He has been a newspaper reporter, a medical photographer, an advertising copywriter, and, in electronic media, has done a great many jobs at the microphone, behind the camera, and in management. He has also been a firefighter, police officer, cowboy, chef, and salesman, in keeping with the variegated pasts that occur again and again in the biographies of writers and other artists.

In the early 1980s, he published three magazine articles; two were on Mountain Man John Colter, about whom he had done a screenplay for his degree thesis. The third was a description of his 2,600-mile horseback jaunt through the Midwest and South in 1978-'79.

"The Gas Man" is his first published story. But there is a feeling in this novelette that it might be the work of a future novelist. We hope so . . . .

PART ONE: THE DEAL

In the starlight, the small flatbottomed boat moved silently through the overgrown swamp, the thick-chestedman seated in front and the slender man standing in the back. The slender man was using a long pole; probing, pushing.

"Water's only about a couple foot deep," he remarked.

"You sure you ain't tired, Dixie Man?" the man in the front of the boat asked.

"No, Sonny," Dixie Man said. "I'm fine."

Sonny rubbed his hands together and looked out into the darkness, where the channel gleamed like new tar in the Florida starlight. He had light sun-bleached hair and a dark beard, and was powerful, with strong hands. He listened to the sounds of the night; mullet jumping and owls hunting and bugs, bugs, bugs.

Sonny had brought the fast ocean-runner in as close as he dared, and tied up to some mangrove. Then he and Dixie Man had camouflaged the big boat. Branson had told them that they wouldn't be able to power all the way, and Sonny had taken along an old wooden flatboat to get them to the meeting.

"When you think we get there?" Dixie Man asked.

"Shouldn't be long. You've been poling for about a half hour."

Dixie Man was lean and dark, not as tall as Sonny, but more wiry. He had an easy Southern drawl that Sonny recognized as coming from Louisiana, but didn't know for sure. He didn't know much of anything about Dixie Man, except that his real name was Charles and he was a hell of a good diver. Secrecy was something that happened often After. Few people told much about themselves, and all he really knew about Dixie Man was what he saw.

Branson had told them to come to a marshy little island about fifty klicks northwest of Cotton Plant Island, where Branson had one of his bases. Sonny had agreed, reluctantly, for although he had sold Branson a lot of fuel in the past, he didn't really trust him.

Sonny was curious. There had to be an extremely unusual reason for this meeting, especially since Branson wanted to hide it from the other island warlords.

"There must be one hell of a load of fuel somewhere," Dixie Man said.

"Yeah. You're reading my mind. Can't think of any other reason why Branson would want us."

"Must be dangerous as hell, too."

"I figured that one myself."

"Hell, if it's too tough, won't be a gas man in the Islands that'll touch it." Dixie Man shouldered into the pole.

Sonny chuckled. "There will be if there's a payoff to match. And there must be, or else we wouldn't be meeting in some fucking marsh."

"I wondered about that. Why way out here?"

"Defense. Shallow water, you can't bring in boats big enough for the firepower to do Branson real harm. If I won't risk my boat, nobody else will."

"Yeah, yeah," Dixie Man said. "You got a point. Place is easy to defend if you know nobody can get anything through at you." He paused and let the boat drift.

In the moonlight, Sonny saw a long shape to the left, horizontal to the water, and on it the silhouette of a man. A flashlight knifed through the dark, signaled once, then three times fast. Sonny grabbed his own light, and shot back one long, then pause, then two long, then two quick.

"Pull it in," Sonny said. "We're here, I guess."

They came to a small, rickety dock made of rough logs and hand-split boards. The signalman caught the rope Sonny threw him. He was dressed in a loose dark shirt and cutoffs, and he looked like he might have come from the Old Islands. Sonny placed his hand on the dock and jumped, his feet silent on the wood.

"Move pretty good for a big man," someone remarked from the land end of the dock.

"That's what all the girls tell me. You always creep up on a guest, Branson?" Sonny could barely see Branson, the darkness hiding his gross bulk. "Let's go somewhere a little more comfortable and talk about this deal you've got planned."

"Sure," Branson's voice said. "But he stays here."

"We both go in, or we both leave." Sonny's voice was even and cold. About six months ago Branson had offered Dixie Man a job as head diver for his outfit. Dixie Man had told him shove it where the sun don't shine, and in Branson's case that could be one of several locations. The same night, Branson set one of his goons after Dixie Man, and the goon was found next morning hung by his heels from a tree.

For a moment there was silence, then a hard scratch as Branson struck a match. In the harsh yellow light Sonny could see the man's face, greasy and pockmarked, the rolls of fat, and the dark shapes of his bodyguards behind him.

"Fine, fine." The red glow of a cigar now bounced in the darkness as the man talked. "This way."

Sonny and Dixie Man were led down the dock across

a narrow stretch of beach, one goon ahead with a flashlight and two more falling in behind. They came to a large hut, and the first bodyguard lifted a blanket that was over the door. The hut was large and shadowy, and an oil lamp burned on a table in the middle of the room. The lamp stank and the light was feeble.

Sonny could see two chairs at the table, and darker shapes towards the walls; old sofas. Off in the corner Sonny saw one of Branson's women sitting on a quilt on the floor. The quilt was used for other things besides sitting, because Sonny could see the stains on it, and in places, blood. The woman had a small candle burning in front of her; her legs were drawn up revealing long slender thighs with bruises on them. She was light-haired, and would have been pretty if not for the strain on her face. Her cheeks were hollow and her eyes bloodshot, and the joint she was smoking looked almost as big as Branson's cigar. Sonny guessed she must live on the stuff.

The goons positioned themselves on the far side of the hut. Dixie Man took a place opposite them. Dixie Man had on a tattered green flak jacket, and underneath Sonny knew he had a heavy automatic in a shoulder holster. Sonny didn't expect any violence, but it was good to know that Dixie Man was behind him.

"Sit down, sit down!" Branson gestured with a fat hand, his hospitality forced. "Rum? How's about a glass? Some fine stuff. Just like from the Old Islands."

Sonny shook his head and sat down. He didn't dare get drunk with Branson. Branson was just too flaky for Sonny, and he wanted all his wits about him. Besides, he knew the island warlord better than he really cared to, and rum made the fat man talkative. Sonny wanted to finish this meeting as fast as possible and get back to his own island.

The woman slipped to the table with a smoke-brown bottle and two glasses, poured, left the bottle and went away without a sound. Sonny ignored the drink.

"How's business?" the warlord asked. He held his cigar in his hand, letting smoke curl from his lips.

"Can't complain. I find an intact gas station when I need to and make the dive. I can pay my bills." Sonny was an independent diver, a gas man. He worked for himself or, if he chose, for hire. He was obligated to no individual warlord, and liked the idea.

"You got the same crew?"

"Pretty much so. You see Dixie Man here."

"You still got the broads?" Branson leaned forward expectantly.

Sonny shot him a wicked smile. "Latina would carve you up like a mullet. And if you were fool enough to touch Boomers, she'd blow up your whole fucking island to get you." There was general resentment all through Island Florida about women on the seas, but little was said about the women on Sonny's crew. Latina was a black-haired Colombian that had an uncanny talent with a machinegun. Boomers was slim, trim, blonde and blue, who got her nickname not only because of her figure but because she was the best Sonny had seen when it came to any kind of explosive.

The remark didn't faze Branson. He tossed down a drink of rum and puffed on his cigar.

"That makes three. Who's new?"

"Picked up a Haitian. Good sailor, hell of a fighter. Name's Adam." Sonny held back on describing the new man. He wasn't sure of him like he was with the rest of the crew. He was very black and lean and too quiet for Sonny's tastes. Sonny had seen him at his worst during a fight. They had hit a gas station and some pirates tried to take the cargo. The fight was quick but he had seen the murderous glint in the man's eyes, and the pleasure he took from the killing.

Sonny looked over at Dixie Man, leaning in a corner,

loose. Dixie Man stroked his moustache and winked at
Sonny, and the big man smiled.

"O.K., Branson. Let's get to the point."

Branson's grin showed rotting teeth. "Impatient, huh?"

"No, just bored. I've got better things to do with my
time than be cooped up with your smelly guards."

"O.K., gas man. Here's the deal. I want to set up a
dive. I've got reason to believe that there is a large gas station with maybe 100,000 gallons of fuel, intact."

"That's a lot of fuel. How do you know it's intact?"

"I have my ways."

"How do you know it ain't been claimed?"

Indignant. "I don't need nobody's permission to take
what I want."

Sonny's mood darkened. "Who else would be going?"

"I got Marlowe to captain the convoy," Branson said.
"I did him a little favor couple weeks ago, and he owed me
a favor back." Sonny did not respond at first. He knew Marlowe and his addiction to poker and guessed what the favor
must have been.

"He lost his boat again?"

Branson just smiled and let smoke drift from his mouth.

"If you've got Marlowe in on this, that means a gunboat is necessary. You expecting some heavy stuff?"

"Let's just say I'm a cautious person."

"Cautious ain't the word. You ain't gonna be on the
bridge when this goes down."

Branson let the remark roll off him.

"Where's this station?"

"Not far, not far."

"Listen, Branson. I don't have to be here. I'm the best
gas man in the Islands and I call my own shots. You tell me
what's going on, or I leave. Got it?"

Branson chewed on his cigar. "It's an old truckstop, lots
of pumps. Diesel and gas. Maybe some kerosene."

"And somebody else thinks it's their territory?"

"You said the word, Sonny. Thinks." Branson's eyes were narrowing and his face turning red.

"Where is it?"

Branson bought some time by putting his cigar in a shell ashtray and slowly refilling his glass.

"South."

"Branson, I'm getting sick and fucking tired of this shit. There's a hell of a lot of ocean south of us, and some pretty powerful warlords."

"And I'm pretty damn powerful, too!" His eyes bulged out of his fat face, angry.

"Yeah, every warlord thinks the same thing. You grab an island, build a fleet, and take as much as you can grab from anybody who has it. It's been like that ever since After."

"All it is is survival," Branson said, his voice growing louder in the still and heat of the room. "The ocean rose and covered everything. I took some of what was left."

"And now you've got some doubts," Sonny said. "What, you think if somebody else gets this fuel, they'll run all over you?"

Branson did not answer, and Sonny knew he had hit it.

"You're gonna start a war, Branson. And I don't know if I want to be a part of it."

"I'm offering you 10,000 gallons of fuel." Branson settled back with his cigar, as if he thought the offer would overwhelm Sonny, smiled and smoked. Sonny put on his best poker face. That was a lot of fuel, but if he was offering so much, that meant Branson was having problems getting a gas man to do the job. Probably because there was a great likelihood of getting killed. High risk and high profit. Sonny liked the combination, even though he knew Branson was probably lying through his teeth about the amount of fuel to bring up. He decided to play it.

"O.K., Branson. Fun and games are over. Now tell me the real offer." The smile vanished from Branson's face.

"I told you. That's it."

"You haven't told me anything except that I'll probably lose my boat, crew, and life so you can get fatter. What's going on?"

"I told you. You locate the fuel station, dive, hook up to it and pump into my tankers. Then we head for home richer than we ever thought we could be.

"Yeah, and how close do we get to Big Island?"

"Look, dammit, if you're scared about a little fight. . . ."

"They've got five times the boats and ten times the men you ever thought about having. And you need me. You need me or you wouldn't be offering me the deal."

"Shit, I can get lots of other gas men."

"Like who?"

"Well, ah, MacIntosh, or Chambers, or that Greek, what's his name, Alexia."

"Fat chance. Mac is dead. Chambers took a bullet and can't even walk yet, and Alexia, hell, he's out of the business. He lost too many sons."

"So where does that leave you? You the last resort?"

"There are only a handful of men who can do what you ask. And you know damn well that I'm better than Mac, Chambers and Alexia put together. I've always produced fuel. Nobody else can say that."

Branson was angry. "What, then? What do you want?"

Sonny sat straight faced and bluffed. "Twenty-five percent of the cargo." Branson choked, coming close to swallowing his cigar.

"And a couple thousand rounds for the M60s. And grenades for the launcher. And some spare parts for my boats."

"That's fucking robbery!"

"No, Branson. It is negotiation. You tell me what you'd

like me to take and I tell you what my life is worth to me. Then, we compromise.''

Branson was not one to compromise. They talked in the thick heat of the hut for over an hour and didn't settle anything. Sonny was getting tired of the shit. He looked at Branson as the warlord bellowed and moaned about the price. Branson was typical of the breed of man who had seized power After. Petty, and paranoid that some other man with a little more strength would come in and push him out. Always looking for the one trick, the one play that would secure him in his little kingdom. Sonny thought it was ridiculous.

Branson had his elbows on the table, the heels of his hands pressing his forehead. He had stayed like that for five minutes after Sonny had refused his last offer. Then his head jerked out of his hands and he smiled. Sonny thought he looked like a pale white toad.

"What about the girl?" Branson asked.

"What are you talking about?"

"The bitch. You can have her as part of the deal." Branson waved his hand and the woman appeared at his side. He put his arm around her waist and stroked her thigh.

"She good, mighty good. And you could have her."

"No, I don't think so, Branson."

"But look at her. Show your stuff."

"She doesn't have to. . . ." but before Sonny could finish her shirt was open and her breasts were out for him to see. As if on cue, she started to walk around the table, her hands holding the loose shirttail back, her hips moving. She stood to Sonny's right, watching his eyes on her, the pale yellow shirt framing her breasts. Her lips puckered slightly as if she was making a decision, then she started to unzip her fly.

Sonny forced his head back towards Branson. "A one nighter ain't in the deal."

"Who said anything about one night? She'd be yours."

"I'm not into slavery, either."

The smile vanished from Branson's fat face.

"You're pissing me off, Sonny."

"And I've had just as much of this as I care to." Sonny stood up. The woman had already retreated to the shadows. "Let's go, Dixie Man."

"Now wait, now wait." Branson was suddenly anxious. He had his hands out, palms down, gesturing for Sonny to take his seat. "We can work something out."

"O.K., but not one more ounce of bullshit." Sonny sat down, and out of the corner of his eye he saw Dixie Man's gun hand relax.

"Name it, gas man." Branson had his fists clenched on the table in front of him.

"Twenty percent of the take, whatever it is. Four thousand rounds for the M60s. Three crates of grenades. And you cover all expenses, fuel, ammo and damages to my boat."

Branson was silent for a long time, and Sonny thought that he had blown the deal by asking too much. What he had asked for was exorbitant, and he knew it, but he wanted to see how far Branson would go. That information would tell him more about the raid than anything the man had said.

"All right," Branson said. Sonny couldn't believe it. Branson must be close to desperation. "But the fuel is payable upon delivery. It's my guarantee that you'll stick around and protect it."

"You know me, Branson. I've never gone half-assed on a deal yet." Branson scowled and chewed his cigar.

Another hour passed and the two men went over the details. Convoy strength in men and boats, coordinates for the site, estimated time for the round trip, fuel consumption, rendezvous. Sonny learned that there would be five boats all together, Marlowe's gunboat, two tankers, and two Cigarette-hull boats, like Sonny's, to run flank.

"Why so few?" Sonny asked. "You've got more strength than that."

"Yeah, but I figure that the fewer I send, the less likely the convoy will attract attention," Branson said. Sonny pressed his lips together and nodded. Branson was right, but if they were seen, the fight would be intense. There was a long pause.

"That's about it, huh?" Sonny asked. "I can get anything else I need from Marlowe."

"Marlowe has been told to get in touch with you to work out any details," Branson said.

Sonny gave a dry laugh. "So sure that I'd agree to the deal?"

"Sonny, you ain't no better than anybody here. You're in it for the same reason. Fuel."

"Damn right." Sonny's smile almost became a snarl, then softened. "Time we were out of here."

Sonny stood up, and felt Dixie Man move in behind him. He shot a quick look at the girl on the quilt, but the blankness had returned to her face and she did not look at him. She was a machine, Sonny thought, and Branson had the remote control. The two men left, pushing away the blanket that hid the doorway.

Sonny could feel the tension. They walked all the way to the beach before Dixie Man spoke.

"Slimy bastard, ain't he?" Dixie Man's voice had an edge to it.

"Yeah."

"Think we can trust him?"

"Only just so far. He'll deliver on the ammo and the rest of the supplies. He has to or else the deal's off, but I expect something to come up later."

"You think he'll send his men to follow us?"

"Maybe, but I kind of doubt it. That would mean some kind of direct confrontation, and he doesn't want to alienate me or the other gas men. Besides, he knows what Latina and Boomers can do in a firefight. He may be gross and ugly, but he's no fool."

They walked down the beach, stepped onto the dock. The signalman was there as if he had never moved.

"El noche es muy plácido, gracias a Dios," Sonny said, but the man acted as if he did not hear, so Sonny did not make another attempt. He got into the boat, then held it steady for Dixie Man.

Dixie Man used the pole, pushing them away from the dock, back through the mangroves to the secret place where the boat was tied.

"Life sure is crazy, ain't it, Sonny."

"How's you mean?"

"Making a deal with a prick like Branson."

There was a long silence.

"Dixie Man, how bad did Branson's goon shake you up?"

He paused and did not speak, and even in the darkness Sonny could see him stiffen.

"The dude had me in his hand. But he wasted time. One of those who enjoys it too much. Like Adam. He had a knife to my throat but started to play the power game, and he played too long. That's when I got him." Dixie Man's silence seemed to add to the thickness, the dampness of the night. Sonny did not press him.

They came up to the cigarette, hidden in a tangle of tree limbs, moss, and mangrove. All was secure. They jumped aboard, pulled lines, took off the camouflage netting.

"Hey, Sonny."

"Hey what?"

"What did you do Before?" Sonny hesitated. Questions about the past were rare After.

"I ran a cruise service. You know. Barefoot adventure in the Islands for the tourists. Had a nice sloop."

"My Daddy and I owned a couple charter boats on Marathon Key, for fishing and scuba day-trips," Dixie Man said. He gave a strange laugh. "Funny. You and me done about the same thing, Before."

·Sonny didn't think much about Before. He still had the sloop and even his crew didn't know about it, but outside of that he wanted no reminders. Too much had changed, too many people were gone.

The sea had risen and nobody really knew why, or how. Some blamed it on the ozone, some on the Russians. Preachers called it an act of God, but as far as Sonny was concerned, it didn't matter.

Sonny remembered the day. He had put in at a pier where the rich folk docked their boats on Miami Beach, to drop off some party types he had taken to Grand Bahama. There was a bar that he liked, on the dock, a dive with a bad reputation that kept most of the snowbirds and the college crowd away. He was sipping a beer when he saw the first wave. He noticed it way out to sea, and watched it as it came in. The line of water stretched as far across the horizon as he could see, an infantry column marching. It was high and fast and Sonny gaped as it got closer and closer. The beer bottle slipped from his hand as he saw the wave hit, foam and crashing power, roll under the boats and toss them about. A small cabin cruiser shattered against the sea wall, and Sonny was on his feet and running to save his sloop.

Already water was over the dock, and Sonny sloshed his way through. The sloop was bobbing but safe, and he frantically pulled lines. He couldn't understand it. The sun was bright, the clouds white and cheery. There was a good stiff wind coming from the mainland and he thanked God for it but that was all the weather there was. Could it have been a tsunami? Sonny doubted it. The huge destructive tidal waves were caused by earthquake or volcanic eruption, and the water took time to gather into the wave. With a tsunami there would have been some warning. This wave came out of nowhere.

Sonny cleared the sloop and had just brought it about when his hand froze on the wheel and he looked out to sea. A second wave, long, high, foaming green death, bearing straight ahead. His sails were down but the sloop had a good diesel and he powered toward the wave, praying he hit it head on, knowing that if the sloop was turned he'd capsize. The wave rushed to meet him and suddenly was upon him, something alive, power that Sonny had never felt before from the sea. The wave lifted him high, high, then shot straight down like an elevator. Sonny looked back and saw the aftermath. There was no dock, no pier. The bar he was at had ceased to exist. A forty-foot Morgan ketch was sitting on top of a condo, its masts gone. And there was water everywhere. He headed for the open sea.

Sonny had two radios on board, and he used both of them. The AM-FM told him that Dade and Broward counties were under ten feet of water already, and the Keys had disappeared. Mass evacuations had been tried in Miami, Fort Lauderdale, New Orleans, Boston and New York, but the water was too swift and there seemed no end to it. Millions were dying. And then Sonny lost touch with the mainland and he could only guess after that.

With the other radio he hailed any ship at sea, any land based operator, but what he got was some long distance gibberish that bounced to him from somewhere far out to sea, and a lot of static. In time he gave it up all together.

The waves continued, massive, but gradually they became smaller and the interval between them greater. He kept the shoreline just in sight, and rode the waves as they came in. Day went to night and back again, and again. He

Illustrated by William R. Warren, Jr.

stayed on the sloop, caught rain on big plastic sheets and took what the sea gave him to eat, rode what was now a constant roller coaster of small swells.

And when it was over Florida was no more than a chain of islands reaching north to more islands that used to be the coastline of Georgia and Alabama. Island Florida was as distant from the rest of the Earth as the Moon. Sonny didn't even know if the United States of America still existed.

And the survivors didn't have a name for it. The sea rose, and there was Before, and there was After, and that was all. It had happened too suddenly, had taken too many lives. It didn't need a name.

Dixie Man gathered up the camouflage netting while Sonny took the helm. The big Cigarette kicked in smooth and strong, and they glided out of their hiding place. Sonny eased the throttle open gently until they had passed the sand bars, then powered up as they hit the open sea. The long, narrow, deep-V hull, designed originally for smugglers, adapted later to ocean racing, bit into the water, then rose up on plane and buried its rudders. The engines shook the decking and made Sonny's teeth itch. Hammering out over the swell, it was a boat to take fatal risks in.

PART TWO: THE JOB

It was sunrise, and pink and orange began to color the eastern sky. The sea was marred with ripples cast from some distant storm, but the Cigarette cut through the swells, skipped, powered through them. Sonny was seated behind the wheel, his denim jacket buttoned to the throat to keep the chill off. The damp cold of the morning air did not suggest the heat that would come later.

The rest of the crew was below, trying to catch as much sleep as possible. Sonny knew that in the next twenty-four hours, sleep would be a luxury.

They had been traveling for about two hours, rushing to meet the convoy and Captain Marlowe, and then get to the dive site. Checking his compass, Sonny made a correction to port, the muscles in his forearm bunching. His hair was further whitened by salt water that had dried there, and the wind carried it stiffly back away from his face.

Dixie Man appeared in the hatchway, hesitated, then pulled himself up and came over to Sonny.

"Couldn't sleep?"

"Hell, no."

"Anybody sleeping down there?"

"Actually, just Adam. He's snored out in the starboard bunk. Latina and Boomers are in the stern talking. Me, I just couldn't stay down there any longer."

"Nervous?"

"I ain't afraid to admit it. We got a hell of a job ahead of us."

Sonny had been thinking the same thing all along. The job had several dangers. The crew of the Cigarette would have to go ahead of the main column, spearhead for the convoy, then connect special couplings to the tanks, and be ready to pump away into the tankers as soon as the boats got there. The less time lost, the less the risk of discovery, and speed was the only thing that might keep them from a fight. Sonny and the crew would be unprotected, vulnerable, but they could save the convoy precious hours. And alone, they stood a better chance of not being detected by ships from the Big Island. The plan was to slip in and then slip out again, but Sonny doubted that they would be so lucky.

The tankers were old trawlers, modified to carry fuel, and they were capable of reasonable speed when empty but were slow and ponderous when loaded. Sonny saw this as a primary danger, because if Big Island found them, they would not be able to run fast enough. They would have to fight or leave the cargo, and nobody was willing to do the latter.

Another problem was the site itself. Sonny had never dived there, nor did he know anybody who had. He had no idea what they would have to contend with below, and he didn't enjoy the prospect. The flood-wave impact might have created a tangle of wreckage. And there was always the danger of sharks. For some reason the shark population had exploded After. Blues and blacktips were everywhere, but what concerned Sonny most were the big guys—mako, tiger, hammerhead. A massive naildriver had hovered near Sonny's dive sites a few months back, its very presence a threat, and it had taken two hits from bang sticks to take the monster out.

"Pushing the boat pretty hard. Sure it's worth all this fuel to get to the convoy?" Dixie Man was smiling his good-ol'-boy smile.

"Really not a problem. We'll rendezvous with Marlowe, then head out to the site. Whatever we burn we can replace when we tap the tanks."

"Have you worked with Marlowe before?" Dixie Man asked.

"Couple times. He's good at what he does."

"He damn well better be." The smile had vanished from Dixie Man's face, and Sonny realized just how nervous the other diver was.

"You ain't gonna crap out on me, are ya?"

"We've been on a lot of dives together, Sonny. No reason for you to say that. It's just that this time we're up against the big stuff."

"I know."

"Damn it. It sure was simpler Before." Dixie Man rubbed the stubble on his chin.

A face popped up in the hatchway, and Boomers came on deck. She was dressed in white painter's pants and a loose orange jersey that said Tampa Bay Bucs on it. Her long blonde hair was pulled back into a ponytail, away from her face. Delicate cheekbones, a graceful curve to her jaw, thin lips and a pert nose. Her face glistened from some cream she had put on, and she smelled of coconut.

"Hey, guys."

"Mornin', Boomers. You get any sleep?" Sonny asked.

"Just a mite." Boomers put her arms above her head and stretched mightily, thrusting her chest out, a casual motion that still drew the men's attention. Sonny had seen her flirt before, setting men off and then leaving them in her wake, but she never played that game with the crew. She was professional and tough, the best armorer Sonny knew, and absolutely stunning in a bathing suit. Sonny wondered for the hundredth time where a woman like Boomers had learned about weapons and explosives. Strange things happened After.

"How's the hardware?" Dixie Man asked.

"We're in pretty good shape," she said. "The forward M60 had a minor problem with the extractor, so I put a new one in yesterday. Everything else is as good as I can make it, seeing how scarce spare parts are."

Sonny smiled. "Don't need to remind me. We should be able to pick up some parts when we're done with this job."

"If certain divers weren't so rough on the hardware, maybe it would hold up better." Boomers poked Dixie Man playfully in the ribs. "And quit leaning on my grenade launcher!"

"Shit, oh dear! I'm not hurtin' the damn thing. You act like it's a pet or something."

"I built it, it's my baby." She smiled at both of them. The grenade launcher was ingenious. Boomers had taken pieces of various machinery, welded them together, and made a weapon that was accurate as well as devastating. She was proud of it.

There was a noise forward, and Adam appeared, leaned against a bulkhead, silent, arms folded across his chest. He was Haitian, tall, spidery, gaunt, dressed in a light blue sweater and torn jeans. His nose was wide with flared nostrils. He had thick lips that when parted revealed bright teeth like white stones. Adam rarely spoke, although Sonny knew he understood at least three languages. At his hip was a long knife in a battered leather scabbard. Once he had seen Adam use that massive knife, in a bar fight on Manatee Island. He had never seen such speed, or such delight as Adam wiped off his blade on the dead man's shirt.

Latina was right after him. She was of medium height, dark from the sun, striking, with high cheekbones and exquisite lips, and an athlete's body. There was a quiet ferocity about her that Sonny found disquieting and attractive at the same time, and he had no idea from where it stemmed. She kept to herself and never confided in anyone. Sonny didn't know her real name, and neither did anyone else, simply calling her Latina and leaving it like that.

Latina's hair was thick, jet black and glossy, brushed and tied back. She came up to the wheel and Sonny found himself caught in her eyes. He just couldn't get past them. Her eyes were so dark that at a distance he could barely make out the pupils, but that was not what affected him. Her eyes were a wall, a barrier that shut out further contact, that made all who looked at her keep their distance. Yet at the same time they were mesmerizing, and Sonny had to remind himself often that she was part of his crew.

"How much longer to the convoy?" Latina asked, raising her voice against the roar of the diesels.

"We should be sighting them soon," Sonny answered.

"Soon, nothin'," Dixie Man said. "Just off to starboard," and he pointed out to sea. Sonny looked beyond his crew, and saw the outline of ships on the horizon. He turned the wheel slightly and headed for them.

As the Cigarette pulled up to the boats, Sonny was reassured and alarmed at the same time. There was a refurbished Coast Guard cutter, familiar from his days in the service. Speed, maneuverability, lots of firepower, but the need for that firepower sobered him. There were two tankers, converted into service by adding long cylindrical tanks salvaged from tractor trailer rigs. There was also another Cigarette, making five boats in all.

Sonny pulled his Cigarette near the gunboat, paralleling it, pulled out a bullhorn and clicked it on.

"Ahoy." The word sounded metallic and artificial.

"Ahoy, yourself." It was Captain Marlowe. He was an older man, a veteran of many fights. Gray-haired, potbellied, he had spent most of his life at sea, and Sonny trusted him.

"What the hell are you doing on the bridge?" Sonny said. "Don't they know to keep you in the bilges where you belong?"

"Yeah, using your head to clean out the sump."

"How'd you get messed up in this?"

"Branson needed a captain who could fight. The old one didn't have the stomach for this kind of game no matter what the payoff. Me? Hell, I'm greedy."

Sonny grinned, and did not mention the poker problem. "Any changes in the plan I gotta worry about?" He and Marlowe had gone over the details long before, but Sonny wanted to make sure there were no mistakes.

"You're to go ahead, according to the coordinates Branson gave you. Set up and be ready. The way I figure it, you'll beat us there by about three hours. These tankers ain't shit for speed. When we get there we'll pump away. And then get the fuck out of Dodge."

"Where the hell is Dodge?"

"Forget about it. Just get your ass in gear. The faster we get in, the faster we get out."

"I hear ya. I'll buy ya a beer when we get back."

"You're on. See ya, Sonny."

While Sonny and the captain were talking, about a dozen men from the cutter appeared on deck, and they shouted and whistled at the women. Latina ignored them, but Boomers laughed and waved back. Some of the men yelled lewd suggestions; one grabbed his crotch and moaned. Boomers fired back a couple of obscenities of her own, and the crews on both ships laughed.

"Hang on," Sonny said, pulled hard to port and buried the throttle. He shot a quick glance back at the men on the cutter, and wondered how many would still be alive when the raid was over.

What a rush, Sonny thought. After all these years diving, the feeling was still the same. The excitement began when he first started to tug on his wet suit, clip on his weights, secure his tanks. It grew as the dive routine progressed; the equipment checks, the last review of planning and strategy for the dive. Sonny contained it, but the feeling was almost overwhelming. He had to remind himself constantly to take his time and make sure everything was as right as he could make it, because a mistake made in haste was something he would not tolerate in himself. And finally that first leap, the shock of the water, the surge of air in his mouth, millions of bubbles, and the sensation. The wonderful sensation of being suspended, floating in a world not his own. There was an intense freedom in diving, where a man could strip off the clumsiness of the surface and become graceful, buoyant. There was a new set of rules here, where airbreathers were at a disadvantage, but he welcomed them as the price to pay for the exhilaration. When Sonny dove, he became part of the sea.

Sonny twisted, tucked his legs in, and dove straight down, away from the bubbles, away from the surface and the light. He moved through the water with practiced rhythm, with smooth kicks. He saw Dixie Man a few feet below him, struggling with a large coil of rope. Sonny reached out, took part of the line and helped untangle it. Dixie Man waved thank you, then turned and headed down. Sonny held the line for a time, to be sure that no other tangles developed, then followed.

The sea was so calm under the surface. No waves, no current to speak of. All there was was the blue of the water and the dark of the bottom. And that was becoming clearer as well. Already Sonny could distinguish the mound of green that was the truckstop.

They had found the site just before noon. Sonny had checked Branson's coordinates, even consulted an old tourist brochure from Before to make sure they were right.

The brochure had a picture of an Amoco station, about a couple of acres in concrete, with trucks and rigs of all sorts and shapes, and passenger cars all around. The main building was a square-looking affair, one story, but sprawling. Built of solid cinder-block, it had lost its doors and windows but stood otherwise unbroken. The brochure said that inside were a restaurant, restrooms, dining halls, short order, showers for the truckers, even a souvenir shop for the visiting Yankees. But what mattered to the divers were the underground fuel tanks that supplied the pumps. The pumps were in an L shape around the building, four islands in the front for cars, six islands on the side for the trucks, and Sonny knew that the tanks would be buried alongside.

And they were going down. Their plan was to hit the truck side first. It should be the easiest to find. The southwest corner of the building was in line with the fuel islands, about fifty feet away. The islands ran parallel to one another, about another fifty feet. When they found one, the rest would be easy. The plugs would be more difficult to find, lying flush with the concrete on the bottom. Sonny's hand brushed against the metal-detector on his belt. The plugs, the access into the riches in the tanks, were all made out of cast iron. That's when the metal-detector would come in handy, because he doubted that there was anything else on the bottom that resembled the plugs. Then just pop 'em, stick on a coupling, and wait for the tankers.

The rest of the crew would handle support duties, watch for ships and sharks, change air bottles. Adam manned the dive boat. The boat was a large inflatable raft, motorized, and his job was to drop tools and equipment, and most important, the couplings to the divers below. The original disaster had apparently swept the fueling area clean, taking even the overhead canopies away. For once, there'd be no need for cutting-torches and the time wasted.

Sonny saw no sign of sharks, or even anything that might attract them. His breath came easier. Both he and Dixie Man had bang sticks, deadly affairs, poles with special tips that contained a live 20-gauge shotgun shell. Set the tip, smash it against the target, and bang. Highly effective on shark. Sonny had used them many times before, but he hated to rely on them.

As the pair dove, the outline of the building became more and more clear. The truckstop was covered with growth, wrapped in a green shroud. A few fish swam about, meandering through the broken windows. The place looked frozen, caught in a living ice, out of time. Sonny checked his wrist. They would be working at just about eighty feet.

Dixie Man took the lifeline he had been stringing and tied it to a stout metal pole near the building. He flashed Sonny a thumbs up, and then whipped back and raced into the building, eager to explore. Sonny went after him, equally curious. There ° was something about these underwater ruins that fascinated him, compelled him, but he knew there wasn't much time for sightseeing. Inside was dark and close, and Dixie Man flipped on the powerful lamp he had on his belt, swept the beam around the room. They were in the main dining area, a large room with broken tables strewn about. The windows were nothing but twisted frames, and the sea had claimed the place. Sand had sifted in, settling like a carpet, and marine growth was springing up everywhere. The bright light startled hundreds of small fish. But Sonny saw the counters and the empty stools waiting for truckers and tourists; could almost hear the waitress barking out orders to the cook. He shuddered in spite of the warm water around him. There was no evidence of bodies. The sea and its creatures had tidied that up.

Sonny grabbed Dixie Man by the shoulder, and signed to him that they had to get moving. Dixie Man nodded his head, and the pair swam out a broken picture window. Sonny took the coil of rope from his shoulder and secured it to the same pole that held the surface line, then swam in the direction of the fuel pumps. Dixie Man followed, keeping the line free of tangles. The pumps were not difficult to find. Even though covered with weeds and growth, they were the only things that were upright. They stood out like sentinels, guarding, marking. Sonny fixed the other end of the rope to the first island to act as a safety line, in case they needed one.

The current was not strong. Sonny could barely feel it tugging his legs. All the better, he thought. With only a mild current, they would not have to tie onto the safety line. They could work without a tether, and Sonny was glad that they would have one less thing to worry them on this dive.

Sonny took out his metal-detector. It was short-handled, compact, with a flat dish on the end and a waterproof battery pack further up the handle. He pointed at Dixie Man, then waved his arm in a circle to his right. Dixie Man nodded and began to search, nose to the sea floor. Sonny took the area to the left and did the same.

The bottom was covered by several inches of sand and silt, but outside of that there were few obstructions. Sonny swam easy, unhurried, the metal-detector making wide sweeps over the sand. A light flashed on the head, and Sonny stopped, took out his knife and dug around the spot. A loose door-hinge, green with corrosion. He jammed it into the sand, a marker, and went on.

A few minutes later he hit it. The light on the metal-detector stayed on and did not blink, and Sonny knew that meant a large piece of metal. Taking his knife, he probed under the sand, could feel the outline of the plug. He pushed the sand away with his hand and found it, like a small manhole in the concrete. Taking a pry-bar, he popped the lid, saw with satisfaction that the nipple and its cap were intact. Sonny inflated a balloon marker, secured a guideline to it and watched it race to the surface.

Sonny looked over and saw Dixie Man swimming to him. He signed to the other diver that he had found the tank for the first set of islands, and that he should start for the Number Two tank. Dixie Man nodded emphatically, then sped to the next island.

Soon, Sonny saw the dark outline of the dive boat making toward the marker. It stopped, and after a moment he saw the coupling begin its descent, small at first, then growing larger. The coupling drifted down to him, and Sonny swam up to it, caught it, and guided it to the tank. The coupling was shaped like a cross, about two feet high, with two open ends and a large valve system in the middle. On one open end was a twist clamp designed to be fitted to the tank. The other end was a bayonet coupling to hook onto the hard suction hose from the tanker. In the middle was the valve system, two water-tight diaphragm closures about four inches apart, like the bread halves of a sandwich.

Sonny slid the open end over the tank nipple and tightened the clamp with a wrench. When secure, Sonny checked the valve system to be sure that the top valve was closed and the bottom one open. He then flipped a lever, and a small bottle of compressed air attached to the coupling flushed the cavity, forcing the water out through a one-way release valve. Now Sonny was ready to pop the cap on the buried tank.

Sonny took a T-bar, a tool similar in shape to an automobile lug wrench. He inserted the wrench though a sleeve in the top diaphragm valve, carefully, and when inside he twisted a knob in the center of the T-bar that extended a three-pronged fastener from the tool. The tool was shaped like a hand, and he groped with it, found the cap, and clamped on.

A shock of fear ran though Sonny, brief but intense, familiar. This was by far the most dangerous part of the job, because a mistake or bad luck now would cost him his life.

If this, if that; so damn many ifs, Sonny thought. If the pressures were too great, if the coupling were not fitted properly, if some unforeseen condition existed, popping the top to the tank was like opening a bomb. And with all that risk, the tank could be fouled or empty, and all the work for nothing. He grasped the handles of the T-bar, took a deep breath and bit down on his mouthpiece. He twisted, hard, heard a familiar and reassuring squeak as the lid started, and then finished unscrewing it. Air pressure inside the coupling kept the fuel inside the tank. Sonny pulled the T-bar out as far as he could, then closed the bottom valve. The second valve sealed the coupling, and it was safe for Sonny to open the top valve. A bubble of air rushed out, and he removed the T-bar and the cap, without fouling the fuel tank.

One was down, Sonny thought, and about ten, maybe

as many as fifteen, to go. He turned and swam in the direction of the fuel islands, saw Dixie Man working with a coupling of his own, passed him and went to the next island, the metal-detector ready.

Sonny swam leisurely through the bubbles, a hand on the lifeline, the surface beckoning. He broke into the sunlight and the first thing he saw was Latina's face above him. He climbed aboard, the aluminum ladder hot to his touch, and she helped him with his gear, her face expressionless. He plopped into the seat next to Dixie Man, drank from a plastic water jug.

"How many more do you have?" Boomers asked. She was stripping an Ingram machine pistol, running a clean rag over it. She had on a postage stamp of a bikini, flashy red, sweat and sunscreen shining on her brown skin. Latina had on a more modest suit, emerald green, and Sonny noted the way she moved, grace and strength in her body.

"Three more," Sonny answered her. It was hot on deck with little wind to cool off the day. "They should be pretty easy, though. All three of them are next to each other."

"How many all together?"

"With those three, it will be fourteen."

"That sounds like a lot of fuel," Latina said.

"I got the feeling that Ol' Mole Face underestimated the find here," Dixie Man said. Everyone, except Adam, nodded in agreement. The tall Haitian was standing away from the group, glassing the sea with a large pair of binoculars.

"There's no real way of telling how much is down there." Sonny took an orange section from a nearby tray. "Some of those tanks could be bone dry. But I think Branson either didn't know the exact size of this truckstop, or he thought he might get away with more of the profits."

"He can't possibly think we're that stupid," Boomers

said, rubbing the Ingram with renewed effort, her agitation showing. "I mean, what an asshole!"

"Asshole is as asshole does," Dixie Man said, a big grin on his face. "You know, I heard once that Branson. . . ."

He stopped short, Adam's cry cutting and forceful.

"Boat!" Adam was pointing to port. The crew jumped up, everyone talking at once. Sonny shouted them quiet.

"Where?" Sonny said.

"There. To the northeast." Sonny grabbed the binoculars and pressed them to his eyes.

"Is it the convoy?" Latina asked.

"No chance." Sonny answered without taking the glasses from his face. The binoculars were powerful, and Sonny could see that the boat was medium sized with a high tower, probably used for sport fishing Before. He could not see any armament, the captain of the boat relying on speed and distance to keep him safe. On the high tower Sonny saw a figure dressed in khaki, the quick flash of sunlight on glass. He lowered his binoculars and nodded his head, smiled grimly.

"Game's over," he said. Boomers took the glasses from him and looked for herself.

"Northeast. Shit!" Dixie Man slapped his thigh in frustration.

"Dammit! Turn on the radio and see if they're transmitting," Sonny barked, and Latina switched it on. She adjusted the frequency, found the signal, and the crew listened in silence to the coded message, not understanding a word but knowing too well the meaning.

"What language are they speaking?" Latina wondered.

"Who cares?" Dixie Man said, running his hands through his hair.

"So it's up. We'll have a fight before this is over," Boomers said.

"But why haven't they hit us already? We are only one

boat." Latina was leaning forward, her hands clenched on a railing.

Sonny gestured toward the north. "They know what we're doing here, but I don't think they'll attack. To do them any good, they'd have to bring up their own tankers, and they'd get caught when Marlowe and the convoy got here. And they don't have enough time yet to gather a task force big enough to handle the cutter."

"So what do you think they'll do?" Dixie Man asked.

"I think they'll let us do all the work and take us when we are out to sea."

"I do not feel so," Latina said. "I think they radioed back to their island for more guns."

"Obviously, they called to base, but I don't think they have the time to mount anything yet. Big Island will need about four hours to muster, and another two or three in order to intercept us. They haven't had the time, and if they throw down on us too early, they'll lose their shot. They can't afford that."

"So what do we do?" Dixie Man asked.

"We get off our asses and finish the job."

The crew was eating a light meal when the convoy steamed into view. Sonny swallowed the last bit of his sandwich, and stood up.

"About fucking time," Dixie Man said.

"Don't be too hard on them, Dixie Man. Marlowe said it himself. Those tankers ain't shit for speed," Sonny said.

They watched as the ships approached, the tankers bulky and slow, the gunboat lean, sleek, wolfish. The radio crackled and Sonny grabbed the hand mike. They talked on extreme low power.

"This is FLA-107385. We have a shadow."

"Affirmative." Marlowe's voice sounded mushy and muffled by the weak transmission, but hard, as if he had not had an easy voyage. "We caught a shadow about 20 klicks north, but he evaded."

"Sport fisher? High tower?"

"Affirmative."

"That's our boy. We have confirmation he is already in touch with home base."

"And ain't that just fucking peachy."

"Marlowe. Dixie Man and I know the setup down below. Send the dive boats over to pick us up, and we can each supervise a crew."

"How many you got?"

"We got fourteen."

"Jesus."

"You got capacity?"

"How the hell do I know? I'm a sailor, not a hydraulics engineer."

"Okay, sailor. See the markers? That's where the tankers go."

"Got it, Sonny. And out."

"Over and out." Sonny put the mike down.

The dive crews from the tankers were efficient and experienced, and there were few problems hooking the couplings to hard suction hoses for the transfer. Dixie Man's crew took the truck side, Sonny's the passenger-car side. Because they had fewer tanks to drain, Dixie Man's crew finished first. His crew came over to help and together they wrapped the job.

It was early evening when Sonny and Dixie Man got back to the Cigarette. Latina, Boomers, and Adam had been busy, and the boat was ready to ride escort.

"Are the fuel tanks topped off?" Sonny asked.

"Yes," Latina said. "We tapped a line into the tanker's hold. I made sure that the fuel was filtered."

"Good thinking. Lord knows what kind of sludge that fuel might have developed in that tank."

Boomers whistled softly. "Look at those tankers. If they were any lower in the water, they'd be barges. How many gallons do you figure?"

"That's the good news and the bad news." Sonny tapped his foot on the deck. "We pumped 24 regular, 25 unleaded, and 22 premium. We even got almost 30 in passenger car diesel."

"On the truck side, we brought up just a little over 72," Dixie Man said. He screwed his eyes shut and clicked his tongue. "That's around 173,000 gallons of fuel, give or take a couple." Boomers and Latina looked at each other, amazed.

"But like I said, it's the bad news, too." Sonny pointed at the tankers. "No way those dinosaurs are gonna be able to run." The crew followed his hand, watched the tankers bob gently on the water. They did not say anything.

After a time, Boomers moved away from the rail, reached for something next to one of her supply crates. She had a mischievous grin on her face.

"Hey, Sonny. Catch!" Sonny looked, and caught instinctively.

"What the hell is this?" She had tossed him what looked like a container about the size of a small milk carton, just the right size to fit in his hand comfortably, with some kind of spring assembly on the top. The container made soft sloshing sounds.

"It's a grenade."

"What the . . . !"

"And it's perfectly harmless. For the moment. I made them up while you were busy with the tankers."

"What are they? Really."

"Grenades. Specifically, gasoline grenades. Kinda like a Molotov cocktail without the bottle. See?" Boomers came over to him, took the grenade, and began explaining how it worked.

"There's about a pint of gasoline in here," she said, tapping the container. "Here on top is a spring-loaded firing system. A pistol primer is inserted here, right underneath the firing mechanism. When you toss it, the grenade is weighted so that it'll land nose first, setting off the spring, snapping the primer, and ka-boom! Instant barbecue."

"Is it live now?"

"Don't go and faint on me, Sonny boy. Look here. This one doesn't have a primer in it yet. But even if it did, see this safety tang? It's gotta be flipped up before the grenade can fire."

"I see. Kinda like a regular fragmentation grenade. It won't go until the tang's released."

Dixie Man walked over and examined one of the grenades, weighed it in his hand. "This," he paused, rolling the weapon gently, "would be pure hell at close range. Do you know how much damage this much gasoline would cause?"

"I didn't make 'em for the afternoon bridge club."

"But you did make them for unexpected company," Sonny said. His voice was grim. "Let's hope our guests don't show up."

PART THREE: THE FIGHT

The convoy ran in the darkness, no lights, no sound except the steady drone of the engines. Marlowe had ordered radio silence during the return home, and Sonny agreed with him. Running from a superior force that might be close at hand, it didn't pay to advertise their position.

The moon was at its quarter, silvery, tingeing everything a light blue like a cheap fluorescent lamp. Sonny could see his crew in the dimness, could make out the phantom black shape of the tanker rumbling to the left of the Cigarette.

The two tankers were in the center of the column, paralleling each other, and the two Cigarettes were flanking them. Sonny had his Cigarette positioned to the starboard of one of the tankers, hugging the outside. The gunboat pulled up the rear. They were headed north at quarter speed, the tankers putting all possible horsepower to use. The tankers, full to capacity, struggled to maintain speed although the seas were calm. Sonny thought of a fat lady trying to swim with her hands tied behind her back. The image did not amuse him.

Sonny wished for a full moon. With clear skies and a full moon he could see better, and that would make him feel better. There was something about fighting in the dark that was especially nervewracking. He looked into the cloudless sky, the stars thick as soup. At least we won't have to fight the weather as well, he thought. His hand was sweaty and he rubbed his leg absently.

The crew was busy, making last minute checks on weapons that did not need to be checked. Wearing flak jackets and old National Guard helmets, Boomers and Latina were making an adjustment on the forward M60. Adam and Dixie Man were in the stern, cigarettes dancing between their lips while they talked in whispers. In the dimness Sonny could see the assault rifle lying on Dixie Man's lap, and he suppressed a dry chuckle. Dixie Man must have cleaned that damn gun five times in the last two hours.

The two men were sitting next to the second M60, Adam casually propped on a metal box of ammunition. Boomers's precious grenade launcher was mounted to port, just about even with Sonny's position.

Sonny kept one hand on the wheel, the other patting his thigh. His hand brushed something hard and metal, and his eyes shifted. A 12-gauge semiautomatic shotgun was in a boot next to him, a strange-looking weapon that Boomers had modified for him. The weapon had a pistol grip but instead of a conventional stock, Boomers had made a molded fiberglass extension. The extension fit the bottom half of Sonny's forearm, and it slipped on like a sleeve. Three Velcro straps allowed Sonny to bind the weapon onto himself, so he could shoot and steer at the same time. He also had his .45 automatic on his hip.

Sonny felt a touch on his shoulder, flinched, and then swiveled in his seat. Latina was standing to his left, a half smile on her face.

"I startled you."

"No, no. I knew you were there. I'm just a little jumpy." Sonny was glad for the darkness, because he knew he was blushing fiercely.

"O.K.," she said, but Sonny knew she knew better. Latina kept her hand on his shoulder, and it was strangely pleasant and disquieting at the same time. Outside of accidental bumps in close quarters below deck, she had never touched him before.

"The damn tankers may get us killed."

"True," Sonny said, "but they're the reason we're here in the first place. We need the fuel."

"Branson needs the gas to keep control of his islands. We need the gas to . . . find more gas. Seems kind of stupid."

"We need it for more than that. Fuel is money."

"And power too. That's why Branson is in it. Piece of fucking scum."

Sonny's eyebrows lifted in surprise. "I didn't know you shared my opinion of him. What has Branson done to you?" Sonny's intensity grew. Latina had never volunteered any information about herself. The coming fight, her touch on his shoulder. Sonny wondered.

She looked away from him, towards the bow, and he stared at her profile. "Before I came to you, just a little while After, Branson tried to buy me from my husband. He offered him food, rum, and drugs. My husband was going to deliver me to Branson, but I found out before he could do it." She paused. Her long black hair was pinned up inside her helmet, but a few wisps had struggled out and they rippled in the wind.

"I found out two days before he was to deliver me. At first I did not believe, but later I did. I wanted to kill him."

Sonny felt her strong hands dig into his shoulder. Still, she did not look at him. Her jaw was set, and even in the moonlight Sonny could see the hardness in her eyes.

"That last night, he wanted me. Maybe because he knew it was his last chance before Branson got me. I let him although I hated it. I had a knife, and wanted to kill him while he was inside me."

"Did you kill him?"

She looked down and shook her head slowly. "I could not. Even though the knife was in my hand. Later, while he slept, I left the bed and got dressed. He always had a pistol at the bedside, and I took it and pointed it at him while he slept, but I could not kill him. Even after all he had done, I could not kill him."

"You must have loved him very much."

"Love?" Her head twisted and she gave Sonny an incredulous look. "No, no. Not love. Killing him like that would have been murder, and that is a sin. I have killed many people, men and women, but I have never murdered anyone."

"What about Branson? Can you work for him like this and not hate him?"

She laughed. "Branson is something I scrape off my shoe." Sonny smiled at her, and before he realized it his arm was around her waist. She did not pull away.

The shrill call of a bosun's whistle snapped Sonny to attention. He looked to the deck of the cutter, behind and to his left, and there he could make out a figure dressed in white standing on the catwalk before the bridge.

"Latina. Take the helm." She looked at him, puzzled; she hesitated. "I know you've never done it before, but see the compass heading? Just keep that needle steady." Sonny got up and she took his place. He reached into his shirt and pulled out his own bosun's whistle, and blew two long, high notes, then grabbed his infra-red binoculars.

The signalman was a young man, clean shaven, and the infra-red lenses gave him a hellish look. He had semaphore flags in his hands, and when he began his wigwag, the waving flags added to the effect. Sonny counted the movements, spelled the words in his head. The message did not last long.

Sonny dropped the binoculars from his eyes, still looking at the cutter and the signalman. He blew a single high note on the whistle, and watched as the signalman vanished inside the bridge. He turned, saw Latina intent on the compass, and put his hand on the back of her neck. She looked at him, questions on her face, and made room for him in front of the helm.

"We move out. Captain has some boats on the screen. Lots of them. They're moving on either side of us."

"What, to cut us off?" It was Dixie Man, clutching his rifle and shifting his weight back and forth like a boxer. Adam had come forward as well, and Sonny could see Boomers in the stairwell leading below.

"I'm not sure, but he wants us and the other cigarette to do a flanking maneuver. We're to run ahead about a mile and parallel his course. When the boats attack, we can double back and hit 'em on their own flank."

"Wait a minute," Boomers said. "How many are we up against?"

"I don't know. Let's see if we can find out." Sonny turned on his radar screen, and the crew gathered around the green light.

"Nothing there," said Adam. His voice was like stone.

"That doesn't mean anything," Sonny replied. "This set has such a limited range we'd never know it until they were almost on top of us. Captain's got a big set high up."

They stood in silence for a moment, then each of them moved swiftly to general quarters. Latina took the forward M60, Adam the back, Boomers the grenade launcher. Dixie Man slapped the side of his Ruger Mini-14, then settled between Boomers and Adam.

Sonny opened the throttle and pulled away, could barely make out the other Cigarette doing the same. He moved fast, and soon the other Cigarette and the tankers were out of sight in the darkness. Sonny kept the throttle open for a long moment, until he was reasonably sure that he was a mile from the tankers, then settled back to one quarter speed. He checked his bearings, and held course.

The green radar screen showed the blips of their own boats, lit up against the sea-return. Still nothing, but he knew it was no false alarm. Marlowe would not cry wolf. He guided the Cigarette in the darkness, no bearings to hold him except his instruments, and waited. The bow made steady, gentle slaps into the sea, and Sonny counted them like heartbeats.

Suddenly, on the edge of his screen, Sonny saw the first green blips of the hostile boats. About a dozen of them on each side of the convoy, aiming at the tankers.

"They're coming in!" Sonny shouted so the crew would hear. Dixie Man was at his side in an instant.

"Oh shit, oh dear!" Dixie Man's mouth was open. "Jesus, look at 'em. Why so damn many?"

"I don't know for sure, but I gotta hunch. Look at the size of the blips compared to ours. They're all small. They ain't coming in with a gunboat."

"That doesn't make any sense. They got us outnumbered, but we've got 'em outgunned."

"It makes a lot of sense, Dixie Man. They can't throw

a cutter at us because of the tankers. A stray shell and they destroy 'em. They want the cargo as bad as we do.''

"They don't trust their own gunners. I like that." Boomers had left her station and was leaning against Dixie Man. "Maybe the rest of them are lousy shots too." Latina and Adam were still at station, had not said a word, but Sonny could feel them listening.

"What the fuck are we gonna do?" Dixie Man asked.

"We wait another minute or so," Sonny said, his voice even and calculating. "The boats look like they're gonna try a pincer movement on each flank. What we're gonna do is time it so that we can hit the last boat coming in on our side, before they see us."

"Kinda like Sergeant York," Boomers said.

"Who?" Dixie Man asked.

"Sergeant York. World War I," Boomers said. "Hero that killed or captured a whole column of Germans single-handed."

"Yeah, I remember," Sonny said. "They charged him once, and he shot the last man first, then the next and the next, until the officer in front was leading a charge of one."

"I bet he was surprised." Dixie Man smiled a wolf smile.

Several quick, muffled thuds came from the direction of the convoy, and sudden brightness hurt their eyes. Marlowe had fired some flares, and the convoy was lit in hot orange light. The flares were high and shot long, and Sonny could see the enemy boats coming, coming, but still he maintained course.

"Back to stations," he said, but the command was unnecessary. He waited, and then the first shell ripped from the gunboat's deck cannon, and he swung the Cigarette in a tight circle and punched it.

If he had a dozen boats this would be different, Sonny thought. With numbers he could break the attack, disperse it before they even got to the gunboat. With only one boat, all he could hope to do is cut off a few of them before they got to the convoy, and then try to stay alive. Keep moving as fast as he could. That would be the difference. He hoped the Cigarette on the other flank would do the same. He couldn't worry about that now. He flipped a switch and small lights came on fore and aft, red, yellow and green bulbs like an old traffic signal. The gunboat would know him by the lights, and not fire on him.

Sonny kept the convoy to his starboard, racing toward the line of boats. The deck cannon flashed, and Sonny's mouth tightened into a line as he saw one of the attacking boats vaporize as the big shell hit it.

Timing and luck were perfect. Sonny saw the last boat in the attacking column, an older, slower fishing boat, saw no cannon or even a machinegun turret. There were men all over it, and Sonny guessed that this was the boarding party. The fast boats to knock out the guns, the boarding party to mop up and take control of the tankers. He jammed the throttle to the max for the intercept.

Latina's first burst of fire swept over the foredeck like a hand, pushing men back. Her second burst hit the bridge, ripping wood and smashing glass, and Sonny saw men inside, their arms flailing. Adam and Dixie Man were firing as well, cutting more down in the confusion. The Cigarette whipped past the bow, all gunners shifting, maintaining fire. Sonny swung the boat in a wide arc and gave Boomers the chance she was waiting for. The fishing boat presented a broadside at reduced speed, and Boomers lobbed three quick grenades. The first hit amidships, blasting out the bridge and cabins. The second and third were back and low on the stern, and blew a gaping hole just below the water line.

A moment, and a new explosion, heat and flame as the boat's fuel went up. Sonny shielded his face, felt the concussion. He blinked twice, and saw the fishing boat break apart.

Sonny made a pass around the dead ship, and Adam opened fire, deliberately, strafing what was left of the deck and the flaming water.

"Adam! Cease fire!" Sonny screamed but his voice was useless against the sound of the M60. Adam kept on firing, the recoil moving his arms like pistons, his face in a snarl.

Jerking on the wheel, Sonny brought the boat hard to starboard, knocking Adam back from his gun. Without looking at Adam, Sonny powered out, headed back towards the convoy.

Flares were everywhere, and in the fire-orange light Sonny could see the enemy boats circling like flies around a dog. One boat was farther out from the gunboat, and Sonny made his choice. More room to maneuver, he thought, but even then it won't be easy. The element of surprise was gone.

The boat completed its turn, and Sonny pointed at it, just off the other boat's bow, practically head on. His crew opened fire; Latina, Adam and Dixie Man. A sharp staccato answered back, bullets smashing into the hull, ricocheting against armor plate. Sonny ducked low with shards of plexiglass flying over him, then quickly cut away.

The grenade launcher coughed twice, Boomers laying in two quick ones just as Sonny turned, but her throw was short and to the side. The grenades landed close in the water, and the concussion threw the hostile boat up then smashed it down again. Sonny saw the helmsmen try to hold on, shake like a damp washrag, then flung into the sea.

The chance. Latina, Adam, and Dixie Man laid in murderous fire as the Cigarette came about. Too close for the launcher, Boomers grabbed one of her gas grenades, flipped the safety tang, and made a high-arced hook shot.

"Gun it, Sonny!" she screamed, and the Cigarette roared, the heat and shock wave washing over them as the enemy boat disintegrated.

Frantically searching for another target, Sonny saw one of the tankers with a swarm of boats and men around it. They had gotten in from the other flank.

"Oh, fuck," he said aloud. "We've got boarders on the forward tanker," he yelled to the crew, and pointed the Cigarette. Sonny held the wheel steady with his knees and took his shotgun. He fitted his arm into the fiberglass extension, palmed the grip, pulled the straps tight, then pulled them a notch tighter. Sonny remembered the fierce recoil of the weapon, but also its effectiveness.

They came to the tanker and hit the near enemy ship on the blind side. The men in the boat were caught unaware and the gunners cut them down with sustained fire. Sonny fired once, twice, the buckshot blasts knocking one man into a bulkhead, another into the sea. Boomers traded her grenade launcher for the Ingram, and she and Dixie Man swept the deck.

Fire from behind. Dixie Man and Boomers went down, Latina returned fire, came up empty, struggled to reload. The Cigarette took a hit in the engine, and Sonny lost power. He emptied the shotgun into the oncoming boat, saw men fall, then stripped it off his arm.

We're dead meat without an engine, Sonny thought.

"Cover me, Adam!" Sonny rushed to the bow, took a line, and without hesitation bunched his legs underneath him and leaped. He crashed and rolled on the deck of the tanker, the line still in his hands. A machinegunner on the other boat saw what he was doing and opened fire. Bullets whistled around Sonny, shattering a porthole. Sonny took the line and secured it just as the slack gave out, the line taut, the Cigarette in tow. His pistol out, Sonny fired once, twice, then emptied the automatic as fast as he could. The machine-gunner ducked, held fire, and when he came up again Adam put a burst into him. One round caught the man in the face.

Sonny leaped again, his knees striking the deck, then off running to the helm. A third boat was coming on them, on the flank, and he grabbed Dixie Man's Mini-14 and emptied it.

"Latina! Adam!" he screamed, ducking down to find another clip. His hand touched something warm and sticky, looked and saw Boomers on her side, her eyes closed.

"Oh, baby," Sonny said, then jammed the clip home and opened up on the boat. Latina and Adam swung around and gave support fire, but instead of veering off, the boat got closer and closer. Desperate, Sonny reached for one of Boomers's gas grenades. He knew they were too close to use it, but he flipped off the tang anyway and lobbed it.

"Hit it!" he yelled, and flung himself on the deck. Blinding flash of light and searing heat, and the screams of men. Sonny jumped up and saw the bow afire, the machinegun crew dark and charred. A man was running along the deck with his arms wide, screaming, burning, and Sonny put two rounds in his chest.

The tanker moved relentlessly, pulling the Cigarette away from the burning boat. Sonny, his teeth clenched and his heart in his throat, fired and fired, no visible targets, just fired into the burning mass until his rifle was empty and he could control his terror.

The fighting was almost over. Sonny saw several burning boats, heard a scatter of machinegun fire, but that was all. He looked towards the tanker and saw men moving, coming out of fighting positions. It was strange, he thought. Sonny had not even noticed the tanker crew fighting.

The last of the flares were dying out. Sonny rushed to Dixie Man.

"Where?"

"Leg. I don't think the bone's hit. I bound it up, but I'm gonna need somebody with a needle."

Sonny looked up and saw Latina hovering over Boomers. The Columbian had taken off Boomers's flak jacket and was working on her. He went to them.

"She took a bullet in the side," Latina said. "Maybe the liver. She has got to get to a doctor."

Sonny agreed silently. He got up, came back with a blanket and an empty ammunition crate. He wrapped her in the blanket, then propped her legs on the crate to help her through shock.

"What about you?" Sonny asked.

She lifted her left arm and showed him a long shallow gash. It was not serious, and wouldn't even need stitches. She gave him a grim smile, then looked down at Boomers.

"Adam!" Sonny called, and he saw the tall Haitian wrapping his arm and tightening the knot with his teeth. He nodded at Sonny and finished tying the bandage.

Sonny went to the helm, grabbed the radio and broke the silence.

"This is FLA-107385, requesting a medical assist for two wounded crewmen. And standing by." He clicked off, waited an anxious minute, and was almost ready to try again when Marlowe's voice came over the box.

"We read you, FLA-107385. Can you transport?"

"Negative. We are without power and in tow."

"Jesus. You took some, didn't ya? When we're in position a skiff will come out. How bad are they?"

"Boomers is the worst. Hit in the side. She's going into shock. Dixie Man needs some sewing and a shot of morphine. Everybody else is dinged up but functioning."

Sonny began telling Marlowe about his side of the fight. As he was speaking, he saw the gunboat pull in behind the tanker. The flares had all died, and Sonny could just make out movement on the deck, then over the side as the skiff was lowered into the water. It wouldn't be long.

"What about you guys?" Sonny asked. There was silence for a moment.

"We took a couple hard ones. The other Cigarette is lost. They rammed after their first run. The other tanker got hit hard too, and I've got her in tow. No major damage on the gunboat, but the medics are busy."

"We lose much fuel?"

"A little, but not much. The biggest they threw at us were machineguns, and those holes we can patch."

"Do you think they'll come back?"

Marlowe snorted. "They just had the snot beat outta 'em. Fuck 'em if they do." Sonny laughed, and he was amazed that he could.

Sonny sat in the darkness, watched the glowing ember at the end of his cigarette. The smoke was harsh in his lungs and made him feel a little lightheaded, but the nicotine calmed him and he needed that.

He did hear her this time, and when her hand touched his back he did not jump. He turned and his face was close to hers.

"I didn't know you smoked those things." Latina had changed into a pair of shorts and a man's workshirt with the tail knotted to one side. She had just brushed her hair and it flowed in the breeze. Sonny put his hand on her bare midriff.

"Not usually. It's bad for diving."

"Do you think they will be O.K.?"

"No doubt in my mind," Sonny said, and he meant it. "Boomers lost a lot of blood, but between the plasma and the donors, she'll be fine." Sonny had a cotton ball and a small piece of tape on the inside of his right elbow. So did most of the people that weren't hit. Blood was life.

"That Dixie Man. After they shot him with the morphine, he still wanted a drink." Latina laughed and brought her hands along Sonny's shoulders. "He yelled and yelled and finally they gave in, but he spit it out as soon as he tasted it. It was sugar cane rum, and he wanted Scotch."

"Is Adam still sleeping?" Sonny asked.

"He's below and his eyes are closed, but with that one you never know." She paused, looked away, her voice lowered. "I do not know about that one at all." Sonny let it drop.

As they were talking the sky began to brighten, and soon the first hints of dawn colored the east, pinks and gold. For the first time they could see the boat, see the damage. There was a great black blotch to port where the flames from the gas grenade had licked and charred. Sonny's eyes shifted to the side, and saw the rust-colored stains where Boomers and Dixie Man had been.

"What do you think?" Latina said to him. "Will we be home soon?"

"Very soon. I bet we spot land in the next couple of minutes."

She paused and looked away, then jerked her head towards him and looked him squarely in the eyes.

"Carmen."

"What?"

"My name is Carmen. But only for you."

Sonny looked back into her dark eyes. Carmen. It was nice to know.

The Fruit Picker

by
Jo Beverley

About the Author

Like a number of Contest entrants, Jo Beverley is a Canadian; thus she joins Sansoucy Kathenor—a fellow member of Lyngarde, the Ottawa SF writers' group—and Edmonton's Marianne O. Nielsen, both in Vol. II.

Born in Morecambe, in the north of England, she came to North America in 1976, is married and has two children.

She has been writing for some time, and was a runner-up in a Toronto Star newspaper competition in 1985. Unusually—we know of only one other successful case—she writes both SF and Regency romances, with a novel in the latter genre scheduled for publication in late 1988.

However she directs her career, it has produced in "The Fruit Picker" a very intricately stylized, realistic rendering of a truly outrageous idea.

It is outrageous, isn't it . . . ?

Lydia McKenzie walked into
Marta Hark-Hogan's salavive with the fluid
grace that never left a fruit-picker even when
off-duty; even when, like Lydia, they were technically
retired. And she kept on walking until she had made a circuit of the vast room.

This was a deliberate move, made to avoid all the other
entrances she had made under the disdainful eyes of Marta's
butler, Slovny. The first time, as she supposed everyone
must, she had just stopped still and gaped. Gaped at the size
of the place, the pink marble, the fountains, the statues, the
quality of the light, both natural and artificial. Marta Hark-
Hogan was not just wealthy in a time when some were very
wealthy indeed, but she had uniquely flamboyant good taste.

The second time she had been careful not to stand and
gawk and had been drawn to look out of the panoramic glass
window at mountains and lakes that were not there, aware
as she supposed most people must be, that these lakes were
actually outside Marta's relatively small country home. To
put false scenery on walls or behind windows was gauche.
To reflect one's own scenery from place to place had a special élan. It had only slowly dawned on her that everyone
who had stopped gawking at the room as a whole must go
to gawk out the windows.

The third time, Lydia had planned ahead and slowly
wandered out of the room looking at the *objets d'art*. She
had sincerely admired a contemporary Chinese white jade
dove, so finely carved that she had been compelled to touch

Illustrated by Moebius

it to be sure it was not covered with feathers. Then she had
touched the companion bird, mounted a little higher on a
green jade tree, and had been shocked to find it warm and
soft. Only after moments did she realize it was a masterpiece of taxidermy, thermostatically heated to play exactly
the trick it had played on her.

This time she would look at nothing in particular and
touch nothing at all. All the same, her eyes could not help
but take in the enormous mirrors now spanning three ala-
baster archways. Something new. Did they also hold a trap
for the unwary? Or was she paranoid? Was the room just
part of the home of an avid collector, not a source of amusement for the jaded rich?

Of course, thought Lydia, as she circumnavigated
smoothly, she too was rich. Rich beyond the dreams of
most, because of her gift for fruit-picking. But compared to
Marta she was a pauper, which was not very important, and
powerless, which was. That was why she was here at
Marta's request to hear an offer of employment that she did
not want.

The tall, thin butler still stood by the door. Was anyone
ever left alone in this treasure house? He watched her every
move with that slight amusement which infuriated her. Was
this steady walking, too, what everyone did? Passing a hol-
ogrammed cabinet, original art by Suvignic she noted, she
remembered that this was the drinks dispenser and stopped.

"Perhaps, Slovny, you would pour me some wine."

The butler's sudden impassivity told her that at last she
had scored. At last she had broken the pattern of behavior
he had witnessed over and over again. He began to move forward but a warm-honey voice from the other side of the
room broke the moment.

"Wonderful idea, Lydia. The humidity must be a trifle
low in here."

Lydia turned to see Marta emerge through one of the

mirrors which were not plate glass but a pliant film that healed itself behind her. She supposed they were also two-way, enabling Marta to observe her guests.

Like everyone, Marta Hark-Hogan had a medically perfected body. But with genius she had preserved the heavy beak of a nose, which gave strength and individuality to her face in a time when perfection was cheap. She wore a high-spiraling white floss wig and a simply flowing red cotton gown lined with costly hologramatic silk, displayed because the dress was cut to the knee in front, to the ground at the back. It was a new style. Lydia rather thought she would copy it.

Marta turned, smiling, to her servant, who had arrived at the drinks dispenser. "The Burgundy, Slovny."

Lydia knew that she must have registered a twitch of shock just as the butler had. Real wine. She gave up the struggle and relaxed, allowing a smile to show. There really was no point in trying to outmaneuver Marta, who could always find a grand gesture to cap any little victory scored against her. But it also made Lydia wonder just how desperate Marta might be to contract her services, how poorly she was likely to take a refusal.

The precious liquid was brought in the tall, finely cut crystal glasses designed to make a small amount of wine seem like a great deal. If she really wanted to impress, Lydia supposed, Marta would serve it in clear plastic beakers. She admired the rich ruby lights playing in the glass as she wondered how many fruit-pickers had labored to filch the grapes from the unwilling French vines just to produce this one bottle. Or, even more impressive, was it a carefully preserved vintage from the last century, from BPS, before the plant-strike?

She had not been able to control the flick of her eyes toward the label, which was covered by the butler's napkin. Marta answered the unspoken question. "It is a modern wine, I'm afraid. I really do feel an obligation to preserve the vintage bottles. We are working on better synthetics and how can we ever match the originals if we lose them forever?''

"I find the synthetics already scarcely distinguishable from real wine," said Lydia calmly. This was by way of a compliment. Marta controlled Synthexicon, the world's leading producer of 'replacement' foods, which had developed the new flour, the new meat, the new cooked fruits and vegetables; and Chateauneuf, the new wines. In an age that had outlawed flesh-eating and then been hit by a withdrawl of services by the plant-world, the producers of microbe-based synthetics held all the power they wished to wield.

Marta laughed, a warm and pleasant sound that was completely genuine. It was the fact that Marta had no need to ever pretend to be anything she was not that made her tolerable. "They *are* indistinguishable. We have run numerous tests."

Lydia raised her brows and looked again at the wine in her hand. She cradled the glass and closed her eyes. When she opened them she took a sip. "Another test, I see."

Marta nodded. "But not of the wine. Word was out that you had lost your touch, Lydia McKenzie."

"I am retired, Marta Hark-Hogan."

Marta walked over to the semicircular window and tapped her foot three times on the floor. Four velvet-covered chairs rose from the smooth surface. She sat in one and gestured Lydia to choose among the others.

"I cannot imagine why," said Marta as if there had been no break in the conversation.

"Perhaps I have no need of money."

"No one in our world has *need* of money, Lydia. But it can be an amusing commodity."

"I do not lack amusement."

Marta regarded her thoughtfully. "What then do you do now for occupation?"

"I grow fruit."

Marta caught her breath and her eyes shone with avid interest for a moment before she shielded them with her lids. "I had heard. . . . You have tame plants?"

"Only because I do not exploit them. They give me a few of their babies for friendship's sake."

"I only need a few babies."

It was Lydia's turn to lower her lids. This was unusually blunt for Marta. Very worrying. After thought she said, "It would have to be very few."

"I need a hundred raspberries."

Lydia stared. "A few! Impossible."

"You picked as many for me not two years ago. I have tried elsewhere. Even with the season coming up, they say it can't be done."

"It can't."

Marta leapt to her feet in the only uncontrolled movement Lydia had ever seen her make. Fear trickled down her spine. Marta desperate was very dangerous indeed.

"It has to be. I have an offer for my son. That is the test."

Lydia knew then that she was in trouble. Among the very wealthy, dynastic marriages were in vogue. The lesser family were invited to show their worth by some test. If Marta had the opportunity of association with a family greater than her own, nothing would hold her back. Lydia felt very like smashing something.

"I do not want to do this," she said flatly. Argument was useless and to force Marta to make the threats she could make would be stupid. But she'd be damned if she'd give in without at least a protest.

The older woman surprised her. She sat down again and

looked at Lydia with genuine interest. "Why not? What is so different now?"

With little hope, but obliged to try, Lydia told her. "My skill at fruit-picking was largely the agility and delicacy of movement common to the trade, but it was also the sympathy I have with plant-life—as you know, since you tested me with the wine. It made me phenomenally successful. It also made the job very unpleasant. As a child, when the full implications of the plants' slow evolution away from slavery to mankind were scarcely understood, I thought it amusing to fool them, to creep up on a twitcher without it noticing me and snatch some fruit before it could jerk away; to project reassurance at a changer so it did not disguise itself before I had a handful of berries.

"Then I realized that I could make a fortune with my gift, and I did so. But working with plants all the time, I could not escape an understanding of their view of the world, their resentment at being twisted out of their natural patterns. Plants have been abused for centuries, but when mankind outlawed flesh-eating the true oppression began. Soon there were scarcely any useful plants that were not hybridized into sterility or so thoroughly harvested that not one seed was left to grow where the parent had once had roots. Is it surprising that they rebelled? That lettuce went back to its bitter ancestor? That beans flooded themselves with oleosaccharides to the point of inedibility? That fruits unable to take that way developed the ability to move away from the grasping hand or disguise themselves as useless plants?

"The fruits suffered most, of course, and they were the ones with which I worked. Even when the synthetic foods removed the extreme demands on the plants, there was no substitute for raw fruits. I could name my price for every berry, every apple or bunch of grapes I poached.

"But even as I grew rich I realized that I was a judas.

The plants learned too. It's true that I lost my touch. The plants discovered that they were betrayed. They sensed the blood on my hands. They will again." She thought bitterly of her apple tree, which last Fall had used its new-found mobility not to twitch fruit out of her grasp but to offer her one of its babies, juicy, sweet and at its prime.

Marta was looking at her with thoughtful intensity. "So you have plants again that trust you. You have rediscovered harmony with them. We need this, Lydia. Perhaps we can repair the damage with your help, learn to live in cooperation with the plant world again. We have brought yeast-based synthetics to such a level that we no longer need to rape the plant world to survive."

"Not if I steal raspberries for you."

Marta had genuinely forgotten. Her grand nose jerked up at the shock of it and she frowned. "You have made up the ground once. . . ."

"Perhaps I can again. It will take years."

Marta studied the gleaming wine in her glass. "Do you not have raspberries you can persuade?"

"A few canes. It would not be enough."

"Can you not explain to them all. . . ."

Even as Lydia laughed, Marta realized her silliness and laughed too. After the mirth there was silence. "I need the raspberries," she said at last. "But afterward, I will give you any help you need to develop your rapport."

"I need nothing except freedom," said Lydia bitterly.

"I will never ask you again and all the resources of Synthexicon will be yours."

Marta's word was good. Someday the prospect of having unlimited resources to develop her ideas might seem adequate recompense for the destruction of her empathy with the plants. But not now. Lydia stood and placed her hardly touched wine on a small table. It had only ever been a test and a symbol.

"When?"

"Two weeks from today. A hundred guests at the wedding. One raspberry for each guest. . . ." Hesitantly she added, "I could fly you to Europe. Surely your plants here would never know."

"That isn't how it works. They would know. Be clear what you are doing, Marta Hark-Hogan. Leave me be and I could put the plant kingdom in your hand."

"You still will," Marta said simply. "I have patience. Anyway, in a few years we will have the yeast synthetics perfected and will be able to woo the plants back with all the delicacy you could want."

Lydia opened her mouth and then shut it with a snap that hurt her teeth. It was useless. Marta had her strengths and her limitations. She had no idea at all of what she was doing, of what this was going to cost.

But as she walked out of the estate, along gravel paths lined with fragrant tame flowers, content with servitude if it included pampering, Lydia smiled a little, if bitterly. Marta would regret this day's work, she suspected. In a few years the yeast synthetics would be perfected? Marta was going to find that she needed harmony with the plant world a lot sooner than she thought. She had obviously not heard the rumors from the yeast vats. They said that the yeast bubbles were forming patterns and there were people who were trying to decode them. The bleeding-hearts who had led the campaign for Vegetarianism and who now refused to eat the reluctant plants would doubtless latch onto this as well. For whatever the message from the yeast was, thought Lydia grimly, it certainly wouldn't be "Eat Me!"

Black Sun And Dark Companion

by
R. Garcia y Robertson

About the Author

Rod Garcia was born in Oakland, California, in 1949. His major writing interests are science fiction and fantasy, and articles based on the history of science and technology. He has contributed to many textbooks in the latter area, and in 1981 earned a PhD in history from UCLA. He has taught at UCLA and at Villanova University.

Currently, he lives with his wife, daughter and parents, and is finishing a novel of historical fantasy. He began writing full-time a few years ago; in 1987, he published an article, "Failure of the Heavy Gun at Sea, 1898-1922" in Technology and Culture, and two SF pieces in Amazing Stories. The one called "Moon of Popping Trees" has been selected for a forthcoming "Year's Best" anthology.

He says he most enjoys writing stories that combine science fiction and fantasy, because he feels there is no real difference between the two. Certainly the following piece does not stay within any one genre. Horror and fantasy cross each other frequently; the other side of speculative fiction is rarely thus employed. But "Black Sun And Dark Companion" is, precisely, a science fiction horror story, for all its upbeat (?) ending . . . .

Ace of Wands: *Beginning, Birth, Creation, Fortune, Gain, Inheritance, Invention, Starting a Difficult Task.*
Reversed: *Decadence, Decay, Emptiness, Failure, False Start, Vexation.*

Black Sun beat down on metaled plain. Keeper's eyes were human and could see no horizon. A vault of stars hung over airless iron with no line dividing heavens from hell. The Planet was immense, with a curve so slight that the distant horizon was swallowed by night.

Keeper's stilts rang in silence on the congealed iron. A hole in the heavens told him that Dark Companion was aligned for another delivery. It was impossible for Keeper to see both Black Sun and Dark Companion at the same time. With his eyes open he saw Dark Companion as a circular blot in the sky, its gravity obscuring and twisting the surrounding stellar images. When he shut his eyes he could see Black Sun as a soft green glow, the glow of hardened X-rays striking through closed eyelids directly onto the retina.

Though it was time for delivery, Keeper did not hasten. The plain beneath his metal feet was pulled flat by gravity, but by no means even. Low undulations rolled through flows of frozen iron. Cracks and chasms opened where the iron had buckled and broken as it cooled. From his breast down Keeper was a terrible tower, and his stilts were tireless engines, but the Planet's pull was even greater. Outside the

Portal he never moved rapidly, for fear of harming his delicate human parts.

As he approached the Portal it flickered into life, a gate of shadows only partly in the world. Its gravity was slight and slender columns supported a pendentive dome, closed above but open on all four sides. Three sides led into halls, galleries, arcades, corridors and storehouses, while the fourth side emptied onto the dark plain. Eons old and largely unused, the Portal's outworks were crumbling. Minor columns supported slumping half-roofs, or only gaping space; rows of spacious buildings were collapsing room by room. Dank air hovered in the dim recesses of the Portal, never daring to drift out onto the open plain.

Ages ago, Keeper had cleared a work area just within the portal. There the latest shipment was waiting, three cubicles resting in a neat row. His seamless metal arm reached down, unclipping the Wand of Life from its place on his tripod. Properly prepared, Keeper pressed a release panel and opened the first cubicle. He removed the occupant, an orange pentapod whose five pale tentacles spread four meters from tip to opposite tip.

The orange pentapod awoke and stared back at Keeper. The beast had been dreaming of soft jeweled seas, their surface lashed into rainbow spray, and cold depths pressed quiet by the weight of many kilometers. Through its tentacles, the pentapod studied Keeper in microscopic detail. The beast saw a hairless human head and half-torso resting on three mechanical stilts, with each amputated shoulder ending in massive pairs of metal arms. Magnification turned Keeper's face into a grotesque landscape. Radiation scars deepened into canyons, plastic patches became broad pitted plains with mountains of raw bone and muscle moving beneath them. A human would have called Keeper's face horrible, but knowing no human standards the pentapod merely found it alien. The pentapod was not a beast that found the exotic frightening.

Keeper lifted the five-legged creature to eye level, then rotated the animal, viewing it from every angle. Calmly he raised the Wand of Life, and with one deft stroke shaved off a tentacle.

There was no loss of fluid; the Wand of Life healed even as it cut. The pentapod writhed and contracted. Part of its world had been stripped away and replaced by pain and horror. The severed tentacle coiled and hopped about the floor. A frown creased Keeper's features as he sliced off another tentacle. This one also leaped about the flagstones, until it twined with the first one. Keeper repeated this process, but found that the orange being lost more than limbs. Each severed member seemed to take some inner vitality with it. The body left behind grew listless, ceasing even to struggle.

This was an uncooperative attitude, and the organism would be dead or useless when the Wand had finished its work. Keeper placed the dismembered being back in its cubicle, needing to ponder the problem before he acted further. Then Keeper tidied up the Portal, taking the stray tentacles and dropping them into the flash furnace. They writhed and twisted until he let them go; then they were gone in an instant of fire and light.

Keeper approached the second cubicle and felt rage radiate from within. Hatred struck him with almost physical force. Holding the Wand of Life ready, he pressed the release panel with one metal hand, while two others held the lid down. Claws lashed from inside the box and poison spines pried at the opening, but Keeper's limbs were not vulnerable to venom and he gave the thing in the cubicle no chance to strike at his human parts.

Here was an animal he understood. Keeper observed the occupant's movements and structure, then resealed the cubicle. He had seen similar creatures before; not the same species, but close enough. Their fearsome limbs came off easily, without sapping the vitality in their armored bodies. They were usually resistant to radiation, and that was an admirable quality on the Keep r's world. Once the rage was overcome, the beast would be highly suitable.

The final cubicle gave off no strong signals, but Keeper took no chances; two arms went into defensive posture, two more gripped the Wand of Life. Keeper slapped the release panel, then rocked back on his stilts.

A human female emerged, rubbing sleep from gray eyes. She swung long bare limbs out of the box and stepped lightly onto the Portal floor. Seemingly astonished by her surroundings, she still took a moment to tuck in her blouse and push her skirt down over her legs. This blouse and skirt were contrasting shades of blue and might have been a school uniform, though Keeper was no judge of such things. Cropped golden hair cupped her face, framing strong cheekbones and soft thin lips. Her hesitant gaze wandered about the chamber, then rested fearlessly on Keeper. "Could you please tell me where I am?"

Keeper heard her words and watched her movements with awe. He recognized at once a female of his own species, but heretofore such knowledge had been very abstract and not at all like the real thing. His memory of things before he became the Keeper had been taken from him long ago.

Getting no answer, she looked around the chamber again. The shadowy Portal, piled with equipment, and its many passageways, formed no part of her mental universe. The mute half-person who towered over her corresponded to nothing she could remember. She gave his cancerous web of scars and plastic patches a frank and searching look. "Then perhaps you could tell me who you are?"

"I am the Keeper of the Portal. This is the Portal."

These responses came automatically; Keeper had never conversed calmly with a new specimen before.

"The portal to where?"

He indicated the arch that opened into starlit waste. "To there, to the Planet."

Perching herself on the lip of her cubicle, she arranged her skirt so it fell neatly over her knees. Each movement was sure and natural, a series of curves flowing one into the other. "Please forgive me, my mind is a total fog. I have no idea how I arrived here, and I feel more than a little out of place."

Keeper realized that he was still in defensive mode, and her easy manner made that seem absurd. Adjusting his stance, he lowered the Wand of Life. "You arrived in the latest shipment."

"Shipment?" She rolled the word over her tongue and ran it through her memory. "None of this makes any sense. Perhaps you had better explain exactly what is happening and why I am here."

What was happening was very simple. Keeper was ready to slice off her limbs and lower torso, then graft her into a metal and plastic body similar to his. He would also have to remove her breasts, since they were quite useless in her future work and especially susceptible to radiation cancers. What was going to happen was perfectly clear to Keeper, yet each wording he came up with seemed somehow wrong.

With a touch of unconscious impatience, she tapped her foot lightly on the floor. "My name is Kara," her tone mixed triumph with misgiving, "but many other things are obscure. I can remember my childhood, my parents, growing up on Farmstead Grange. My tutoring seems very recent, and I remember leaving for the Academy; a strange city, a new apartment—then nothing. So here I am, no

Illustrated by Alex Schomburg

longer a child but with no idea about my adult life, my current friends, or how I make my living."

She searched the scarred mask above her. "You would not care to refresh my memory?"

Keeper's human parts shifted a bit, but metal and plastic remained locked. He was trying to think how he could turn the conversation back toward her imminent dismemberment.

"I thought not, but you can surely tell me about here and now. Are there other people around?"

"There are others, out in the world beyond this Portal." Keeper gestured toward the empty archway.

Kara hopped down and strolled over to the entrance. Black Sun and Dark Companion lay in the center of a stellar cluster, and stars by the thousands hung like holes in heaven letting distant fire shine down on the iron plain. Nothing barred her from stepping straight out onto the plain. Only ancient instinct held her back. She could not see the hard rain of radiation, nor feel the gravity that flattened iron, but the ragged metal and cold stars hardly seemed inviting.

"I can't just walk out there, can I?"

"No, in your present condition the gravitation would smash you against the ground and the vacuum would rip apart your lungs." Keeper's tone became encouraging, "But once you have been altered and equipped, you may roam as freely as I do."

He had strived to put things in the most positive light, but found the effect was just the reverse. Her eyes went wide, looking over Keeper's mutilated body.

"Altered? Does that mean like you?" Kara fought to keep her voice neutral. Fear or contempt could sound like she was insulting him, and she felt in no position to offend this tall clockwork horror. "Thank you for your concern, but I do well enough the way I am. The memory needs assistance, not my body."

Keeper's human parts twisted in their harness. "This is merely the Portal, a place of transit. Out there lies the world. How can you make yourself useful in your present soft state? You cannot take measurments and gather samples, you cannot even move about the surface."

She gave his world a withering glance. "I can see quite enough of this world from here. I feel no need to chart its dimensions and sample its wonders. I grew up on Grunwald, a planet with deep forests and tawny steppe. My world has air, warmth, and life."

Pictures from the past, half-memories, surfaced and submerged in Keeper's brain. He ignored them. "None of this alters circumstances. We are what we are, this world is what it is. Your present form is clearly unsuitable."

"I find it very suitable. I never asked to be brought here."

"How do you know what you have asked for? You have no recent memories."

A knot of truth tightened in her chest, but Kara continued as best she could. "I do not need memories to know that I never asked to be hacked apart on some dead dark world."

Keeper's limbs were tireless, but his brain was human and had reached its limit. "It is not my duty to debate with specimens. In due time you will feel as comfortable as I. Any errors in shipment must be discussed with the Director."

"The Director?"

"The Director reviews all routine beneath the Black Sun and Dark Companion."

"Good, then I will see this Director." Such certainty seemed absurd even to Kara, but she knew it was her only weapon against the multi-armed colossus.

"Perhaps you will, but first return to your cubicle."

"I am comfortable where I am." This was another

absurdity; Kara was increasingly uncomfortable, but determined not to retreat one micron.

"If you fail to return to your cubicle, you will soon be far from comfortable. I am about to release the monster confined in the cubicle next to yours. His claws and venom will do me no harm, but they will damage that frail body you are so attached to."

With ill grace Kara consented to being sealed in, and the Keeper turned to confront the contents of the second cubicle.

The monster in the box called itself Chi-ella. A single glimpse of Keeper had filled Chi-ella with hate. Loathing was Chi-ella's normal reaction to the unknown, but Keeper's wicked combination of cold metal and weak flesh evoked a special disgust.

As Keeper prepared to open the cubicle, neither antagonist felt the least uncertainty about the outcome. Keeper was pleased to put Kara out of his thoughts and concentrate on routine tasks. Chi-ella found a repellant fog hiding recent memories, but the basic outline of Chi-ella's life was vivid. Hundreds, perhaps thousands of times, Chi-ella had taken weaker creatures into his claws, squeezing till they ceased to squirm. Not once had one escaped. Chi-ella's armored carapace flared from deep blue to crimson. Crushing claws and barbed tail trembled with anticipation. Keeper might mean to dismember, but Chi-ella was going to kill.

Keeper's metal limbs snapped into combat stance. He slapped the release panel and sprang backward. Chi-ella came roaring out, head down, claws wide and low to the ground. A hurtling thicket of poison spines threw itself at the legs of the metal mantis. The Wand of Life mowed through the poison thicket, scattering spines and spraying death about the chamber. Chi-ella had expected this; spines were meant to be expended. In the confusion, claws seized on Keeper's stilts. The Wand of Life flicked down, and a clawed arm came off at the shoulder. Chi-ella braced its mighty tail against the flagstone floor and heaved. The tripod toppled and Keeper came crashing down.

Kara shrank from the sounds that shook her cubicle. She had not a shred of hope to pin on the struggle. One monster might kill her, the other intended to cut her up and confine her in a living hell. If both died she would starve in a locked cubicle. Kara shut them out of her mind and hugged her body. Her flesh was still hers; she had to hold to that.

Chi-ella crawled over Keeper's metal parts, trying to reach the soft flesh. Movement became more difficult as the Wand of Life methodically shaved off limb after limb. With short chopping strokes, the Keeper whittled his specimen into shape. Finally even the massive tail came free. Chi-ella's head and torso twisted on the floor, mandibles screaming soundless defiance.

Relaxed and reassured by this return to orderly routine, Keeper snapped himself erect. Stalking about the chamber, he collected Chi-ella's scattered limbs and dropped them into the flash furnace. Each part took only an instant to burn, though the barbed tail and giant foreclaws lit the entire Portal. Then he picked up the somewhat reduced Chi-ella and returned it to its box.

King of Wands: *Devotion, Education, Friendship, Justice, Maturity, Sympathy.*
Reversed: *Austerity, Dogmatism, Exaggeration, Excess, Severity.*

Keeper shuffled over the plain with Kara cradled in three of his arms; her gravity-weighted limbs were as useless as Keeper had claimed. Gravity distorted her eyeballs, blurring the stars. X-rays ripped from the Black Sun by Dark Companion cascaded onto the plain. Though she was shielded by Keeper's metal parts, Kara could still taste the raw-metal flavor of radiation.

Beneath its dead sun, Keeper's world was etched in iron hues; black, silver, gray and slate, smudged in places with dull red-orange oxides. Keeper's voice, carried by conduction through his metal body, sounded low and far away. "You spoke of forests and steppe?"

The rebreather that covered her face and chest helped Kara push air past heavy lips and thick tongue, and into her aching lungs. "Grunwald looks green and gold from orbit, colder and drier than Old Earth, without oceans and so much cloud cover. Water lies locked in muddy lake beds, time-worn rivers, and blue-green marshes. Forests are there, but they are separated by brown deserts, tundra, and grasslands."

Secret fears surged through her. Would she see any of that again? "You can lie on Long Mere Steppe listening to the wind whisper over the tall grass, knowing that the grass goes on and on, bending over the edge of the world."

Keeper pondered this description. "The world you see around you was never like that. It was a gas giant before the explosion that created Dark Companion. That explosion took everything; moons, atmosphere, crust, mantle— everything but the metal core."

"I wish it had taken it all," she hissed.

"You will learn to see its beauty."

She thought the chance of that was miniscule, too tiny to waste her labored breathing on.

In silence they entered a natural amphitheater formed by a frozen iron whirlpool. With infinite caution Keeper decended, spiraling toward the narrow shaft that sank into the eye of the metal vortex. Ripples in the metal formed crude steps, enabling Keeper to carry Kara downward.

Once they were well into the shaft, wind whistled from a thousand openings. When they touched bottom Kara found she could let her oxygen mask slip, though her lungs were as heavy as ever. She kept the rebreather strapped tight to her chest, forcing air in and out. Even lying in Keeper's arms, she had been exhausted by the trip. Gathering the strength to lift her head, she watched the stars wander over the mouth of the pit.

A voice brought her back to the business at hand. "Why have you brought an incomplete specimen to me?"

Kara craned her neck to get a look at the Director. "She would speak to you," Keeper answered. The air in the pit made his voice almost normal, though it was still slurred by gravity.

"Speak." The Director's voice was computer-modulated and electronically correct, but Kara could see that the Director had once been human, or at least living. Scraps of flesh still beat amid a maze of wires and tubing. The Director had been augmented, rebuilt and repaired, bit by bit, until his bulk half-filled the cavern at the bottom of the shaft.

"Why am I here?" asked Kara.

"You were purchased."

"Purchased? From whom?"

"From your people, your planet."

Kara let her head fall, forcing blood into her brain. "From Grunwald? That makes no sense."

"If reality were sensible, there would be no need for science."

"Why would they sell me?"

"That is their way of dealing with heinous criminals."

"Criminals?"

"Yes; you were convicted of a capital crime. The mind that commited the crime was destroyed, burned down to the level of innocence. What is your last memory?"

"I remember my life as a child."

"Exactly. What could be more innocent? It is the most

humane and lenient form of execution.''

"But what was my crime?" Kara wanted to cry out the question, but lacked strength to do more than whisper.

"We did not inquire. There are many universes, each with billions of suns and planets. There are so many crimes. What is polite behavior on one planet is a capital offense on another. I do not waste memory keeping track of changing moral values. Rest assured, however, that your punishment is complete.''

"Then why am I confined to this awful place?''

"There still remains restitution. Your sale price helped to compensate any victims and to cover the expense of administering justice.''

Kara struggled against gravity and the keeper's grip. "To punish me for a crime I do not remember is not justice, it is unspeakable cruelty.''

"Who spoke of punishment? The mind that committed the crime is gone. That price has been paid. What goes on here is not punishment but honest labor.'' The Director went on to describe the work to date: the heroic microscopic mapping of the Northern Hemisphere, the daring descents toward the core. "It will take many millennia to fully measure this world. With care and luck you will live through it all, spending many lifetimes working for a worthy cause.''

Kara could say no more. She ceased struggling and lapsed back into Keeper's arms. In school she had debated crime and punishment with classmates, but never applied it to herself.

"We sense an inner willfulness in you, a core of resistance that respects neither our routines nor the justice of your own planet. No doubt this is the source of your criminal behavior, a kernel that the mind-probes failed to find and destroy. Conquer this willfulness and your life here will be productive; give in to it and you will be found unsuitable.''

The mechanical voice modulated itself, shifting to

another tone. "Keeper, you have broken routine by bringing her here. The Portal was not meant to be a source of disturbance. If you allow another break in routine, the Portal will be closed until a more suitable Keeper can be found. Be vigilant and consistent, uphold the routine; otherwise close the portal and terminate yourself."

The Director was finished and Kara could say nothing.

Keeper climbed out of the pit and slouched back across the heartless plain. The black rain of radiation had ceased for a time; Black Sun and Dark Companion were down below the invisible horizon. The planet's pull remained as terrible as ever and Kara hung limp in his arms, dragged down by necessity and crushed by circumstances.

Queen of Wands: *Femininity, Honor, Love, Practicality, Purity, Sympathy, Understanding.*
Reversed: *Deceit, Envy, Fickleness, Infidelity, Instability.*

Kara watched Keeper work over Chi-ella's inert form. She noticed the deft determination with which he wielded the Wand of Life, exposing Chi-ella's motor neurons, grafting them into electrochemical circuits. These circuits were in turn connected to heavy gravity treads. The parallel layout of Chi-ella's medial and posterior motor neurons made this task easier. As he worked, Keeper kept looking at Kara, hoping familiarity would ease her contempt. He fixed massive levers to the exposed roots where Chi-ella's forelimbs had been, levers that terminated in sturdy magnetic clamps. Keeper then fused the clamp-control cables to the nerve fibers that had controlled Chi-ella's foreclaws.

Stepping back, he criticized his work. "This beast has no sympathy and its neural structure is coarse. It will learn to use its new limbs quickly, but it will never be fit for more than brute labor. The hostility we saw reflects its fundamental nature.''

Kara said nothing and sat hugging her arms to herself.

Chi-ella began to react. The clamps opened and closed, treads began to grind on the paving. Keeper lifted the beast and put it quickly into its cubicle. ''Soon it will master its new limbs. Breaking its violent spirit will be another matter.'' Chi-ella's cubicle rattled.

''What can you do to alter a creature's spirit?'' Kara's question was listless; she pressed her hands hard against her thighs.

''Synthetic glands can be grafted onto the nervous system. These glands secrete sedative hormones, but they will dull the brute's wits until he is fit only for following commands.''

Kara said nothing, turning vacant eyes toward the empty archway.

''What are you thinking?''

She closed her lids. ''I see black-purple leaves against a rusty sky. I hear sunset wind in the high foliage. I smell wood smoke and dinner cooking, mixed with the odor of dank soil and new-mown grass.''

''Do not persist. None of that has any meaning here and now.'' Keeper turned his attention to the first cubicle in the shipment. The remains of the pentapod were slack and listless; its orange color had become a mottled pink. Any movements were without focus. ''Now here we have abject failure. There is nothing to do but send it back.''

''Send it back?'' Kara's voice sharpened, her eyes came alert.

''Yes, when Black Sun and Dark Companion have crept back into position a shipment may be returned to its universe of origin.''

''How so?''

"Dark Companion is the bridge. It is a hole in the heavens, existing in many universes at once."

Animation swept over her. "Send me back also."

"What?"

She brushed stray hair from her face. "I am not suitable. You said so yourself. Send me back to where I came from."

Keeper slammed the cubicle closed. The limbless pentapod did not bother to shudder. "Stop this nonsense. The Director explained your people do not want you. They will return you here or do something even worse."

Her lips became a tight determined line, her gray eyes flared. "I will chance it. Nothing could be worse than this."

"You are rash and willful." The Keeper's limbs were rock steady but his human parts quivered. "Many things can be worse; the Wand that will cleave off your limbs can cut down your will as well. Do not force me to carve holes in your mind. I want your intelligence for the tasks we have to do."

The silence that followed was broken only by the rattling in Chi-ella's cubicle.

Beyond the Portal, Black Sun and Dark Companion climbed through the shining cluster. The Keeper prepared the first cubicle, explaining the routine to Kara. When all was ready they rested, and in low tones Kara told stories of Grunwald. Keeper let her talk, hoping that saying the words would help free her mind. He set his mind to picturing the world she described. When Dark Companion was in position, Keeper signaled that the time was almost at hand.

Kara nodded and stepped back. As she moved she snatched the Wand of Life with one hand, while with the other she slapped the release panel on Chi-ella's cubicle. For an instant the two humans stared at each other, sharing shock, anger, and sadness. Then an avalanche of hate came crashing out of Chi-ella's cubicle. Chi-ella had learned from its first defeat. Spinning on new metal treads, the beast made no attempt to grapple with the great mechanical arms. Instead, Chi-ella sped straight to the flash furnace. Clasping the oven in its magnetic clamps, Chi-ella tore the furnace from its base. Then spinning about on one set of treads, it flung the furnace at Keeper.

Keeper was caught off guard and lunging forward, blinded by the flash from the flaring circuits. The massive furnace crushed one stilt completely and knocked another out of line. Only his four long arms broke his fall.

Kara cowered behind her cubicle, clutching the Wand of Life.

Chi-ella screamed in triumph, running back and forth over one of Keeper's metal arms. Then Chi-ella saw the open gateway and the Wand in the Woman's hand. Choosing escape over another meeting with the Wand of Life, Chi-ella charged out toward the beckoning plain. Forward treads hit the heavy gravity and ground to a halt. Momentum flipped the beast-machine over and gravity slammed it down. Chi-ella came to rest just outside the gate, grounded on an iron shoal and crushed by the weight of the treads.

Holding the Wand of Life between them, Kara came over to where Keeper lay. His human parts were undamaged, but his stilts were broken and one arm had been mangled by Chi-ella's treads. He looked up at Kara. "I must close the Portal."

"You will do nothing until you send me back. Reject me and return me, for I am completely unsuitable."

Rising on a good arm, Keeper scanned the carnage. An electrical fire was beginning to spread from where the furnace had been. Smoke drifted into the galleries and upper passageways. "Yes, you are totally unsuitable; your willfulness is truly criminal.

As they prepared the cubicle, her gray eyes softened and dampened. Each labored movement Keeper made was a silent reproach, mute testimony to how she had wrecked him. When the cubicle was ready she knelt beside him, taking his corroded flesh in her arms. "Come with me, Keeper. You can no longer do anything here. Somehow I will see you are repaired. You can be reborn in a better world than this one."

He shook his scarred head. "Your folly is beyond belief. You destroy my routine, then ask me to desert my post. For what? So that I may join you in some unknown fate. Leave me. Let me atone for my own folly, while your people punish you for yours."

"Perhaps they will," whispered Kara, "but first I will make them tell me why." She climbed into her cubicle, holding tight to the Wand of Life. The Keeper closed her in, then sent off his final shipment.

Dragging himself about the chamber, Keeper went through the routine that would close down the Portal. One by one the fields collapsed. As atmosphere went whistling out into the void, gravity pressed him to the ground. With his last measure of control he managed to raise an arm and turn himself off.

To the Next Generation

by
Ramsey Campbell

About the Author

Ramsey Campbell is famed as the most meticulous living craftsman in the field of horror fiction. Born in Liverpool on January 4, 1946, he makes his home there in Merseyside still, with his marvelously unflappable wife, Jenny, and his two bright-eyed children, participating in an often riotous household. He is a boon companion to many, he laughs often and loudly, and surely all's right with his world. Which is a way of telling you that an (often unreliable) cliché is true in his case, for no one doubts that unsettling ruminations coil and uncoil behind his open, ruddy countenance. In a frank autobiographical appendix to his extraordinarily believable slasher novel, The Face That Must Die, he testifies to a hair-raising childhood. But to know Campbell the man is to know that he is bearing up splendidly.

The newest W.O.T.F. finalist judge, Campbell is markedly thoughtful about his craft and the predilection that attracts some artists especially to this form. Notable earliest for his short stories, he is aware that the novice horror fiction writer has few major markets for short fiction. The emphasis is all on novels, and there is a shortage of places in which to hone one's skills competitively—which is the only true way to hone one's skills.

Should it contain some element of fantasy . . . or science fiction . . . a deft horror story is perfectly welcome here. L. Ron Hubbard, after all, is the author of "Fear," a classic in the genre. From its beginning, this series of books has published horror fiction, with Dennis J. Pimple's "Arcadus Arcane," Victor Rosemund's "The Thing From the Old Seaman's Mouth" (Vol. I) and Jean Reitz's "Monsters" (Vol. III) in addition to "Black Sun And Dark Companion." It is to be hoped that the following expert advice from an unusually expert source will help increase those numbers. . . .

Why do we write horror stories?
If you write in this field you're bound to be
asked that question, and in any case it does no
harm to know your reasons. It must be the question I've
been most asked in my career, and I've amassed quite a few
answers. However, I don't think it's possible to answer the
question until we have defined what we mean by "horror
stories," and so here goes my neck on the block.

Horror fiction is the branch of literature most often concerned with going too far. It is the least escapist form of fantasy. It shows us sights we would ordinarily look away from
or reminds us of insights we might prefer not to admit we
have. It makes us intimate with people we would cross the
street to avoid. It shows us the monstrous and perhaps
reveals that we are looking in a mirror. It tells us we are
right to be afraid, or that we aren't afraid enough. It also
frequently embraces, or at least is conterminous with, the
ghost story. It flourishes here and there in the fields of
science fiction and crime fiction, and not infrequently it
bobs up in the mainstream, whatever that is. Despite its
name, it is often most concerned to produce awe and terror
in its audience, but it is not unusual for a horror story to
encompass a wider emotional range.

All these reasons (and maybe more that you can think
of) justify one answer I give anyone who wants to know why
I write what I write: that horror fiction seems to me to be
an extremely broad field—quite broad enough to allow me
to deal fully with any theme I want to deal with. Another

answer, perhaps the one most likely to strike an echo in any aspiring writer, is that I want to pay back some of the pleasure which horror fiction has been giving me almost since I learned to read. (Indeed, my very first memory of anything I read is of being terrified by a story, presumably intended to be charming, in a British children's comic annual, where a Christmas tree dissatisfied with its lot uprooted itself from the tub and creaked back into the forest, scattering earth on the carpet as it went.) Even simpler, and as true, is the answer that I write horror fiction because I'm proud of my field. If you aren't proud of the field you write in, I can see no point in doing it at all.

Pride in a field involves knowing its history. I've no room here for a reading list, but let me recommend two fine fat anthologies as representative: *Great Tales of Terror and the Supernatural,* edited by Phyllis Wise and Herbert A. Fraser in the late 'forties and still triumphantly in print, and David Hartwell's more recent *Dark Descent.* One reason to become familiar with the traditions of your field is to discover what has already been done; another is to learn from the masters. A field whose writers relate only to their own peers is in danger of disappearing up itself.

I've seen it claimed that Lovecraft and earlier masters are irrelevant to today's writers in the field, on the basis that if they were working today they would bring themselves unrecognizably up to date. In Lovecraft's case that claim is demonstrably rubbish, and I have my doubts about Arthur Machen and M.R. James, but that's not the point. The techniques of these writers have been imitated, but they have never been bettered as far as I'm aware. Study M.R. James if you want to learn the technique of the glancing phrase of terror, the image that goes by almost before you notice and shows enough to suggest far more. (It's worth knowing how to do that.) If you want to examine the model of the tale of supernatural terror where carefully graduated hints and glimpses build to an awesome pitch, Lovecraft is where to look.

Lovecraft is a classic instance of the writer who constructs strengths out of his weaknesses. He had little interest in characterization, or talent for it, and so he wrote stories in which the insignificance of humanity is the theme and the source of his power. No wonder that his novels were essentially extended short stories. Here I should admit that I first saw print by imitating Lovecraft slavishly. With the benefit of hindsight I feel there's nothing necessarily wrong in beginning by imitation, since if you have any originality of your own to be brought out you will soon become aware of the limits of your model. The aim of any literary apprenticeship is to allow you to tell the stories only you can tell, but it can be useful to develop the rudiments of technique by imitation, in order to gain some fluency before you begin to write more personally.

I hope that doesn't sound more daunting than it is. I'm simply asking you to build a solid foundation as a means toward being true to your own imagination and experience. By all means read voraciously, and don't limit yourself by confining your reading to your own field; but read as a means to finding your own voice. There's only one Stephen King, for instance, but there are far too many writers trying to sound like him. Show us what only you have seen—tell us your secret thoughts and wildest imaginings. Above all, be honest. I believe that fiction at its best shows us what we hadn't seen before or what we had forgotten. Sometimes it makes us look again at what we had taken for granted. I recall how shaken I was by L. Ron Hubbard's classic story, "Fear," one of the most vividly imagined inner landscapes in horror fiction.

It seems to me that, despite all the claims I made on its behalf at the beginning, horror fiction as yet often takes for granted conventions that the field needs to examine in order to develop. Who better than the next generation, yourselves, to do so? Let me suggest a few clichés for you to attack.

Take the theme of evil, as the horror story often does. Writing about evil is a moral act, and it won't do to recycle definitions of evil, to take them on trust. Horror fiction frequently uses the idea of evil in such a shorthand form as to be essentially meaningless: something vague out there that causes folk to commit terrible acts, something other than ourselves, nothing to do with us. That sounds to me more like an excuse than a definition, and I hope it's had its day. If we're going to write about evil then let's define it and how it relates to ourselves. In my view fiction should disturb, and especially disturb the reader's prejudices rather than seek to reassure by indulging and confirming them.

All good fiction consists of looking at things afresh, but some horror fiction seems to have an inbuilt tendency to do the opposite. Ten years or so ago many books had nothing more to say than "the devil made me do it"; now, thanks to the influence of cheap films, it seems enough for some writers to say that the leading character is "psychotic," no further explanation necessary. But "pychosis" itself is only a catchall label for many sorts of behavior. It's the job of writers to imagine how it would feel to *be* all their characters, however painful that may sometimes be. Perhaps it's a lack of that compassion that has led some writers to create children who are evil simply because they're children— surely the most deplorable cliché of the field.

Some clichés are simply products of lazy writing. Tradition shouldn't be used as an excuse to repeat what earlier writers have done; if you feel the need to write about the stock figures of the horror story, that's all the more reason to imagine them anew. For instance, we might have believed there was nothing new to be written about vampirism until

Karl Wagner wrote "Beyond Any Measure," whose stunningly original idea was always implicit in the vampire tradition and waiting for Karl to notice it. Again, generations might have thought that the definitive haunted house tale had been written, but it hadn't been until Shirley Jackson wrote *The Haunting of Hill House* (a statement guaranteed to make some of you try to improve on that novel, perhaps).

Put it another way: I believe one reason folk feel deep emotional reactions to my own novel *The Face That Must Die* is that it confronts you with how I imagine it might really be to be a killer with "abnormal" motives, rather than keeping a Halloween face or ski mask between him and the audience as an easy device to turn him into a mere bogeyman we can dismiss as being nothing like ourselves. It's only fair to warn you that some readers and publishers would rather see imitations of whatever they liked last year than give new ideas a chance. But I've always tried to write what rings true to me, whether or not it makes the till ring. And the result has been that the till *does* ring. If you feel involved with what you're writing, it's likely that your readers will.

There's another side to the field which is overdue for attack by a new generation: its reactionary quality. A horror writer I otherwise admire argued recently that "it has been a time-honored tradition in literature and film that you have a weak or helpless heroine" implying, I assume, that we should go on in that vein. Well, tradition is a pretty poor excuse for perpetrating stereotypes (not that the author in question necessarily does); time-honored it may be, but that doesn't make it honorable. In fact, these days so many horror stories (and, especially, films) gloat over the suffering of women that it seems clear the authors are getting their own back, consciously or not, on aspects of real life that they can't cope with.

Of course that isn't new in horror fiction, nor is it new

to use horror fiction to define as evil whatever threatens the
writer or the writer's lifestyle. But at the very least one
should be aware as soon as possible in one's career that this
is what one is doing, so as to be able to move on. I have
my suspicions, too, about the argument that horror fiction
defines what is normal by showing us what it isn't. I think
it's time for more of the field to acknowledge that when we
come face to face with the monsters, we may find ourselves
looking not at a mask but at a mirror.

Now all this may sound as if it requires some discipline
and dedication, and my experience is that it does. After all,
the best way to compete is with oneself, to do better than
one did last time. I'm not the first to say that the most important thing for a writer to do is to write, but I'll add that you
should work on whatever you're writing every day until it's
finished; to do otherwise is to court writer's block, every
blank day adding to the hurdle that prevents you from getting back into the story, making the task seem more impossible. An example of this is my story "Litter," where six
months elapsed between my first day's work and my return
to the story, which I took up by writing the line "That's how
he enters the story, or this is." I should have rewritten the
story to improve its shape, of course. Now I rewrite more
and more severely, and take great pleasure in cutting thousands of words out of first drafts; I think that's a pleasure
worth learning as early as possible in one's career, not least
because realizing one can do it helps one relax into writing
the first draft, where it's better to have too much material
for later shaping than not enough.

Learning to relax enough with the technique of writing
novels comes easier to some than others; you may feel you
need to plot a novel in advance (maybe all the way to breaking it down into chapter synopses) before you begin the first
chapter, but it's worth trying to regard the synopsis merely
as a safety net once you begin writing, trying to let the novel

develop itself as it takes on more life. I did that first in *Incarnate,* and since then I've avoided plotting or constructing too far ahead, trying to know only as much as I need to know to start writing and head in the right direction. It can be fearsome to find yourself losing your way halfway through a novel, all by yourself in the unknown, but I find that the solutions are usually somewhere in what you've already written, and I can tell you that the bad days are worth the days when you feel the novel come to life.

I'm still stressing the arduousness, but let me see if I can pass on some tricks I've learned:

We all have an optimum period of creativity each day, and it's worth beginning work then if you possibly can. Mine is from about seven in the morning until noon or so. It's easy to get distracted away from your work, but music may help; my desk is between the speakers of the hi-fi on which I play compact discs (which last longer than records and keep me there longer) of all sorts of music from Monteverdi onwards. (Steve King uses rock, Peter Straub jazz.)

Don't be too eager to feel you've exhausted your creative energy for the day, but if you sense you're close to doing so, then don't squeeze yourself dry: better to know what the next paragraph is going to be and start with that next time. Scribble down a rough version of it rather than risk forgetting it. Always have a rough idea of your first paragraph before you sit down to write, and then you won't be trapped into fearing the blank page. If you must take a day or more out from a story, break off before the end of a scene or a chapter, to give yourself some impetus when you return.

Always carry a notebook for ideas, glimpses, overheard dialogue, details of what you're about to write, developments of work in progress. If an idea or something larger refuses to be developed, try altering the viewpoint or even the form: if it won't grow as a short story, it may be a poem.

Sometimes two apparently unproductive ideas may be cross-fertilized to give you a story. Then again, you may not be ready technically or emotionally to deal with an idea, and it can improve with waiting.

What else can I tell you? Only to write. Surprise us, astonish us. Enjoy your work. Above all, don't despair. The frustration you will inevitably experience sometimes, the feeling that you don't know how to write, may be the birth pangs of something genuinely new. I know I still suffer that experience every time I write a story. Believe me, it's preferable to playing it safe with a formula. Good luck! I look forward to reading you!

6770: The Cause

by
Mark D. Haw

About the Author

Mark D. Haw is twenty, English, and lives in Cam-
bridgeshire. This is his first published story, a winner
in the second quarter.

Part of the continually increasing number of United Kingdom entrants, he was England's first winner, and subsequently attended a special 1987 W.O.T.F. workshop at the
Dickens Museum in London. There Ian Watson and I worked
with a selected group including Vol. III author Christopher
Ewart of Scotland. One of the other attendees has since been
a finalist, and another submitted a finalist story to the Workshop. Haw thus graced a first-rate group, working hard in a
setting where no one could take writing lightly.

Nor does Haw appear to take it so. Even at his age, he
has a good collection of rejection slips from various SF magazines, and says in a letter to the Contest administration that
he spends his spare time reading through them. Yet he says
it in a remarkably cheerful way, probably a sign that though
he is serious, he is hardly gloomy about his eventual prospects.

We think he has good cause to be optimistic about them.

"Space is made out of trian-
gles," Frish said to her as she opened her eyes.
His face leant close to hers—seen from the corner of her eye loomed his elbow, where he leant on it, pushing an enormous dip into the mattress—and she could pick
out all the crags. He had a face like the Moon. Dee could
hear his breath; he had breath like the ocean. "Some," he
went on as she yawned, "say time, too. What do you think?"

It was dark in the room. Shadows abounded. "Is it
morning?" Dee yawned again, twisted out from under his
gaze a little way to peep at the window. "Or did you just
want to do it again?"

"You're not really just a sextripper." He leaned back,
off the elbow—the bed quivered back like elastic, into the
greater curve formed by the rest of his body—and lay on the
pillow, hands now behind his head. "Have you ever done it
with a whole family?"

Dee wondered what he wanted to hear. It had been that
way for her for a long time; I can't act on my own, she
thought. I have to do what they want, exactly, without even
knowing what they want. For the Cause. She decided:
"No," she said.

"'No'?" His eyebrows rose with the corners of his lips.
She smiled too. "No. But I spent a week once tripping so
that this stuck guy got to do it with me every year of his life."

He laughed, then looked amazed. "Every year? He
waited—"

Dee nodded. "June twenty-first. Regular." She slipped

out from under the bedcover and moved toward the gray square of the curtained window. "The last time around it killed him. He was eighty-four." She peeped out of the window, lifting a corner of the curtain.

Frish laughed and she heard the bed shake with him.

Dee turned back from the window, smiling. You bastard, she thought. And kept smiling.

Finally Frish quietened and got a look in his eye. It *was* morning, but he wanted to do it again anyway.

She needed information, but she had to be subtle. She grimaced lightly in the shower and rubbed hard. It was only psychological. And Dee already had her pay-off set up for when she left him; Frish was going to die.

He lived out in a desert. Once, Dee thought, I could have said '*the* desert' and everybody would know where I was. But *when* I was? When she came out of the bathroom she saw his box lying on a side table, in the sort of casual position that said it was well-used, like a pair of shoes or a TV control unit. She grimaced again, and got the feeling that the box was grimacing back.

"I can order you a new box over the phone," Frish said, appearing from the kitchen.

"What?"

"You were looking at my box." He smiled, coming up to her. "Like you wanted to steal it. I . . ." But he wasn't about to offer again. The longer I have no box, Dee thought, the longer I stay with him. The loyalty of the age. Having no box was her excuse for being here and it was certainly a good one (thought up by somebody faceless back in 6750); her story was that she had dialed the desert by mistake and then dropped her box down a cliff somewhere. Frish would have believed anything; eclipsed by my tits, she thought.

They ate breakfast. "I have to shop tomorrow," Frish

said around a mouthful of something. Everything here tasted of sand to Dee. "I shop once a—"

"You told me." But she smiled, because she still needed her information. She ate some more sand.

"Well, I was wondering where you'd like to go." He ate sand too.

"Go?"

He shrugged. "You don't have to."

"What do you mean, go?"

"Shopping."

"*Shopping?*"

There were frowns flying everywhere. Both stopped eating, sat with elbows on the plastic table (lightly dusted with sand) and stared. "I mean," Frish said, with great deliberation and twisting eyebrows, "Where would you like to go shopping? I mean, *if* you'd *like* to go *shopping?* With me?"

After a moment, they both laughed.

As they resumed eating, Dee thought, this is too convincing. We're almost real, together.

She didn't fancy the shopping trip at all, so she decided to try to get it over with that evening. All I will see—she thought as they climbed into bed and the heating system rumbled and the stars were very clear outside—in those shiny shop-windows and demo-men in suits—all I will see are the faces of those kids beside the streets and the blood at the corners of their mouths and the crushed-down faces. She tried not to think about 6750; it might show on my face, she told herself. Frish started in on her neck and worked down. He had never kissed her *lips*.

"Frish," she said afterward, even though he sounded asleep (she had to start somewhere), "What are we doing? I mean, technically."

Maybe he was awake. Dee half hoped he wasn't. But

finally he rolled back over so that his face leapt out in shadowed relief and he lay there, possibly annoyed, staring at the ceiling.

But he didn't sound annoyed. "We're technically screwing. Reproducing, only not reproducing. If you want to free it from its more artistic aspects." He stuck his tongue out; now he was smiling.

He thinks I want to do it again, Dee thought. He thinks this is my polite way of begging. "I didn't mean *that*," she said, putting just the touch into 'that' that a sextripper ought to. "I mean, the tripping. The boxes. Traveling here and there all over the place."

"From 1998 onward," he reminded her. He sounded like a schoolteacher suddenly—Dee was glad, and excited, thinking this ought to be it. "And past 6770 it gets nasty. Don't forget that."

Or he was just being obvious to fend off her question. She could hardly remember herself exactly what she'd asked now. Don't forget, she thought, and saw the crushed—

—faces. On a whim: "How nasty does it get, Frish?"

He laughed. (*Laughed.*) "You think *I* want to find out?"

I could show you, she thought. I could show you.

And that is where your whims get you. Take perverse pleasure. She found that, for once, she was getting turned on; she didn't stop to wonder why. Perhaps, somewhere in space-time, she really was a sextripper, tripping in space-time.

"Ever meet yourself?" she whispered to him, afterward again, but he *was* asleep this time.

Life is so cryptic, Dee phrased in her mind. It sounded a sensible thing to say but she could say nothing because she was holding his hand and he was dialing carefully, screwing up his eyes and peering at the box in his other hand as if he wasn't used to going shopping once a week. She could only think of the hours ahead, which she didn't want to face. We can never escape, she thought to mask some of the images, even though we can beat Einstein; we can travel anywhere and when, but we still move forward, when we get there, at that same mortal pace.

She would have liked to have continued in such a profound manner, but he'd finished dialing and they were—

—there, an invisible gap between times. Are we really anywhere different? she found herself thinking in that disoriented mind which spun down inside her disoriented head.

She gripped his hand tightly, to keep from falling.

He misinterpreted it, as he always did everything, and squeezed back, as if they were really in love or something. And led her into the throng, thronging the lit streets.

"Where are we?" she asked him three times, only getting heard on the last. People buffeted like winds out on the desert. Christ, she thought, where *were* we?

"It's a place I know," was all he said. He pointed to the night sky; it looked overcast first, then her eyes, picking up photons eventually, identified stars, until she could see almost the whole universe. It was even more full than the universe over the desert; Dee was amazed. There were still some things that could amaze her.

"It's an asteroid," Frish said. She stood still while staring up to keep from walking into people. "We're on an asteroid. You haven't been here before?"

They'd never told her about this, back in 6750. "No!" she gasped. And then she thought, am I in the future? Maybe I'm ahead of 6770; maybe they lied about *that* too. Maybe I—

She wished she could have seen what he'd dialed. Then he said, "2345," and she knew. "It only exists for five years. Maybe you missed it," he went on. "I mean, five

Illustrated by Leo and Diane Dillon

years like this. In 2348 it gets holed by a suicide-man in a space rocket. Or so they tell me.''

Dee shivered; it was cold here, under the stars. The plastic sky that had to be there was invisible and possibly not there at all; just thinking about the vacuum made her chest tighten a little. And that made her hand tighten; we're getting really serious about this, she thought, meaning to grin wryly but for some reason not managing it. She wondered who the suicide-man was (had been, would be) and she thought she knew. The Cause, again.

In the school of the revolutionaries, where they were/are/will be only trying to safeguard their future:

her task was probably the most important ever. If of course a phrase such as 'ever' had any meaning in the years sandwiched between 1998 and 6770. At their hideout under a mountain it was 6750, or something like that; already things were becoming a little nasty. There were—she'd seen, on her way here—people in the streets whose time was compressing, who were reflecting from the 6770 barrier, who had lived up to that year and *bounced* and were living their lives backwards. Oh, it didn't bear thinking about. Nobody was about to theorize. But they wanted her to take out the time machine.

"The *source*," they said—because, you see, when your time compresses so does your head—it's all in the mind— and you begin to hurt and your blood begins—"is what you have to get. The boxes are just boxes. We want the machine; we want you to destroy the machine."

Of course she was confused—they'd always told her not to think about it. "What will happen?" she wanted to know.

For a moment they might have seemed unsure, or maybe not. "It'll give us our time back," they said. "It'll stop this traveling. It'll tip the light-cone back forward. It'll let us live properly again. It'll get rid of 1998 and 6770.

It'll give history back its early years, and the future back its late ones."

She nodded and tried not to think about it.

"We know who built it," they said.

The Cause.

"You're shivering."

Dee stopped shivering. They gravitated to a coffee-bar at the top of a cliff, and sat by the window—it was midnight and there was room—and stared downward. It was a very long way down. At the bottom there was mist.

"I think that's sulfur," he said. "But I could be wrong. How do I know what sulfur looks like?"

"Do they serve tea?" Dee wanted to know.

"I suppose so. You look frightened."

Well, she felt frightened. She smiled thinly but didn't try to hide anything; something inside was telling her that she was through hiding, and she was running out of arguments. She wanted to tell Frish about how long she'd been looking for him, how many places and times she tripped through, traveling, doing her bit to further crush heads back/forward/sideward in 6770. "Don't you have any friends?" was all she said. Perhaps it was by way of build-up. I have to kill him, too, she thought, drinking tea.

Frish was shrugging. Then he said, putting his coffee cup down and spilling a little in the saucer, "Well, maybe not now. I used to," he added, then realized that 'used to' was a meaningless phrase in a non-time-based culture but could do nothing except laugh.

"You don't mind? Why not?"

"Why not I don't mind, or why not I don't have any?"

"What?"

"Why—"

A comet passed by, far brighter than the sun. The sun

was only a star and hardly looked like a comet at all.

"I like to keep to myself." He shrugged.

"You invited me in."

He laughed.

"I want the source," she said.

"I've come a long way," she said, with a gun pointing under the table at his stomach. "It's taken a long time. Things can still take time, even with those boxes, and the more time we take the more time the souls lose in 6770. You're going to tell me where the generating machine is and I'm going to destroy it. And we'll be free of each other; everybody will be free of each other. Nobody will have to be crushed anymore." That was the Cause, after all. "It's unnatural. What you've done is unnatural."

Frish looked very surprised. And a lot of other things besides. And then his face fell as if it had been a mask and he just looked resigned and regretful. Or so Dee interpreted it. "Dee," he said.

After a moment, while teacups clinked in the background, she waved the gun around a little—even though he couldn't see it—and said, "Is that all you have to say?"

He drank some coffee. She wondered if he'd actually seen the gun at all; it began to feel a little ridiculous in her hand. "Dee," he said again, as if it meant something—

"My name is Suxanne," Suxanne said.

"I don't suppose they told you."

"What?"

"They didn't tell you about the others."

"The others?"

"The others who've tried to get me like you're trying to get me. You're not the first, Dee or Suxanne or whoever you are. They've been trying for a very long time. Why did you think I lived in the desert? Why don't I have any

friends? The last friend I had"—he drank coffee—"was the
first one who tried. She told them that I invented the
machine and then she tried to tell them where it was and
then she tried to kill me." He drank coffee. "Is that the
plan?"

Suxanne wavered with the gun. Frish wasn't looking
too concerned. The crushed heads in 6770 were a long way
away, and receding. The word was betrayal, or something
like that, sort of mixed in with other things, some of which
had been on *his* face earlier.

"Well?"

"Well, what?"

So maybe it was accidental, so maybe not. He had a lot
of blood in him. I had to kill *someone* was how she defended
herself to herself. And it was hardly going to be *me*. Anyway, the blood burst forward—not what she'd expected—and
spread out on the table and the floor and spattered across
her front; speckles even got onto her trigger finger, where
they felt warm and sharp, like pins. They say sometimes that
you learn something when you kill someone. Suxanne, or
Dee, or whoever she was, dropped the gun and drove her
chair back and as she stood quickly, his body, after teeter-
ing, fell to the right and hit hard against the glass of the picture window. She thought for a moment that he'd go right
through and tumble down the cliff into the sulfur or whatever it was. But the crack she thought was glass breaking
was only the steel gun hitting the floor. Frish's eyes weren't
even open. Maybe, she thought as she flew toward the door
and eyes followed her, he knew what was going to happen.
She wondered if by some strange telepathic mechanism he
hadn't actually engineered his own death. Maybe it was accidental, maybe not. The people in the midnight cafe didn't
really know what had happened and she made it out onto
the street in the ensuing silence. Where, standing there, she

realized she'd forgotten to take his box.

Looked back, saw realization taking place inside where people crawled like flies over the body in the corner, looked forward, saw a few straying heads turning her way, ran. Ran. Ran. 'Til exhausted.

I could leave the Cause behind, she thought, and become a *real* sextripper.

Picking up another box had been absurdly easy; he was probably still sleeping it off somewhere while Suxanne flitted here and there semi-aimlessly on the stolen machine. Only semi-aimlessly because she was actually looking for someone, somewhere, as well as running. She'd sat shivering in countless cafe windows watching streets, mostly night streets because she had an idea she might be more at home there, wondering at alternative times whether she'd left prints on the gun, on the body, in the house, anywhere. The only solution to the murder seemed to be her own non-existence.

She was always like this after a kill.

I've destroyed their bodies, she thought, and I've destroyed my own, but I can't escape like them. I wonder, she continued in her mind as, wherever she was, it began to rain. I wonder how many people I *have* killed. For the Cause. Through the endless searching. To wind up here, another one dead, the closest one so far, and still without what I need to know; I still don't know where the source is.

A waitress wanted to know if she could help; Suxanne asked her about the machine; the waitress smiled and shrugged and offered her another cup of tea. Suxanne smiled and said no and left and stood outside in the rain, until the feelings she always had after a kill finally died down. She got very wet. But it made a change from sand.

"You have to go back," they told her when she finally

found one of them, who took her to more of them, in a shadowy dripping cellar more like a cell, a floor that creaked and leaked, a light bulb that burned her eyes and fizzed when water drops fell on it.

"Back where?"

"To the desert. His house." They were all as shadowy as the room; she'd never really known who she was working for. She wasn't working for these; she was working for the people in 6750, who should have been in 6790, who were living their lives backwards, who were clasping their shrinking heads in despair, whose lips were dripping blood from the corners. In the corners of the cellar there were dark stains that were probably blood, too.

"Why?" she said. Her voice whined and rattled. There was a puddle on the floor around her chair; they'd found *her*, in fact, standing in the rain. "I can't go back; they'll be covering it; the cops—"

"Forget it," they said. "Forget cops. Christ, *think*. The cops won't know when you and he came from; they'll go back to—" They looked around at each other, waiting for a date.

"2345," Suxanne said.

"Yes. 2345. So you go 2346, and they're not there. Nobody else will be, either."

"I'm confused. I'm *tired*."

"Don't try to think. Go back and search the place; find the source. He must have something there. Papers, clues we could interpret." They paused for a moment, seemed to change tones, almost considerate now. "Don't worry about killing him. He would never have told you. He would have shot you first. We wanted him dead; we wanted that. At least."

She shuffled out, following one of them to where they

said she could sleep for a couple of hours. Thinking, *at least?* What more is there?

She was dreaming of how disjointed everything might become someday soon when gunfire in the hallway woke her and sat her up straight and left her staring blindly at the wooden door; a silence as sharp as the shots cut in; she blinked; the silence blinked with her. She began to fall asleep again, sitting there amidst tangled blankets, until more rapping bullets pulled her eyelids open. This time she jerked her legs off the bed, half stood, fell back as the crucifix pinned to the door flew across the room and landed on the bed, along with splinters and bullet-smoke. There was a small hole in the door, but no light came through. Instinctively Suxanne scooped up the box at the bedside. She began to dial, lost her concentration when cries she thought she recognized came through the door, lost it again when a body she thought she recognized came through the door, back first, black steel machine gun last. More bullets followed, ripped into the body on the floor, scissored up and across the back wall above the bed, dragging ever toward her; she dialed and began to spin up, seemingly in slow-time—in her sleepy shocked state she found her mind wondering how many different kinds of time there actually were, out there— and amazingly, as the room faded, she felt heat in her stomach where an only-half-there bullet arrowed through her. She wondered now if it would spin up with her, materialize at the other end of the line and carry on through, flying out of her back into whoever was close. It would be a hell of a puzzle for the cops: no weapon, two bodies, one with a bullet in it and one with an exit hole and no entry hole. But of course everything gets confusing in a non-time-based world; it's better not to think at all. She came out, in a room, in the middle of the desert, whichever desert it was.

There was no pain and no bullet. All her reasoning had been in vain.

Frish, the man who she'd shot to pieces herself in 2345, stood facing her, with a pitying frown and a strange smile all mixed together on his face.

Suxanne wanted to fade away again; she desperately wanted that disjointedness which had been with her since 2345; but she stood, and faced him, and was unable, this time, to disappear.

She dropped her box, and it lay forgotten. She had half expected it to smash into black fragments, and when it hadn't she had assumed it had anyway. For a moment she seemed to be in three times at once. One of them was very cold and one of them was too far away to reach.

"Hello, Dee," Frish said.

Her gun wasn't where it was supposed to be; she looked at herself and saw that she was naked. Her bleary eyes reminded her that she'd only just got out of bed, however long ago it had been. Now, she thought, I really *feel* like a sextripper.

"I—"

"Here." He handed her a thin flannel gown shaped like a cloak, with a high collar and big buttons. Vaguely she remembered seeing it before. She twisted her way into it, and it, being too large, folded itself around her. She noticed the desert heat on her skin by its sudden absence as she wrapped herself. Sun streamed in through the picture window that made up the wall behind a sofa.

"I—" she began, and she still didn't have anything to say.

"Sit down," Frish offered, waving at the sofa. "You look tired. Cup of tea?"

"Coffee?" She moved over to the sofa slowly, not turning her back to him in case he disappeared or something. She sat down, stood up again, said "I—," sat down. Frish did disappear, into the kitchen, but he carried on making sounds and crashing cups and kettles, so she assumed he was still there. Finally, as she heard the kettle buzzer buzz, she said loudly, "I *shot* you."

Then she thought, absurdly it seemed, what if he doesn't know? The one I shot may have been a decoy—a test. What—maybe he hasn't heard that I—

"I know," Frish said, coming back into the room with a tray. "Or rather I know that you didn't shoot *me;* you shot another one of me." He put the tray down, carefully, onto the table in front of the sofa, and began to go about the business of pouring.

"What?"

He finished, handed her a cup. His face, leaning toward her, still had that same expression, a kind of confused confusion, mixed of course with absolute knowledge and control of what was going to happen. It didn't fit together properly, as if he had a cleft lip or something, so she tried not to look too often. She stared at her coffee, swimming around.

"I'm sorry," he said, "I've forgotten your real name. You told me, but—"

"It's Suxanne."

Frish nodded. "Yes," he said. "I didn't have time to remember it before; you—"

"I *shot* you!" Now she looked at him, incredulous and hoping that he would have time to explain before she finally went mad and ran off into the desert and lay down on a rock until the sun fried her like an egg.

Hot coffee dripped in tiny streams down the side of her mug, scalding her fingertips with tinier pinpricks. She looked down and saw her hand shaking and quickly put the cup down on the table and then found her hands wandering around, looking for something else to do. They fell like hawks onto one of the gown's big round buttons. She left them to it and looked back up at Frish, who, it appeared, was staring into his own coffee, or tea, or whatever it was. Suxanne said, after he didn't speak or look up himself, "Didn't I?"

Now he looked up. His face was still all twisted up, but now she hardly noticed; she'd gotten used to getting used to things. "You shot one of me," he said at last. "It's hard to explain."

"Explaining must be easier than coming back alive with a slug—" She didn't continue. How, she wondered, do you talk, civilly, to someone you've just *killed?* She tried to think of what they would say, back in the cellars and holes in 6750 and wherever else; something about the Cause, no doubt. Nothing helpful. Then she remembered that, in the last cellar she'd visited at least, they were probably all dead themselves; it was possible, she realized, to conjecture that she herself had killed *them* too, assuming the cops had been after *her.* Being the only one allowed liberal use of her own box, she had of course escaped. It saves me, she thought, while it kills the people from 6770.

Frish, it appeared, was explaining. "—but there're more of me. I mean, they're all *me.* But they're everywhere, and I"—faltering—*"I,* my mind, I suppose—*I'm* only in one place at a time. I mean, one place and time at—"

They stared at each other. It was a morose scene; there were barriers between them everywhere; it was seeming to drag on forever.

Finally he managed it. She was almost ready to believe anything anyway—and, for that matter, he was almost ready to say anything.

"I seeded all the time—1998 to 6770—with copies of me. They're living; I can invade them any time. It only took a little tweaking of the machine. I could do it for you. I had an idea who you were, but I hung around, seeing what would happen. It's all happened before. They didn't tell you that—they never told any of the others, either. The others rarely got as far as killing me; I'd lost them long before. I didn't lose you—partly because I thought you seemed different, or maybe I'd just had enough of running. Partly because you acted faster than I expected. You shot me and I changed to another of me—to *me*, here—and I dialed this place and time, being pretty certain somebody would turn up and try to search the house. There's nothing here; go ahead and search. I wanted to show them that killing me, even chasing me, was doing no good; I wanted to explain."

"About this?"

"About 6770."

The Cause, she thought.

"And the cause of it all," he said.

There is, after all, she admitted to herself, more than *one* cause. As such. Maybe that's what's wrong; maybe confinement—

"You're here," Frish was saying, "because of what you've seen in 6770. I suppose you are."

She'd almost forgotten about that.

"And I'm here," he went on, "to tell you that you're wrong; what's happening to the people there is good, not bad. And not painful." He seemed to confer with himself. "Maybe a little painful. But worth it, for them. Ever seen"—He was questioning now, she realized—"anybody with a crushed head before 6740?"

She shook her head, thought about it, shook her head again. "6750," she said. "No one before then."

He poured more tea, or coffee, or whatever it was. He was nodding. He handed her her cup back, then when she didn't take it he put it down carefully, silently, on the table. Steam rose, twirling around itself. He sat down, then sat forward intently, hands wrapping his own mug. "It takes a

bounce of thirty years. Maximum. And that's only to *us:* the
people themselves, with their crushed heads, experience it
as"—shrugging—"maybe an hour. Then they're gone completely. In that hour they're . . . rotating. Out of our space-
time. It's a kind of Lor—a transformation. They hit 6770
and rotate up out of our spacetime." He was looking excited.

All she could think of to say was "Why?"

"6770," he said, as if '6770' were a code-word to end
all code-words, an ultimate explanation, a final absolute
meaning. Thankfully, he enlarged. "6770 is the barrier.
Time ends at 6770."

"Because your machine—"

"No!" he shouted. Suxanne felt as if she were back in
the cellar-classroom indoctrination of 6750, or whenever it
had been, getting shouted at by crippled (failed) ex-terrorists
now flying desks, long-nosed high-foreheaded people who
wanted to be out killing for the Cause. *"Not* my machine!
My machine didn't create the barrier; *the barrier is natural.*
It was always there, in 6770." He scanned her eyes with his
eyes, trying, she supposed, to gauge how much she believed.
She in fact believed it all, in the same way that she'd
believed it all back in 6750; she was used to believing.

"I'm tired," was all she could say. And the sun was
going down, across the desert. She began to feel chilly,
inside her gown.

"I've got to *explain.*"

"Let's fuck," she said after a moment. For once, it was
an answer.

I was a sextripper all along, she thought. And, in the
cool darkness and quiet, half in the dip his body made in
the bed, she chuckled and her body chuckled with her. Ripples spread out; he woke up.

"I was a sextripper all along," she said to him, smiling.

"Your destiny," Frish said.

He appeared to be going to sleep again. "Explain some more," she said, lying on her side and balancing her head on her hand and nudging him with her knee.

He rolled onto his back and put his arms behind his head, on the pillow, staring up at the ceiling. He glanced at her. "I built a time machine."

"I *know*." She laughed.

"A *small* one. Like your box. Your box isn't a machine—it's just a remote unit." Her box stared back at him from where it sat, on a table in front of a mirror. "But the first box I built was a real machine—I built it around . . . 1986. Somewhere like that. And I flew into the future; spent some years finding out."

"The past?"

"Not the past. You can't go into the past. The earliest I could go—anybody can go—is the date the machine is first used. It's technical." She shrugged, or at least tried to, making the bed rock lightly in all different directions. "And I found—eventually—the barrier. At 6770."

"Time ends?"

"Time ends. No more. Our time and space just shut down. Lives just cease; everything ceases. So I thought about it, built a large machine that would operate over all space and time—that's what you tap into when you dial on your box. I built it and started it up in 1998—"

"1998."

"Yes. 1998. Now you know." Now Suxanne was staring up at the ceiling too, but he went on anyhow. "And I . . . *angled* it so that at 6770 our time/space component . . . so that we're—the people there—are rotated into other dimensions. Which *do* continue. You can do it—just dial 6770 and sit back. From here I can't see through that rotation; maybe those new dimensions end too, somewhere. I don't want to go through; if you go through, you don't get back. Despite what it looks like, time only flows—really flows, up here—"

He twisted a hand out from under his head and tapped his temple. "one way."

I never would have thought, Suxanne thought—but had nothing else to think. I never, she decided finally, would have thought *anything*. This is too large to think about. That's why they tell you, she realized, not to think at all; it doesn't bear thinking about.

"I'm sorry I shot you," she said. At least, she thought, I think I am. Does it matter?

"It doesn't matter," he was saying. He rolled his head on the pillow to look at her. "I've been murdered five times."

"By—?"

"Four of them were from 6770. Or wherever it is they come from. The first was some punk kid who stole my boots and my original, pre-1998 box. It could be anywhere now. Don't ask me to take you to 1986."

"I can stay here," she said. The Cause? It had faded, the way people faded when they dialed.

"That sounds like a line from a film," Frish said. "The last film I saw—my last visit to 1986, when they still had films—was. . . ." He thought for a moment. "'The Blue Dahlia.' Do you *know* what a *film* is?"

"Is it morning yet?" she asked after a small silent while.

"Let's do it anyhow," he said, grinning.

Suxanne thought: we have four thousand seven hundred and seventy-two years in which to live.

"What *year* is it, Frish?"

"I've *no* idea."

She saw her box reflected in a mirror. There was another whole world behind *there,* too.

Mother's Day

by
Astrid Julian

About the Author

Astrid Julian was born in 1952 in a small community near Dortmund in West Germany, then at the age of four came to Canada with her family and lived in Edmonton, Vancouver and Toronto. In 1967, her family moved to Cleveland, and she is now a professional typesetter there.

Along the way, she has attended Simon Fraser University, Université Laval, Cleveland State University and Kent State University. She holds a Master's degree in German and a baccalaureate in French. She has a teen-aged daughter and is expecting a son on precisely the same day this volume is first being released.

She began writing as a newspaper contest winner published on the front page in Oakville, Ontario, when she was 13; has "always" been an SF reader, and in September, 1987, met Vol. II author Jay Sullivan at a Cleveland-area convention devoted to serious treatment of writing. She is now a member of the same writers' circle as Ken Schulze (Vol. II), Paula May (Vol. III), Mary A. Turzillo and Jay. What she brings us here is her first published story, containing an SF idea I have never seen before.

Aboard the interstellar pirate vessel *Nancy,* Michelle St. Gille sang in the shower.

"Mich-ch-chelle . . ." The spider-like face in the mirror coughed. Two large segmented arms lifted the shampoo and washcloth up in the air, while the four atrophied limbs along the inner thorax rinsed the shampoo from the spiracles lining the bottom jaw of the face. "That's better," ten tinny voices, one from each spiracle, wheezed. *"Ah, Michelle, comme tu est belle aujourd'hui."* A feathery arm-tip reached up and flicked soap from the five left eyes. "Not your typical Montréal *mademoiselle,"* the face whistled, "But not bad."

Was her daughter's hair still as blonde as Vassily's? St. Gille wondered as she bent her hairy face down, next to the bathroom wall. Warm jets of sterile air stretched and swirled the short fur into black daisies. She looked back into the mirror. Fluffed up like this, she could almost call her powderpuff of a face attractive.

How St. Gille loved to remember that other face, the sweet young face of Annette Kurilnikov, her five-year-old daughter, and the promises that had been exchanged as she pressed Annette back into her nurse's arms! "Grow up strong and smart. Study hard. You're going to be a very wealthy, very powerful young woman some day. Make me proud of you."

The little girl's light brown eyes had glittered with

tears. St. Gille, expecting to be killed, had felt like a tea-kettle about to explode, she wanted so desperately to leave her baby with some words that would guide her into adult-hood. ''Be good,'' she had said feebly. ''Be good, my daughter.''

What had happened to that little girl during the last twenty years? St. Gille wondered. Would she understand why St. Gille had done what she had done? Would she for-give St. Gille for consenting? And if she did that, would she then also forgive St. Gille for all the years in which the *Nancy* had carried on with its vicious trade, impossible to capture at star-spanning speeds, impossible to find among the myriad solar systems when she hove-to to take on or dis-charge cargo.

The proboscis was what really disgusted St. Gille, even after almost two decades of cohabiting the slink body. The proboscis hung limp, down across her thorax, matte-black and hairless, its sharp bony tip cracked and yellowed from overuse.

It was when the proboscis slid into the soft neck seg-ment of a warm lutscher; when the lutscher wriggled and squirmed uncomfortably, that St. Gille most regretted her deal with Chlerk, the outlaw slink. Taking the washcloth, she swabbed the proboscis clean, roughly, not caring that it hurt. She brushed toothpaste over the horn tip. The splayed bristles of the toothbrush splattered white droplets on the naked proboscis. Finally, St. Gille used the end of the small gold crucifix that hung about her hairy thorax to unclog the two stingers at the very end of the tip. The venom they shot paralyzed the lutschers.

Lutschers reminded St. Gille of Terry sowbugs. Four-foot-tall sowbugs. Chlerk was getting sloppy lately, not car-ing if the dim-witted little creatures were properly anesthe-tized before she sucked them dry. St. Gille would make sure they had that small gift. A glimpse of a heaven, before they joined her in the hell of Chlerk's mind, she thought, remembering the death of her own body.

It had taken eighteen years to find a weakness in Chlerk's carapace. And only in the last six months had St. Gille been able to plan the mutiny.

Her antennae stiffened when she thought about it. Today was the day she was actually going to see her daughter again. At last, the plotting, the conniving and the killings, especially the killings, would end.

The shower, the steady pelting of hot water drops mashing feathery antennae against her hairy head, hadn't been enough to erase the nagging queasiness at the pit of Michelle St. Gille's hind-gut. Her accomplice Billo, the ambitious captain of *Nancy*'s cutter . . . would he hold true to the plan? If he did, would he be able to carry out his part successfully?

In spite of all their precautions, the *Nancy*'s alarm had gone off the night before. It had been Billo's task to bring the police and Annette through the fields of detectors Chlerk maintained around this sun and its planets, especially Rondo, the crucial one. Despatched on a casual errand by St. Gille, then arrowing to the authorities, Billo had almost but not quite been perfect. The police had obviously found and entered the Rondon system, but had not been able to evade detection after all. Chlerk, who of course had no idea what it might be, had been hysterical with suppositions. It had taken Billo's ingenious radio calls from the cutter, and herself in Chlerk's brain, three hours to calm Chlerk again.

It was probably just some old pirate who shared Chlerk's taste for sentient creatures, St. Gille had told Chlerk. He had bought himself a new ship and forgotten to enter the proper codes as he flew by the sentinel probes. And even if it might be vice cops instead, so what? What could the cops know? The slink accessories to the *Nancy*'s enterprise weren't fools. Hadn't Chlerk and St. Gille even sent Billo to Terra to be educated? There was nothing for

Chlerk and herself to do but keep cool, St. Gille'd told her.

Thanks to Chlerk's dissolute appetites, it had worked. Even with the alarm still clanging, Chlerk had caught the mushroomy smell of wild lutscher from the fresh shipment just up from the planet's surface. She had stalked and killed a lutscher while it was still in the holding pens, abandoning herself to dreams of the hive and leaving the mundane affairs of the ship, and of their body's daily hygiene, to St. Gille.

Now St. Gille skittered out of the bath cabinet on four legs, abdomen thunking along behind. Still befuddled by the morning muddle of her many appendages, she tottered on into the captain's cabin. She'd had it panelled in knotted pine. Outrageously expensive, but worth every penny to a homesick *Canadienne*.

Her parents' cottage in Lévis, across the river from Québec, had been panelled in pine. Warm and cosy pine, so different from the cold high-tech of the family house in Montréal where her parents had been forced to move when St. Gille Enterprises, the family company, went into receivership. St. Gille had been only eight years old, but she still couldn't forget the accusing stares her aunts Elisabeth and Marie had directed at her father. As if the war had been his fault and poverty his just reward. It was the self-righteousness that St. Gille remembered best. One does not forget being judged, and then pitied, coldly and with sly enjoyment, for one's unfortunate choice of parent.

How had they treated little Annette? she wondered. She saw by the ledger that they hadn't skimped on her clothes or on fancy girls' schools. But the numbers were as cold and silent as St. Gille remembered her aunts being.

St. Gille's hairy black head swivelled to one side as she looked out into space.

The *Nancy*'s orbit was moving her into the dayside of

the planet Rondo. The edge of the dark disc that blocked the
starlight from the window of the captain's cabin was crust-
ing into a pink-and-cream crescent of reflected sunlight.
The lip of the planet kissed an abnormally bright star; the
platform that St. Gille had built on her second trip to
Rondo. Faint wisps of light flickered between Rondo and the
platform. Firefly freighters, bringing up the lutscher larvae
that formed the heart of a St. Gille biologic computer. All
perfectly legal, as long as the larvae hadn't been initiated
into the Rondon hive yet. The larvae would form their own
hive under the umbrella of St. Gille Enterprises, the largest
computer network known.

The other shipments were what made Chlerk and St.
Gille pirates. Trade in adult, fully sentient lutscher was the
only crime that still carried the death penalty on the slinks'
home world, Sheelar. It was not the enslavement, so much,
as the soul-sucking . . . and that not so much as the addiction
to it. Buyers were avid for it, nonetheless. St. Gille had
wondered, often enough, if vices were inevitably linked to
intelligence . . . whatever its embodiment. But so were vice
squads, then.

The flutter of blue, red and yellow ship lights appeared
ordinary enough. It would keep Chlerk calm when she
roused herself from her stupor. The alarm of the previous
night would seem like a bad dream. Billo was doing well.

The hairy black creature turned away from the window.
The hooks of her right hind foot snagged in the shag carpet
and she stumbled. *"Viage!"* St. Gille swore. The dark
brown carpet reminded her of home, but it was dangerous
to slink feet.

She flicked on a video terminal and swung her abdomen up, into the webbed bunk. Lately, it seemed to weigh
as much as one of Grandpère St. Gille's antique computers,
she thought, as ticker quotes flashed across the screen. She
pulled black leather boots onto her four feet. "Come on.

Viens. Where is it?'' she said to the monitor. A long line of numbers and letters streamed from left to right.

While she waited, St. Gille squirted her usual three puffs of perfume on her antennae and upper thorax and decorated the slick, black- and gray-striped abdomen with the green and yellow body paints Chlerk insisted on. Finally, there it was, almost the last listing on the Montréal Exchange. "St. G. 43-3/4 up 1/2." Good. When it was all over, her daughter would be one of the richest women on Terra. It almost made her bargain with the slink soul-sucker worth it.

"What . . . ?" St. Gille heard the sleepy voice of her bodymate pop from the spiracles. Chlerk was too lazy to fight her way through the buzzing static that fogged her mind and neuronal pathways. It was the residue of thousands of lutscher kills. She spoke aloud to St. Gille, as if they were in two separate bodies.

"You still watch stupid numbers?" Chlerk squawked as she took in her surroundings. "Is sick to waste time like this."

"Are all slinks this bitchy in the morning, or just the soul-suckers?" St. Gille whistled her usual retort through the spiracles.

"Numbers. Bah. Numbers means nothing." Chlerk answered.

"Yeah, sure. And you supply all the snuff parlors on Sheelar with adult lutscher for free. Out of the goodness of your heart. *Va te faire cuire un oeuf*," St. Gille wheezed, knowing that Chlerk's French was so poor, she'd never know she'd been told to go to the devil. It had taken Chlerk many years to follow her thoughts in English. Still, the gap from English to French was not as wide as that from English to Slink. Finding out how private her thoughts remained was critical.

"Cooks egg? Why would we wants to cooks egg,

Michelle? Sick it is, to kills something twice before you eats it.''

Ah, St. Gille thought. Chlerk had not yet learned not to translate literally. But her French was improving. If St. Gille waited much longer, Chlerk's torpid occasional excursions into the hive mind might soon be the only time she had left to think her own thoughts.

"What has Michelle done to my belly?" Chlerk pointed at her abdomen in the mirror. "You makes Chlerk an office worker with yellow stripe like that. Warrior stripe goes straight across."

"Crapaud! Even the lowest plebe of a warrior would spit on our antennae if she knew you were a soul-sucker.''

St. Gille felt control of the arms shunt to Chlerk as the slink body picked up the jar of yellow paint.

"But they can'ts be knowing that, Michelle." Chlerk struggled to paint a straight line across her shiny paunch. Almost daily, now, with each descent into the hive mind, Chlerk seemed less able to control her own body. St. Gille congratulated herself on the timing of the imminent mutiny. Chlerk seemed unaware how dependent she had become. The *Canadienne's* presence in the body freed Chlerk to indulge her appetite's every craving. After all, St. Gille was there to bathe the body, rest it, exercise it, even snap it back to reality when necessary.

"The way you've been swilling the whiskey during those poker games, they could well know that, and a lot more." St. Gille took pity on Chlerk at last, and wrested back control of the arms to give her bodymate a proper warrior's stripe.

The cabin lights flashed on and off, then glared red, as the ship's emergency klaxon blared. *Ostie!* The alarm wasn't supposed to have gone off until Chlerk was in the stock rooms. St. Gille steadied herself as she switched the link from the financial wire to the bridge. Well, it had had to start sometime.

"What news?" Chlerk whistled at the monitor.

One of the lutscher servants typed on a keyboard: "Gamma Sector report. Three vice-police sloops, maybe more. A Terry yacht." That the hive would let its members work on Chlerk's ship, when it knew how Chlerk used them, amazed St. Gille.

"The hive grows curious," Chlerk answered St. Gille's silent thoughts out loud. "Soon hive forms own network for messaging," Chlerk said. "What you does then, Michelle?"

St. Gille felt the booted feet tug the slink body toward the door. In spite of her teasing, Chlerk was suddenly worried enough to start moving their body herself.

St. Gille rolled her thoughts up into a ball and silently recited French nursery rhymes.

"Comes, Michelle." Chlerk paused while St. Gille took over control of the feet. "It stinks. Terries and vice cops together. Gives order. Alerts platform." Chlerk's English whistled through the spiracles of their shared face.

"I've done that already," St. Gille answered.

"Wakes Kurilnikov," Chlerk ordered.

St. Gille felt relief she dared not put into thoughts, not even French thoughts. Kurilnikov was far too vulnerable in cold sleep, but if she gave in too easily Chlerk would be suspicious. "Can't we wait? See if it's really necessary?"

"Chlerk curses day she makes you friend of people, Michelle. Cannot Chlerk makes simple decision without it becomes argument?" Chlerk asked. "It's Chlerk, the slink, he is hating. He doesn't knows you are my visitor." St. Gille/Chlerk pushed the call buttons for the domestic lutscher to wake Kurilnikov. "Too long it takes to be waking him out of cold sleep," Chlerk continued. "He needs be on bridge already, if cops are in Gamma."

It had been years since St. Gille had last spoken with

Vassily Kurilnikov, her husband. She longed to see him
again, but part of her was afraid. She would have to control
the proboscis, something Chlerk had never allowed the *Canadienne* to do. Chlerk never tired of doing the killing herself. The twenty years would be wasted if St. Gille couldn't
keep Kurilnikov alive, in his own body, a long life ahead of
him.

The former company battle tactician still thought St.
Gille had left with their child. She could bear the hatred for
Chlerk that showed in his face. But today she would see the
pain that her betrayal had caused. Even that wouldn't matter, if only she could see Annette and Kurilnikov reunited.

She should have driven a harder bargain, she scolded
herself, in French, for the hundredth time. One that
included freedom not only for the child but for the husband
as well.

The shared body was shuffling through the library past
a computer console when the klaxon sounded again. Chlerk
punched some keys. "Damn! What goes on on bridge?" she
asked. The monitor filled with large green mathematical
symbols, then blanked. "No read-out!" She kicked the desk
with two booted feet.

A lutscher servant came into the library carrying a
bowl of laser spheres. The pale gray chitin of its armor
plates clacked softly as it scuttled to the shelves. Passing the
slink, it bowed its head and inadvertently exposed the soft
neck. Chlerk precipitously grabbed onto the small body
with both her large segmented arms and before St. Gille
could stop her, she slid the proboscis into its neck. St. Gille
scrambled to separate herself from Chlerk with static. Too
late. As their proboscis noisily sucked out the warm body
juices of the lutscher servant, St. Gille found herself trapped
in Chlerk's feeding frenzy and the subsequent rush of ship-
board impressions as seen through lutscher eyes. Lutschers
formed a hive mind, she reminded herself. They didn't

really exist as individuals. The static in Chlerk's mind
buzzed with denial. "Murder, murder," it crackled.

Images of the bridge flashed through Chlerk/St. Gille's
awareness. In seconds, they knew all the events taking place
on the bridge up until the moment they killed the lutscher.
The ship was Terry, a Class Yacht. A commercial cruiser. It
lagged behind the other intruder ships.

Billo, where are you, Billo? St. Gille wondered. The
vice sloops are already in Delta Sector. Slow them down.
Don't let the cops come before I have at least one look at
Annette.

"Damn!" Chlerk swore. She shouted at the lutscher finishing the dead one's errands. "Brings Kurilnikov on the
bridge as soon as he is wiggling legs." The lutscher bowed.
They never spoke, but as part of the hive mind, each one,
down to the last individual on the surface of Rondo, instantly
knew what all the others knew.

Chlerk/St. Gille scurried on through the library, ignoring the bows of the two additional lutscher who had come
to carry out the dead husk. "Thinks cops sees us?" Chlerk
wheezed through the spiracles.

"Who knows? Twenty years ago, vice cops wouldn't
have had the technology to do it. Not from as far away as
Delta Sector. But if they have Terry help? We should change
our orbit. The small moon on the other side of Rondo. The
radiation from the burned-out company warehouse should
hide us until we find out what they want." St. Gille didn't
gibe at Chlerk about how the slink had been forced to use
atomics to defeat Kurilnikov and herself. Best not to remind
her of former days.

"Chlerk agrees." The slink lightly brushed the warrior
stripe with a feathery arm tip.

Kurilnikov's hair was a blonde tangle when he arrived

Illustrated by Frank Kelly Freas

on the flight deck. Wrinkled olive fatigues with sweat-stained armpits accented what years of cold sleep had done to him. His pants barely hung on his hips. His frailty tormented St. Gille. As he looked at her, the puffy slits marking his eyes widened, and the *Canadienne* could see the redness caused by the eye drops that kept the lenses moist during the hibernation.

Good human hygiene remained a mystery to his lutscher caretakers, St. Gille thought. She bent the slink body, pulled a comb from her left front boot and handed it to Kurilnikov.

"We has no time for this," Chlerk told St. Gille silently.

"You want him to work, you can't treat him like your lutscher animals," St. Gille flashed back. He was going to meet his daughter today, she thought in French. Unless Annette had sent someone else. St. Gille was suddenly horrified. They had specifically demanded her presence. But if the police had told her to keep away? Annette had to be there. She had grown up believing both her parents dead. Could she resist a chance to meet her father? Or her mother?

There was gratitude in Kurilnikov's blue eyes as he reached for the comb. Gratitude where there should have been disappointment and sadness, even hatred. St. Gille had traded away his freedom and her own life. Perhaps, if she hadn't insisted on keeping St. Gille Enterprises' cut of the legal Rondon trade, he too might have gone free.

"Never," Chlerk interrupted her thoughts.

St. Gille started. Chlerk had been eavesdropping. How much had she understood? "You needed the Company, too," she told Chlerk, trying to keep her off balance. "If I hadn't appointed you as agent for St. Gille Enterprises, you would have had no legal reason to be here."

"So . . . you makes deal because you likes Chlerk," Chlerk thought at St. Gille sarcastically. "You likes money, Michelle. You makes deal to keep money, and you keeps Kurilnikov because he keeps money safe, first from pirates,

then from Vice. What you does when daughter comes?
Thinks he keeps it safe then, too?''

Annette. Chlerk had caught something about Annette.
St. Gille's thoughts retreated into the regimentation of the
rhymes she'd recited to the infant Annette. She watched a
shadow darken Kurilnikov's face and his puffy eyes widen,
as he looked up from the feelers to the furry thorax. The
crucifix! *Merde!* She'd forgotten to take it off. He must have
recognized it. Her mother had given it to St. Gille just
before her first visit to Rondo, when St. Gille'd been crew on
an exploration ship. Doing manual labor on an expedition
financed with every last cent of her mother's savings.

Chlerk had ripped it from her neck, she'd say if he
asked. Kurilnikov looked away, embarrassed, and sleepily
took the comb from her feelers.

St. Gille couldn't help thinking of the first time she'd
met Kurilnikov. The slink soul-suckers had run out of thrills
and new sentient life forms. When they discovered Rondo,
suddenly it became the rage to explore hive minds; not the
dull experiences of the domestic lutscher, but a wild hive,
one that covered an entire planet. The war between rival
gangs of soul-suckers had been in full swing by the time the
battle tech arrived.

St. Gille had expected a Russian, of course. Some old
general left over from the last war, who hadn't been able to
find a job in the private sector.

The Company had sent Kurilnikov. A feast for the eyes
and the soul, who spouted melodious Russian songs and
poems as easily as he fought off slink raiders. All the
women had loved him.

St. Gille still couldn't believe that he had wanted her,
unrepentant capitalist that she was. How could she have
repaid him like this?

She watched Kurilnikov stretch and walk over to the control panel where five lutschers were busily plotting their

orbit around the moon. St. Gille was surprised that after almost twenty years, the sight of his slim, boyish hips could still excite her.

"Soon, s-s-soon," Chlerk fought through the accumulated lutscher static to tell her. "Soon we finds male and makes Kurilnikov friend of people, too."

St. Gille hid her disgust in French thoughts. "A nice fast one," she said to Chlerk.

"Yes," Chlerk agreed. "Fast one. Shameful it would be, to lose Kurilnikov in first mating. Noble warrior he is. Ah, ah! Such feelings I then shares with you, Michelle." She sighed loudly.

"Stop it, you old lecher," St. Gille said. "I remember the last time you got to feeling romantic. You got drunk playing poker with that slow-footed jerk Chaust and you almost lost Kurilnikov to him."

"Michelle is right. Next season Chaust was caught. And female was not so fast as Chlerk."

"Maybe he was in love," St. Gille offered consolingly.

Kurilnikov's voice ended the internal dialogue. He was seated at the controls. "How long was I being in cold sleep this time, you hairy devil?"

"Fourteen Terry months," Chlerk lied.

The look in his eyes! St. Gille watched him make mental calculations. He still hoped for a reunion with her. It was cruel, but necessary to let him believe such a thing was possible. He knew her fear of poverty. That fear had been his favorite point when he lectured her on the many flaws of capitalism. But he also loved her. As long as he believed he was protecting her assets on Rondo from vice cops and rival soul-suckers, he would keep on.

St. Gille hadn't told him about the earlier meeting with Chlerk, where she'd agreed to become a friend of the people. Kurilnikov had gone into cold sleep thinking he had saved his wife and daughter and dreaming of a reunion that could never take place.

St. Gille had wanted to die. The electrical patterns of her brain should have been pulled apart and probed as Chlerk discovered what it was like to be human. Instead, the neuronal circuitry had replicated itself inside Chlerk's brain, and no matter how Chlerk had tried, she could not erase it.

Kurilnikov punched codes into the computer. "One Terry Class A Yacht and three slink police sloops." He tapped a yellow triangle on the monitor. "There is Billo in his patroller, checking them out." Kurilnikov swivelled his seat around. "Why have you awakened me?" He looked up at Chlerk. "Your fellow creeping crawlers have situation in control."

"Billo?" Chlerk's chest limbs wiggled happily. "Yes. Chlerk forgets about Billo. Billo will finds out what they wants."

The gray and black slink body slid into the seat next the human. Both were transfixed by the traffic screen.

"What does he do, that young fool Billo? Why doesn't he turns them away?" Chlerk fingered her belly paint nervously.

"Nee znayu," Kurilnikov mumbled to himself. His body stiffened as he punched trajectories into the *Nancy's* computers. "But I think something is very rotten in your organization, Chlerk." He tapped the screen with his fingers. "Yes, there," he said pointing at a series of flashing numbers. "He's leading them right to us."

"What kind of deal is this?" Chlerk wheezed.

St. Gille hid her elation in French thoughts. The biggest deal of your life, Chlerk, she hoped secretly. She tested the neural networks. Arms and legs twitched nervously. Good. Chlerk didn't notice.

"Slink cops and Terries together. Baah. This stinks," Chlerk said.

As a message from the convoy flashed on the screen, pixels illuminated a hairy slink face. "Billo!" Chlerk whistled her disgust.

"Party-time, Chlerk. What's wrong?" Billo scratched his proboscis with arm-tip feathers.

The signal. Annette was here. Now . . . to get Kurilnikov off the *Nancy* and to her.

The monitor flashed again. "You look kind of intense, Chlerk. Eat someone that didn't agree with you?" the young, Terry-educated slink asked. His garish pink-and-blue body paints glowed like a navigation beacon.

"Baah!" Chlerk snorted lutscher body juices from the proboscis onto the flight deck. "So he goes respectable, does he? Stupid kid." Her armtip pushed the reply button of the control console. "Just says what you has to says and gets on with it."

"The game is over, Chlerk. The vice cops are throwing a party and you're the guest of honor. But before the fun can start, there's a little matter of Lieutenant Colonel Vassily Kurilnikov. There's an exec at St. Gille who wants him. I'd hand him over, if I were you. Things'll go easier for you."

"Michelle," Kurilnikov whispered.

What was Billo doing? St. Gille wondered. Why hadn't he left, the way they'd planned, clearing the way for the police to act?

"You would, Billo," Chlerk whistled to herself. "You slow-footed spawn of a lutscher toilet monitor. You thinks if with me there's no mating, there's still to sees me crawl. Well, comes here to me, then. Comes to your Chlerk," she wheedled, parodying. St. Gille saw Billo shiver with killing rage, and suspected it would kill him.

St. Gille watched as four yellow triangles headed for the *Nancy*. Slinks loyal to Chlerk were coming to warn her. Billo had disabled their communications and weapons systems, but everything could still go wrong, if they reached the *Nancy*. Kurilnikov fired. One by one all the yellow triangles but Billo's winked out. "An attack," Kurilnikov said. "I have them all but one."

Chlerk honked belligerently. She turned to Kurilnikov. "Well? And him?"

"He's coming in range."

No. St. Gille's French thoughts froze. A flick of her segmented arm and Billo could be saved. But Chlerk would know everything.

"Just another second. . . ." Kurilnikov said. His fingers hovered above the controls, then pushed four buttons, one after the other. "There."

The yellow triangle disappeared.

St. Gille wrung her chest limbs in spite of herself.

"What goes on?" Chlerk wondered aloud.

The sirens on the flight deck howled. Screens showed a Terry yacht rising between the large pink-and-cream disk of Rondo and the black horizon of the small moon behind which Chlerk's ship hid.

Chlerk/St. Gille's chest limbs writhed with agitation. "Shoots it!" Chlerk hissed hysterically.

"No. Stop!" St. Gille spoke directly to Kurilnikov for the first time in twenty years. "Look!" She pointed at the nose of the ship. Light from Rondo's star bounced off the metal hull. An etched green and white shield, which only members of the St. Gille family carried on their ships, glowed in the starlight.

"The crest of St. Gille!" Kurilnikov whispered. "It's Michelle." He turned around and grinned at Chlerk. "I knew she'd be back."

"Shoots it!" Chlerk ordered Kurilnikov again.

"Neekugda!" Kurilnikov got up to push away a small gray lutscher edging toward the controls.

Chlerk's proboscis waved menacingly toward Kurilnikov. "No! No!" St. Gille screamed silently at Chlerk. "Wait. We have one hostage. Perhaps we can get another."

Just one look, she thought desperately behind a bit of camouflaging lutscher static. *Un dernier regard sur mon bébé.* St. Gille reached up and held her mother's crucifix with the weak chest limbs.

Chlerk didn't notice. She was a whirlwind of conflicting thoughts. "No...Chlerk thinks not," she told St. Gille silently. "Dangerous it would be. Chlerk remembers last time Michelle, Kurilnikov and Annette was together. Chlerk must using atomics to win."

"But I was always the strong one, Chlerk. And now I'm on your side, the way I never was before. You know me, now. You know that I'll do anything... have done anything to keep from being poor. Prisoners are poor, Chlerk. That's what we'll be, prisoners. No more rides into the hive. With hostages, we can bargain."

The yacht moved in alongside the *Nancy*.

Two shapes, one human, one slink, appeared on the videoscreen.

"It's her!" Kurilnikov said, as he watched the screen. "Michenka! At last!" His voice cracked. "No. There's something different."

"I am Annette Kurilnikov," the human said.

Kurilnikov ignored the rest of the transmission. "Annette! You tricked me, you hairy old nightmare! That's my *daughter!* How long have I been here? What have you done with my wife?"

"S-s-safe. Safe. Michelle is safe," Chlerk wheezed.

"Hello. Hello." Annette's voice called from the communications screen. "This is Annette Kurilnikov, Chairman of the St. Gille Foundation. The slink standing next to me is Chirondelle, Director of Slink Special Investigations. You are holding a prisoner, Lt. Colonel Vassily Kurilnikov. We request permission to board and speak with Captain Chlerk."

"No," Chlerk answered. "No one boards *Nancy*. Especially not stinking-a-lot vice cops. Makes deal. What does Terry gives Chlerk for Kurilnikov?"

"No deals, Chlerk," the slink policeman said. "Not until we see Colonel Kurilnikov alive, in person."

Chlerk looked from the videoscreen to Kurilnikov. Sizing him up.

"Enough. Chlerk decides." Cold sleep had left Kurilnikov too frail to be a threat.

"Comes," Chlerk said out loud. "But leaves slink there. The little Kurilnikov comes alone."

Annette was shorter than St. Gille remembered being. Had her own stride been that sure, her own eyes such a light brown? St. Gille wondered. The young woman walked through the entry lock, past the spot where St. Gille/Chlerk waited.

Kurilnikov hovered in back at the entrance to the flight deck. Annette marched right up to him, ignoring the hulking slink. "Hello, Father," she said.

"Nanushka." Kurilnikov groaned and pulled his daughter to his chest in a rough hug.

They stood motionless for several minutes. St. Gille patiently waited her turn, admiring how beautiful her daughter had become. She felt the slink face fur moisten beneath the ten eyes.

"Ee tvaya mat?" Kurilnikov asked at last. *"Kak*
. . . how is your mother, Annette?"

Annette pulled herself away from the Russian and walked toward Chlerk/St. Gille. "Why don't you ask her yourself? How are you, Mother?" She looked up into the slink face. Billo had told her, then. St. Gille fought down her own emotions. Chlerk—

The proboscis waved dangerously close to Annette's

white neck. St. Gille wanted to warn her to move away. But she couldn't force the words past the spiracles. She wanted just as badly to touch her baby. St. Gille reached out a forearm and brushed her feathers across Annette's cheek.

"Isn't it a little crowded in there, Mother?" Annette asked. Her upper lip pulled into a sneer.

St. Gille felt her antennae stiffen.

"Next you'll be telling me that you've missed me. Or that you're lonely."

The loathing in Annette's voice! St. Gille pulled her armtip away.

"Don't be absurd, Mother." The young woman looked up into the slink face. "The only thing you're capable of missing is your money. Couldn't you at least have let him go?" She pointed at Kurilnikov.

Kurilnikov's hand clenched the stair railing.

"I'm sorry," St. Gille's voice groaned through the spiracles. "It was the only way."

"I don't believe you, Mother."

"Money over everything, *veedeesh lee,*" Kurilnikov's voice was a husky whisper, "Capitalism rears its ugly head once again. How could I have been so stupid?" He looked back and forth from Annette to St. Gille.

Did he remember that her own hair had been brown, not blonde like Annette's? St. Gille wondered.

"This is dangerous. Chlerk doesn't like," Chlerk interrupted St. Gille. "We must kills them now. They knows too much."

Chlerk reached out to Kurilnikov and Annette with the proboscis.

Now! St. Gille stiffened the proboscis and held it straight down in front of her thorax with the chest limbs.

"Traitor! Traitor!" the spiracles suddenly whistled. "Chlerk trusts you!" she screamed at St. Gille.

"Salaud! Who do you kid? You were as surprised as I was, to find me still alive, inside you."

"Chlerk protects you. Chlerk helps you build Mom and Pop shop into big business. Chlerk makes you rich."

St. Gille didn't answer. It took all of her concentration to keep Chlerk from using their body to attack Kurilnikov and Annette.

Why didn't they understand? What kind of business-woman was Annette? Couldn't she see? St. Gille had made the best of a bad situation when she could have abandoned herself to dreams of the hive with Chlerk.

"Vassily," St. Gille wheezed through the spiracles. "Please."

Her husband turned toward her.

The tears in his eyes gave St. Gille the courage she needed. She shut Chlerk out of the neural circuit that con-trolled the slink arms and legs. Chlerk was left with only the atrophied chest limbs and the voice.

"Bitch!" Chlerk's whistle pierced the air. "After all Chlerk does for you. Keeps mate alive. For twenty years. No matter it uses too much fuel."

St. Gille shuffled their body back toward the airlock. Give in now and every sacrifice she'd made had been for nothing.

"No!" Chlerk screamed. "It's crazy you are. It's too much trouble you make. All this for one egg." Her voice pleaded. "Lets Chlerk go and we finds nice mate. A fast one. You have hundred eggs. Thinks, Michelle! One hun-dred babies. If you lets us live. What's one puny human baby compared to 100 slink warriors?"

St. Gille pulled the body through the airlock doorway. The small chest limbs struggled to pull the arms back out. The air spiracles along the jaw screamed unintelligibly.

The airlock door whooshed shut.

St. Gille quickly scrambled forward on all four legs to

the airlock window. How handsome her young husband looked, even though he badly needed a shave. She remembered the feel of razor stubble brushing against her human cheek.

"Now!" St. Gille yelled into the microphone. "I don't know how much longer I can hold her. "Please," the spiracles wheezed. "Do it !" she whispered.

He stood motionless, staring at the airlock window. Tears streaked through the grime years of cold sleep had left on his cheeks.

"*Démerdé-toi!*" She shrieked and pounded on the window. Why didn't he move? "*Cochon communist.*"

He shivered as if he were suddenly cold. But, at last, his hand reached for the switch.

Air sished.

The furry face pressed tight against the glass and Michelle St. Gille greedily looked out at her daughter for as long as her ten shiny black eyes could see.

Buffalo Dreams

by
Jane Mailander

About the Author

Jane Mailander is bright, articulate, and sure she has something to say. Among other aspects of her self-expression, she makes a practice of attending West Coast Science Fiction conventions with a cardboard carton from which she dispenses examples of her origami. (For some delightful reason, a number of SF fans on both coasts of the U.S., at least, have in recent years been taking up the Japanese paper-folding art, at which Jane is rated a master.) Her story here, too, folds into a succession of intricate shapes that tantalize with hints of what is to be, and then suddenly complete, and surprise.

She discovered in high school that she could write well, and that it was a joy. When her college degree in English led her only to marginal jobs, she began seriously freelancing. Currently a typesetter-proofreader in Rancho Palos Verdes, California, she entered every Contest quarter in succession for two years, then abruptly was judged the First Place winner in the first quarter of this year. After this fact was publicized, she suddenly sold a radio play the producers had been considering for two years. "Buffalo Dreams," too, turns out . . . well, not quite as you'll expect . . . .

It was very long ago, in Nebraska, and far stranger things have since happened to me. But in that place, at that time, when my life's ambitions were paltry things, how I helped the talking buffalo of Broke Plow was the strangest adventure I had experienced in my thirty years as a carnie and magician.

It began at the Broke Plow station on September 14, 1896. I was left to contemplate the ugliness of the jerkwater-turning-boomtown as my train went on to Kearny without me. From where I stood on the watering platform, I could see nearly the entire length of the mile-long town, and it was far too crowded with people in the middle of the day to be a farming town alone. The road was powdered silt from sheer human and horse trampling, but not even the dust would rise in that midday heat.

A real jerkwater. But they had the talking buffalo, and they had crowds. They needed me, and I them.

I felt in my breast pocket for the quarter knotted in my kerchief, but decided against getting lunch. My best bet was to get straight to work. If I was lucky, I might shill enough money out of the crowd to get a night's bed and board in one of the three hotels I could see as I walked through the people, toward the crowd at the far west end of the town.

Who knows, I thought. I could even make enough for the rest of my train ticket to North Platte in time for Colonel Cody's return there, and I wouldn't have to be stuck in this raunchy town.

The heat was very bad; I ducked under the awning of a grocery store and set down my leather case blazoned with ZOROASTER THE GREAT in green on the side, and sat on it to watch the people flock to the great walled enclosure. I had heard rumors of the talking buffalo as far east as Grand Island, and I knew it was my best shot at making some money to carry me all the way to North Platte for Buffalo Bill's return to his hometown. Trying to catch on with his Wild West show was in all probability the last time I could try for the big time; there is very little call for forty-year-old carnie-wizards when younger shills will work for half the pay. George had been reasonably kind when I left the Omaha State Fair, though—he had let me keep my case and my magic tools.

I gave the old leather case a pat. I could have gone on to my intended destination, but only if I had forfeited my baggage.

I couldn't sit for long, heat or no heat; a crowd of marks with money did to me what the smell of honey does to ants. In two minutes I was strutting into the very thick of the throng, arrayed in my green silk hat and sash, and shouting of the wonders the Great Zoroaster had achieved before the eyes of Queen Victoria and the Kaiser, and I was off and running. It was a pretty good crowd; these folks had come prepared to see the buffalo, they weren't just hanging around, and anything to add to the carnival atmosphere seemed welcome, judging from the amount of cash I raked in in over three hours.

The site itself was typical of a small-town oddity show; the high board wall was unpainted and looked fairly rickety, the sign advertising "The Ghost of Sitting Bull, Reborn As A Buffalo With Human Speech!" was hand-lettered in faded red and the barker, a red-faced man with a Swedish twang, wasn't dressed as gaudily as his station required. But crowds went in, and went out happy with the illusion.

"How marvelous!"

"The gunman must throw his voice," one man grumbled.

"Someone ought to feed that poor creature," a woman said.

"Can you believe what he did to Custer?"

I must confess that my curiosity began to get the better of me. I rationalized my desire to see Sitting Bull's Ghost by saying to myself, Well, if it's a fake, it's still a buffalo. It's worth two bits to see a real live buffalo. So I folded up my case and doffed my hat and sash so I could keep them near me. As I neared the gate, I felt the money I had made, then untied the kerchief and removed the quarter.

At first all I could see and smell was that solid mass of people coming and going; the enclosure was only about the size of a large silo. The sun beat down, and screams broke out here and there as people fainted; babies bawled and children shouted. The enclosure formed a ring around a paddock hemmed by rail fence, guarded by a small thin man with a shotgun who kept pointing it at random people and who said nothing.

As I was swept into a clear spot near the fence, I caught a glimpse of a large dark lump in the center of the small paddock. The buffalo reclined in the straw, and it stared back at the ogling marks. Its jaws moved, and noise came out, but I couldn't discern words above the jeers of disappointed children throwing straw at the animal.

I was disappointed. This sorry thing didn't even *look* like a real buffalo, a Currier and Ives buffalo. Still, I supposed the big Swede and his gun-toting friend were lucky to find any kind of buffalo at all in the state.

There were, of course, the tame ones in Buffalo Bill's Wild West Show. . . .

In the mood for a little sport, I shouted, "Hey, Sitting Bull! You remember Annie Oakley?" The buffalo sneezed, and I froze for a minute before I could rationalize again. For a second, the sneeze had sounded like "Cicilia." "Watanya Cicilia" was Sitting Bull's pet name for Annie Oakley; it meant Little Sureshot in Sioux.

I was still telling myself it was only a sneeze when I extricated myself and my satchel from the stifling pen, where I was met by two large men of the blacksmith's-apprentice variety.

"Mr. Erikson wants to talk to you after we close," a ginger-haired behemoth told me. He and his tow-headed friend disappeared back into the crowd.

I had a feeling about what Mr. Erikson would want to speak to me about, so I plied my trade with greater vigor than ever for the rest of that afternoon.

Once in a while I would shout a few phrases in Sioux (there were some Dakota Indians in the Omaha State Fair, and they were not above reverting to their native tongue now and then). They made very handy magic words for making a pea disappear and for pulling cards out of ears and so forth; but what I was really trying to do was contact Sitting Bull. There was no reply—I probably couldn't even be heard through that racket.

And so I sweltered, and smiled, and bled green down my face from the hat, until milking time, when Erikson and the thin man with the shotgun scattered the crowd and the two big apprentices boarded the door.

I had made seventeen dollars and forty-five cents in a little under six hours.

Erikson and the little man walked over, frisked me, counted my cash, and removed thirteen dollars at gunpoint. "You wouldn't have no crowd in this jerkwater to make money off without my buffalo," Erikson said in a smooth, soft voice. The thin little man pointed his gun and gulped a little, his eyes bugging at the sight of the money; he received three dollars, and took up his position at the boarded door. As Erikson began to walk to the nearest hotel, he said, "One more thing, carnie. Rent's four dollars a night here. And don't try any of the other hotels, 'cause I own them all." The two mastiffs trotted to keep up with their boss and to receive their cut. Except for Gun at the door, I was practically alone on the streets; the crowds had returned to the hotels and farmhouses to feed their squalling children. And I just stood in the street, as cleaned out as any other mark. But I had measured and tested Erikson and his gang, as surely as I had measured the crowd. There were ways around them; they were pure amateurs in their handling of me. If I played my hand right, I would surely make back my losses and be on the next train to North Platte.

And I was no stranger to hard times. I knew the ways around spending money for food and board. So I headed into the setting sun along the bank of the Platte, stopped for a drink and a quick swim at an eddy, and began beating the grass for a good place to sleep. It was like walking through a furnace; all the trapped heat of the day, prisoned in the gold grass, would be set free all through the night. The air was glassy hot still, and it would have shimmered if there had been light to see it. I knew the ground would not cool till past midnight. The brittle grass crackled under my thin shoes, and blades scratched my hands.

I wasn't quite sure what I was looking for, but I found it by stumbling into it. I stood in a great convex saucer of prairie, nearly as deep as a short man's height, and as big around as the buffalo pen. Short grasses and violets lined the bowl, free of the wind and the long grass. An old wallow, where the great shaggy buffalo had once rolled the winter wool from their backs, rolled until the land had become imprinted with this evidence of their sheer weight of numbers.

I put my case at my feet where I could feel it constantly, bedded down in the violet plants (the blooms had long since gone, but the sweet smell remained), and was settled cozier than if it had been a bedbug-infested tick at one of Erikson's hovels.

(The rumbling was like thunder, an earthquake; the purple flowers trembled and the very ground quivered as the great brown thunder rolled over me. I lay flat, terrified, as the huge beasts swept around the wallow, some leaping right over it. They smelled like cattle, like prairie dust; flecks of sweat or spittle pattered on my face and clothes; their own lowing was swallowed up by their hooves. The numbers thinned; then only a scattered few galloped past; then a man fell into the wallow next to me. He was a white man like me, but short curved horns protruded from his black curly hair and a shaggy beard hung in long brown ropes from his chin and neck. He panted, open-mouthed, and his sides heaved; his breath smelled of violets. I looked where his hands should be and saw a pencil sticking out of the cleft in one immense forehoof. I reached out to it, and the pencil-point pricked my hand.)

I snatched the hand back, and was awake. The sun was just dipping into the wallow, and the air was still cool. My hand still hurt, and I examined the ground, where I found the point of a flint arrowhead sticking nearly straight up from the ground. I took a better look at the wallow; there were more arrowheads, and a brilliant round white object at the far west point of the wallow winked in the sun. Upon observation, it turned out to be a large round flat plate of bone, with a crude sun symbol scratched in it. Some Indians must have used the wallow as an encampment, then. I pocketed five or six of the arrowheads, retrieved my case and headed back toward town via a nearby field, where I gleaned a handful of wheat heads for my breakfast. I had a feeling that breakfast at a hotel in town would just come to four dollars. On my way back into Broke Plow, I formulated my arguments to Erikson.

Fortunately, Erikson was greedy enough not to do much bickering. I spoke to him, even as the crowds rematerialized and Gun pried up the boards on the door, and told him bluntly that I wasn't going to do any more shilling that day.

"The way I figure," I said, and flicked a bit of chaff off my traveling case. "it just isn't worth my time to work for you. Train's coming in another three days, and I can sit this little hickdom out till then." As Erikson began to swell and turn red like the frog in the fable, I added, "Or, I could keep hitting the marks same as yesterday, and we split the take, sixty-forty, till I leave."

"Fifty-fifty," he said; his eyes shifted to the mass of people waiting, to the numbers trickling in from the other side of town.

"All right. 'Course, I *may* not work as hard as I did yesterday. Might just make five dollars today. Fifty percent of that's, um. . . ."

Like I said, he was greedy. And the kind of man who keeps blacksmiths around as lapdogs is the kind of man who's never had to fight by himself, for himself. If he had me killed or beaten, he wouldn't get any money off my tricks. I even got my room and board thrown in, but resolved to sleep in a different hotel each night so as to remain alert.

Then I set to work. With a full day to perform, especially the morning, when people are eager, cool and fresh and have all their money . . . I made twenty-one dollars, five of that in the first hour, and the disappearing arrowheads were a favorite of the children.

When Erikson and Gun came by to collect their take at dusk, I asked to see Sitting Bull again, and produced another quarter before they could ask for it. I dropped the watermelon rind I had been chewing on and accepted a lantern, as my case occupied my other hand.

When I saw the animal, I understood the pitying murmurs from the women and men, and the sad children leaving the pen. It was flat on the dirty straw; only the heaving sides showed me it was alive. By the lamplight, the hair looked pale and was coming out in chunks, and sweat plastered what wasn't falling out. Mucus runnels down the eye I could see made it look as if it had been crying. It made no move toward the pan of water Gun must have just put out. By the time I would be halfway to my goal, Sitting Bull would be dried up and gone like the prairie grass.

I hate to see a dumb animal suffer. A mouthful of water here and there couldn't change what was going to happen. Nevertheless I set the lantern down on my case and climbed over the rail fence, and I dragged the water pan closer to the buffalo's mouth. I cupped a double handful over the lolling tongue, and then another. "Poor Tatanka Yotanka; won't be long now."

The tongue withdrew back into the mouth, the jowls moved. "I'm not Sitting Bull," the buffalo whispered. "So you don't have to talk Indian to me."

I stared at him for a long time before the questions tumbled out of me.

His name was Jackson Priest. He had been a man in April. "Naturalist. Chicago magazine. Artist." His train had stopped for water, and he had gone off into the prairie to draw. "Gorgeous plants. Beautiful violets. (Another gulp of water.) A big hollow spot." I shivered, remembering the dream I had had there. "Then a blizzard, out of nowhere. I was trapped, light clothes." Priest tried to heave himself into a sitting position; I helped push him, and he thanked me quietly. "Wasn't all helpless. I knew West dangerous. Had gun. Colt 45." I hid a smile; a dude. The great shaggy head dropped, staring at the large cloven hooves on the ends of his forelegs.

"Then, buffalo stumbled into wallow. Big. So big. We stared at each other." Priest bent to the pan and drank it dry. "Thank you, Mr. . . ."

"Diggs, Oscar Diggs." I patted the damp shoulder. This was too important for anything but my real name. "Keep talking."

"More water?" He was still panting.

"Finish your story first; they might not let me back in. I'll tell the gun to bring more in."

He gave a sigh that sounded like a sob. "He won't. I've been here since May, when they built this damned thing. They give me just enough food and water to keep me alive. Keeps me weak. Too cheap to make the wall stronger. I don't think I can stand up any more."

"Keep talking, keep talking," I hissed. "I'll do what I can." The bastards. Did they really know what they had?

"I killed the buffalo. Shot it right between the eyes, like Alamo Long in the dime novels. Heard about the ox and the blizzard. That's what I thought."

I nodded. Everyone had heard about the man in Nevada or Kansas or Kentucky who had killed an ox and had stayed warm in its carcass through a fierce snowstorm.

"Had my Bowie knife (I couldn't help smiling again), and I opened it. Ughh." The buffalo face twisted and the tongue lolled out. "Like stockyards. But hot. I got in. Blood. So warm. Fell asleep. Dream."

Again I thought about my dream, and shivered. What horrible thing had happened out in that wallow?

"I saw Indians. Lots. Angry. Sitting Bull . . . I've seen his picture. He said, 'Last one. Last one. You last. You last.' Then he yelled something in Indian, and I woke up. Like this." The massive head twisted, the eyes rolling down the length of the animal body.

I looked up, where the stars were appearing in the sky over the dank pen. "How did you wind up here?"

A scowl looks black indeed on a bovine face. "I was shot by Erikson when I appeared near the town." I noticed the white scar on the flank. "And I yelled something in English before I remembered I didn't look like a man any more. I made it into a grunt as fast as I could, but I was at his mercy. I don't think he knows I can really talk; he thinks I sound like a man talking."

"If Erikson knew, he'd charge fifty dollars a head to see you, not two bits," I agreed. Then I was fixed by the wide brown eyes, and they glowed gold in the lantern's light.

"Get me out of here," he whispered. "Please. I can't live like this much longer."

"Hey, carnie, get the hell out of there!" Erikson's voice roared from the opening door. "You been in there near half an hour! You better have another quarter with you."

Half an hour. Was that all the time I had been with Jackson Priest?

"I'm coming!" I yelled, leashing my anger. "But this thing needs more water! You want it to die on you?"

Erikson and his apprentices were waiting for me when I emerged, and I produced another five dollars without questions. The farmhands vanished with their dollars after boarding the door, and Gun was soon dozing at his post.

"Listen," I hissed, "that thing's near dead. If we're gonna keep making money off it, you gotta give him more food and water."

He looked at me exactly the way he looked at the marks.

"What're you, carnie, stupid? Season ain't gonna last forever. Can't keep this thing through the winter, that costs money. He's got maybe a week, two weeks? So? So we tell 'em, right at the gate, he ain't gonna last long. We charge 'em double, triple to see the last of the talking buffalo and take the next train out when it's dead. Eh? That's how it's

Illustrated by William R. Warren, Jr.

done, carnie. And we find something else at the next town.
We'll find another buffalo.''

(What had Sitting Bull said about the buffalo Priest had
killed? Last one.)

The first casualty of a career in a carnival is pride. I
proved it that night by sleeping in one of Erikson's hotels.
I'm almost ashamed to say it, but I slept very well indeed.

But I woke before dawn with a craving for an apple.
Barely before I could finish dressing, I had slipped out to the
general store. The shopkeeper was milking his cow in the
barn behind his store, but I wouldn't wait for him to open.
He grumbled, but wasn't too unhappy at selling something.
He emerged from the locked shop with a large red apple.
"Two cents."

Then I looked into the store and saw the barrel full of
apples. Sweet, juicy . . . food and drink both. "How much
for the whole barrel?"

All that day it was apples. I juggled nine at a time, made
them disappear and reappear, pulled them from children's
ears, made one into two and three into one, balanced them
on my head and feet and hands and nose, and sold them for
a penny each. To each one, adult and child, I made it explic-
itly clear that they were *not under any circumstances* to feed
the talking buffalo with those apples. And some of them
didn't feed the buffalo; I saw perhaps nine or ten people re-
emerge from the pen, still gnawing the cores. All the rest
were empty-handed and guilty-looking. God bless human
nature!

I didn't make much that day; with the apples and the
Danegeld, I was nearly broke again. Erikson was in a jovial
mood, though, having made twice the usual take (he had
kept his word about raising the entrance fee). I was not so
jovial. I still had a few apples left, but my train would come
in another two days. If I bought more apples I wouldn't have
any money left; if I didn't, Priest would die anyway, and my

source of income would disappear. If I saved what I had for train fare, and didn't eat, Priest would die; if I did tricks and didn't bother with the apples at all, Erikson would still get me. I couldn't get Priest out of my head. It was bad enough now. But maybe it was better like this, than for him to really speak and be trapped forever to that Swedish slug.

Gun hadn't been very conscientious about making the farmhands clean the paddock, I had noticed, and I volunteered. Erikson was in a good mood and was more interested in getting a drink than in supervising; he accepted my theory that Priest might last a little longer with clean straw.

The stench was worse before. The pen always smelt of sweat and urine and manure and tobacco, and the reek hit me. But now, the smell of crushed apple cores was mingled with the other foul odors, and I forgot clean about the smell when Priest actually staggered to his feet to walk over to me. "God bless you, Mr. Diggs," he whispered, his voice not quite so hoarse and faint. "Everyone mentioned the apple tricks you were doing. I feel like I've been reborn." Have you seen your dog's face when you've combed the fleas out of his tail? I discovered the gratitude an animal's face can show in another way.

"I'll buy more apples tomorrow." There. "And I'll keep it up for as long as I don't get caught." Why tell him that I barely had the funds for a half-barrel now? And then a quarter-barrel, a bushel, a peck . . . Erikson was charging double, and folks weren't going to be so generous any more.

The buffalo nodded his huge head, a deep and solemn bobbing as if he were consenting to a religious ceremony. "Just for a couple more days. Then it's over."

"No," I said, feeling a stab of pain, "no, for as long as you need. I can stay on. There'll be other trains."

"No," the animal said, and swung the heavy head, chin to shoulder, as if he was brushing flies away with his beard. "No. Two days. I've pretended to be weaker than I felt today; I stayed down. But keep sending me apples for two more days.'' Then he put that enormous muzzle right next to my ear; I could smell the apples on his breath. His voice dropped even lower. ''Then I'll be able to break out of the wall.''

The next day was a nightmare. I spent my last cent on pears (I had bought all the apples, and pears were the only thing available in bulk), and they were more expensive. The heat was even worse than it had been the previous days— most people wound up eating the pears before they reached the pen. Erikson now demanded sixty cents from each visitor, young and old alike. The green in my silk hat by now was only a memory down my neck. Yet I sweated, and smiled, and offered the shell game and the rope trick and the magic hoops to tighter-fisted people, made sullen by the heat and the price of admission, and I tried not to lose my smile even when I heard folks whispering about the dying animal inside the cage. By the day's end I had made forty-five cents. Erikson was sure I had held out on him, and his butcher-boys shook me down. I was always a small boy, and I knew better than to fight them by now.

But when Erikson reached for my case, I yelled and charged like a mad bull, shoving him away from my satchel. All that did was to delay my drubbing for five seconds. When I could open my eyes again and sit up, they had retreated, all but Gun, who kept this weapon trained at me from the door of the pen. That little bit of a smile he wore hurt worse than the punch to my eye had. Finally, I knew exactly how Jackson Priest felt.

''Find another town, carnie,'' Erikson had said through my dizziness and pain, when his ox-yoke had finished their work. ''Old men shouldn't be shilling.'' I'd been drawn in like any other mark.

I managed to pull myself to my feet and walked past

Gun with some dignity. At the outskirts, I fled, leaving my silk hat in the dust. I ran past the noise and stink of the depot, where men were stacking coal and filling the water-tower for the train's arrival the next day, past the farthest western reach of the town. I fell full length on my stomach on the riverbank, and plunged my head into the Platte; the rush of that deep water said "Hush, hush," in my ears. Then I stood, dripping, and followed the deep blues and reds of the setting sun out onto the prairie. The heat rolled up from the ground, drying my bald head and stabbing into my brain, but I kept following that faint red glow. I could feel the west pull me, as a magnet pulls iron. Somewhere there, just past the horizon, North Platte lay, as near as a two-day train ride. It might as well be at the North Pole. But I kept going west, unable to stop walking. I was leaving them all— the bloodthirsty marks, the greedy con men, the dying man-animal.

A waft of cool air hit me an instant before I stumbled and fell into the wallow. Once down, I couldn't get up; it was as if my limbs had soaked into the ground, and my head become a stone.

The stars above my head wheeled round until my exhaustion caught up with me.

(Fire—a sheet of crimson flame and smoke a mile high tore across the prairie, roaring past the wallow, whipping its way to Broke Plow with the speed of a panicked horse. People ran in the streets in every direction, and a terrified captive squealed and battered feebly at its prison walls as the crackling death swept upon the paddock.)

I jolted upright, gasping in the hot air. It was still night, and the ground was cooling, but I staggered out of the wallow and began going back to the town as fast as I could, stumbling as I came awake. As I began to affect a stiff trot, I dug into my pockets and scattered the arrowheads. I thought of the markers in the wallow, the sun-plate that caught the first light of the morning sun. Deep magic, old magic, *real* magic. Sitting Bull, the great medicine man-turned-warrior, killed in a Ghost Dance while trying to res-urrect the buffalo taken by white men, killed seven years ago, Ghost Dances held in circles, in sacred places. . . .

I could hear the rustling of the creature from outside the back of the pen, and a groan.

I crept around to the front. Gun was dozing. I gave him a good wallop on the head with the big rock I had in one hand, but I hampered my own aim by grabbing for the rifle with the other hand at the same time. I got the gun, but he was awake, and yelling with pain. He had a very high voice, like a girl's. He was running to get Erikson, so I whipped around and blew the bolts out of the door with both barrels.

The buffalo was on his feet; even in the starlight I could see him stagger. "Diggs?"

He was too big for the door. "Now!" I yelled. "Butt the damned wall in!"

The rail fence splintered aside, but the wall didn't yield when he rammed his head. "So weak . . ." he gasped.

I started bashing the wall with the gun butt. We took turns at one spot. Only a weakling buffalo or a human could be stopped by that rickety thing. A weakling buffalo *and* a human smashed through the boarding, to yells and torches, and Erikson screaming for my blood.

In a move as natural as mounting a horse, I grabbed a fistful of hump wool and scrambled onto the buffalo's back. "RUN!" I screamed.

Priest had been kept in a pen for three months and more, starved and overheated. He ran like a greyhound. We plowed through Erikson's bulls and scattered the torch bear-ers, and then the light was gone, and I couldn't see any more. Wind whistled in my ears, the jolting threw me back and forth across that skinny spine of Priest's, and I clung for

dear life to the hump pelt. A mass of cold splashed up to
seize me, and I was in a grip of water, being dragged down.
I let go in blind panic, kicking back up to the surface to gasp
and spit water. The river current was pulling me back
toward Broke Plow; I tried to paddle free, but only swam
in loops as the lights grew brighter downstream. All he'd
have to do was line his men up with guns along the bank
and wait for the duck to swim by. Then the lights were gone,
the stars whirled, and I slammed into a great black wall. I
flung an arm out to hang on, and my fingers tangled in wet
wool. I let Priest tow me to the opposite bank and practically drag me out of the water.

I could barely see him, now that there were no lights
from town, but I could hear him sob for breath. He probably felt worse than I did, which was hard to believe.

"Get back on, Diggs," he wheezed. "We gotta hide."

By the time Erikson could have organized a decent
search party, we were lying low in the long grass about
a mile west of the town and three-quarters of a mile south
of the river. Erikson could comb and comb, but Nebraska
prairie is the best place in the world to lose something you
don't want lost.

Once I got used to it, buffalo-back wasn't the worst way
to get to North Platte. Of course, it was easier as Jackson
Priest began making up for all the lost meals, and that sharp
spine was hidden under a good layer of back fat. I was
amazed at his appetite for grass and weeds—he had a buffalo-
palate as well, I gathered—but lost my squeamishness when
he, as a naturalist, was able to find a few plants that I could
eat as well. Fire was provided by a flint arrowhead and my
jackknife. Priest even hunted for me, approaching unwary
rabbits or quail and delivering a fatal kick.

Finally free of Erikson, we spoke freely. He wanted to

join Col. Cody too, once I had told him about my plans, and carry me.

"You saved my life, Oscar," he said, when I questioned him. "It's the least I can do. Besides, it's not safe out here any more."

"Yes," I agreed over a mouthful of cattail root. "Best get signed on with a traveling enterprise."

In all our travel to North Platte, we never saw another buffalo, and we looked hard. The Sitting Bull in Priest's dreams had been right—perhaps he was being punished for killing the last buffalo in the state. But even Sitting Bull could have mercy. The old shaman must have thought that Priest's fate at Erikson's hands was too cruel a punishment, worse than living as a free buffalo. He must have sent me the dreams.

Like I said, we made it to North Platte. And behind us, we left a trail of near-sightings and rumors that beat the ox-carcass story all hollow.

October 21, 1896, was a day of wild riding, fancy shooting, bloodcurdling reenactments of Little Bighorn and Col. Cody's own fight with Yellow Hand, grand heroics and daredevil stunts, all Buffalo Bill's way of thanking the town where he grew up. Priest watched from near the buffalo pens, his mouth hanging open at this grand Old West on a silver platter.

It seems Col. Cody had heard a few rumors himself concerning the buffalo rider, and Priest and I auditioned before his very eyes that afternoon. At my voice commands the animal paced, trotted, galloped, rolled over, sat up, and pawed the earth in response to mathematical questions. We were signed up at once.

That same evening I saw Cody reject a conjurer who had auditioned as well.

"This isn't a circus, Mr. Marvo," he said not unkindly.

"Folks come to see the Wild West, not side-show per-
formers. Can you shoot, or ride, or throw bulls?"

But if you've seen the Wild West show and don't remember seeing Omaha Jackson and His Trained Buffalo, don't
feel too bad. I was with the company only two seasons. During that time, though, Jackson Priest and I traveled to New
York, Missouri, Philadelphia and parts of Canada, and we
were acclaimed at every stop. Priest, who as a tame animal
was free to roam, became good publicity, and was very popular with city kids. Over the months he spoke less and less,
and then he stopped altogether. But he still responded to my
voice, right up till we returned to Omaha in 1898, in August
coincidentally. It was time for the State Fair again, and I was
welcomed by my old manager as a returning hero when I
went over to visit.

"I see you've got the same old balloon." I remarked.
I gave it a long look, and my face must have revealed a little
homesickness.

George laughed. "Go ahead, Omaha Jackson. One
more time."

So I went up, in the old balloon where I had promoted
the fair and which still bore the initials of Oscar Zoroaster.
But those freak Nebraska storms can hit any minute, and
well, here I am. I just hope Jackson Priest fared all right
with the common buffaloes in the show from then on.

SF Illustration
As an Art
by
Frank Kelly Freas

About the Author

As a special feature of this volume, Director of Illustration Frank Kelly Freas has created our unprecedented gathering of major SF illustrators. This is a spectrum of masters from the great days of pulp on to contemporary days.

The illustrations on these pages are new. Their spirit is in a tradition that is now classic, and is offered for your enjoyment and appreciation. It would be hollow to enlarge in words upon what your eyes can see; no one else but Kelly Freas could have caused it.

He published his first SF magazine cover, for Weird Tales, *in 1950, but shortly thereafter became strongly associated with* John Campbell's Astounding Science Fiction, *where he swiftly became the definitive ASF black-and-white and cover illustrator of the post-War period.*

It was not so much a group of writers who sustained ASF's identity in the 1950s; it was Kelly. Many major new illustrators were appearing, in ASF and elsewhere, with now fondly remembered work. But Kelly, at his board through long nights, working seven days a week, ably assisted and upheld by his marvelous wife, Polly, did almost as much work as all his peers combined. He holds more Hugo awards for Best Artist of The Year than anyone, and at mid-century the awards came year after year after year. His work established and held the "look" of Astounding *for a decade, and frequently lent valid extra dimensions to the stories.*

After a sabbatical to do fine-art painting in Mexico, Kelly returned to SF and swiftly broadened out into book and record-album covers as well as magazine illustration, including dozens of depictions of Alfred E. Neumann on Mad *magazine covers.*

Over those two periods, he captured the total respect of his peers and established a lasting influence over successive generations of younger illustrators. Concurrently, he pursued an interest in high technology that would lead him, in time, to the design of NASA mission patches and work with the U.S. Navy. He can be seen from time to time wearing an Issue jacket and nuclear-submariner's badge presented to him on one of those occasions.

In his frequent attendance at SF conventions—often as Artist Guest of Honor—he is widely, admiringly and affectionately recognized as the *authority on SF illustration.*

As a practicing commercial illustrator for nearly 40 years, I have naturally
developed some strong opinions on the subject
of illustration in general, and speculative fiction in particular. Fundamental to my viewpoint is that the innate, trained
and well-developed skills of the artist are the essential foundation but *only* the foundation upon which the illustrator
must build.

The responsibility of the illustrator is to the story, not to
a fashion, a theory of art, or the presumed demands of a market. When, as sometimes happens, the esthetic values of a
given picture clash with the illustrative requirements, the latter should take precedence.

Illustration is a communication art, and as such
requires the illustrator's grasp of all factors significant to his
or her audience, i.e. human traits, emotional orientation,
educational level, relevant symbolism, and especially an
awareness of the environmental and technical elements his
audience will expect him to understand.

From the above, it will be obvious that for an illustrator
all human experience, all human emotion, and all human
knowledge are raw materials. This, rather than specialization in a style, is what determines his or her particular area
of expertise.

In my own experience, I have found that speculative fiction (science fiction or fantasy), while offering the illustrator by far the greatest scope for his knowledge, his abilities,
and his imagination, is at the same time the most demanding

of his total application. The western-story illustrator, the mystery illustrator, the love story illustrator, et al. have sharply defined areas in which their knowledge must be accurate and exhaustive: outside that area, a smattering of general information and a bit of research is enough. The SF illustrator on the other hand *must* be adequately competent in these and any other areas the story demands, and be a quick-enough study to become an "expert" on radio-telescopes this week and microbiology the next. He must also have the ability to forget as fast as he learns: unlike the engineer or technician, carryover from one field into the next is more likely to dilute than enhance his effectiveness.

Effectiveness in art is primarily communication—and one communicates with his readers in their language. This is the reason abstraction, surrealism, expressionism, etc. have had little success with American readers. A Mondri-anesque framework for a composition can make an excellent basis for a high-tech type of illustration; an Yves Tanguy or a Dali approach can set a good mood for a psychological illustration—but in each case, the esthetic approach must be kept almost subliminal to be effective. The reader wants direct, clear, visual information.

The problem is further complicated by the fact that SF readers are by and large as little interested in academic es-thetics in their illustration as they are in formal literary val-ues in their reading. Those are icing on the cake, at best. Like writers and editors, readers are primarily verbal, and they have a strong tendency to prefer a strong story, however plainly written, over a literary masterpiece with a weak story. So, overall, they are pleased with a piece of art if it does its primary job of enhancing their enjoyment of the story.

It must be kept clearly in mind that the STORY comes first. The job of the illustration is to enhance it. The illus-tration must first catch the reader's interest—show that this is a story to enjoy. It will set a mood, give a flavor that tells something of what to expect. And it will give just enough information—"Hey, that's a 1947 Dodge truck!"—to whet the reader's curiosity without satisfying it—"But what the hell is it doing on the Moon?!?"

Ideally, an illustration should complement the story so well that neither story nor picture is as satisfying by itself as the two are together. The picture can vastly improve a story simply by showing the reader an environment or setting that would take several paragraphs to describe, in a few subtle brush strokes that communicate without detailing the nature of the setting. Or it can unobtrusively provide the reader with a significant detail, which will add immediacy and clarity to a situation otherwise difficult to express verbally.

This is especially valuable in characterizing. SF readers in particular tend to see their story-characters defined VISUALLY. The generic pirate, cowboy, railroader, etc. of yesteryear—a style which still, by the way, has a valid and useful place in general illustration—is not usually satisfactory. The most popular characters in SF have invariably been well-defined individuals. The usual handsome hero or pretty girl, as done in "slick" illustration, turn readers off.

All of which is not to say that SF does not have its accepted signs and symbols as evolved by the field's master illustrators over the years. Together, these familiar touches make up what readers recognize as the "feel" of a "true" SF illustration. We have all seen artwork full of spaceships and/or wizards, technically well executed, that is obviously the work of someone who has no idea of what SF is all about and what attracts readers to it. Work of that sort does not draw the reader in—no matter how elegant, it pushes the reader away, because it is the work of a stranger. The new SF illustrator's job is not to avoid the familiar, but to be aware of it and to find new ways of presenting it. The tension of working within the boundaries and pushing outward against them is good for the illustrator...and success under that tension communicates to the reader.

Keep in mind that the very nature of SF is one of endlessly finding new aspects of a reality that exists within unbreakable rules, whether they be the rules of science or of magic. The thoughts of the SF reader reach out beyond the stars, but what is found there is measured by a reality anchored in life on Earth, which constitutes the whole experience of an audience of sharp observers with strong ideas on what is true, what might be true, and what is highly unlikely. The audience wants pictures it can FEEL.

The SF audience is truly a great one to work for, and worth all the effort it may take to please it, simply because it is in fact so broad while intensely aware of its boundaries; and so open to new thinking while retaining what it finds best in the old.

The illustrator could do much worse than to take the typical SF reader as a role-model.

Heroic Measures

by
Paul Edwards

About the Author

Paul Edwards graduated with a degree from the play-wrighting division of the theater department at UCLA in 1970, having also directed and acted in many productions of works ranging from Euripedes and Shakespeare on through Samuel Beckett and contemporary Los Angeles playwrights. Two of the plays were his own.

Pursuing a childhood ambition, he then began a study of medicine. Without the time to simultaneously work on the stage, he seriously took up blues piano, first as a hobby and then as an increasingly intense avocation. At one time, he practiced medicine by day while playing with some of the major blues artists in Chicago; now he is an emergency-room specialist but still finds time to play in local clubs on occasion.

An avid reader throughout his life, with a particular interest in science fiction, Edwards returned to his first love, writing, in 1984 and made his first professional prose sale two years later. The following year, ''Heroic Measures'' was awarded First Place in the third Contest quarter, and is thus among the four candidates for the year's grand prize.

As this is written, no one yet knows who that winner will be. It might be a librarian from New England, it might be an entomologist from Zimbabwe, or an origamist, or. . . . But, in fact, it will be a writer.

The botulinus toxin they've been sending me recently has been almost worthless. The solution is so thick that I can hardly ever keep out an air bubble when I load the pellets. The gun could explode in my face any day, but that's the risk we all take, I suppose. There's almost always a precipitate. I scrape it out of the vial and save it in a double jar. I used to wonder why I didn't throw it away. Maybe I'm afraid of the foming nitric acid I'm supposed to denature it with.

I wish I knew for sure that other doctors have been given one of these pellet guns, but it's not possible to ask. How can I approach a colleague and say, "Busy, isn't it? How many did you get last week?" Guesses are pointless, for, after all, who would pick me for "armed and dangerous?" I'm a quiet man, I keep to myself. I keep to myself so much that I lost Kathryn, my ex-wife. Maybe the powers that selected me for Epidemiology knew that vengeance wasn't a high priority in my life, for considering her continual infidelities, who has been more provoked by a philandering wife than I?

Of course, I'm not surprised she left me. When the government stepped in after the Doctors' Strike of '94, the appeal of being a physician's wife evaporated. In sickness and in health is all right, but being exiled to the very bottom of the middle class would pretty much guarantee the end of her media career. I would never put my needs before Kathryn's, and anyway, you can't cage an eagle. There were plenty of rich, eligible men in the world of the arts to take care of her. I suppose she stayed with me as long as she did out of a sense of obligation, as I had supported her ambitions when she was unknown. She wept when I was denounced, and waited for me to tell her to go, which of course I did. A phony argument from her would have been maudlin, and she didn't give me one. I loved her too much to drag her down with me. The love she gave me that last night has sustained me through all the dark days I've lived through since.

Not that I was ever jailed, no, for I had never joined the AMA, so I couldn't be indicted for conspiracy. Still, they put in me in uniform, just like every other practicing physician in the country, destroyed my lifestyle, confiscated my bank accounts and portfolio, even my retirement accounts, and with a stroke of a pen, my HMO vanished, and along with it, my deferred income, vested interest—but I'm not bitter. Really, I'm not. I could have ended up like some arrogant, privately practicing specialists I know, dancing at the end of a rope from below the skylights of the local shopping mall while a Muzak orchestra played "Raindrops Keep Falling On My Head." Family practitioners like me suffered the least of *that*, thank God.

These days, I put in twelve to fourteen hours at the Quiklinic, a parade of whiners with no discernable illnesses demanding drugs, then go home to bed, unless the console has printed a vector assignment for me, which it usually does. I make enough for the rent, and an occasional lube and oil for the old Iacocca.

Of course, there's nothing quite so valued as a good scapegoat, so even when we'd been squashed, there were still a few doctors who condescended to protest in public. Fools! That's when we began to get blamed for everything, especially the Epidemic.

Reverend Morgan called for universal blood donation from the pulpit of his television station, and it seemed like such a good idea that the profession took it up. But who

remembers Morgan now? It was such a good idea: relieve
the blood shortage and find every AIDS case in the nation
at the same time. Things were getting desperate. Fully a
third of my patients had a red card for the full-virulence
"A" strain. The projected death rate from the Epidemic was
grossly underestimated, as usual, owing to a gross underes-
timation of the American sex drive. We all stood up in our
white coats and applauded when the President signed the bill
into law, never dreaming that the American public was so
afraid of needles that they would never consent to this. It
was also common knowledge that the bad old AMA had
squirreled away the secret knowledge which might have
made a difference If Only We Had Known In Time. . . .

But since the law is the law, the National Guard came
to rescue local police and health departments, and now you
can't take out a loan, get a job, cross the Bay Bridge, or even
go out on a date without being forced to stick your finger
out and produce a little heme for the Govlab. And doctors
are the bad guys, of course. We're the ones who get the lab
results. The console gives us the encryption codes—no one
else can get your AIDS test results, I'm still pretty sure of
that.

It would have been nice to have Kathryn on my side
when the riots started. But now—I keep a low profile, bitter
only enough for an occasional prayer that she wraps those
perfect legs around the wrong hips.

Once doctors had become quasi-military, we were subject to orders and court-martial if we chose not to obey. A
close friend suicided; at the time I thought it was just
divorce depression. There were so many divorces, another
blow to our collective ego.

I remember my day precisely. After securing the console room, as usual, I keyed into Omaha Central, but instead
of my usual daily schedule clattering out of the printer, an
insistent beep blatted at me. I thought it was a breakdown,

but the screen was filled with red letters: "ELECTROMAGNE-
TIC PRECAUTIONS." I had to dig through the papers on my
desk to find the privacy defense manual, and do everything
it said before the noise would stop. Then came the message
that changed my life forever.

National Security Council et cetera. Mandatory solitary
confinement if I blabbed et cetera. Pursuant to Presidential
Order et cetera. I was used to threats by now, but this seemed more stringent than usual. Then came the Muzak legal-
ese: the duty of physicians to society, the failure of genetic
research to find The Answer despite billions upon billions of
dollars, the moral turpitude of the promiscuous, the vilifi-
cation of the infected promiscuous. There was nothing new
in this, either. Prostitutes with AIDS were summarily incar-
cerated for the rest of their natural lives, which, in the
prison environment, averaged from a few weeks after arrival
to immediate murder.

Then the kicker: I had been selected for Vector Elimination. I had proved I could be trusted. There could be no
legal action against me. The method selected was humane:
the infected ones would never know what happened, just
have a peaceful, instantaneous death. Society would be
spared the further spread of The Virus. Morality would
increase. Population would once agàin increase. Life would
be better for everyone.

The tone of it was apologetic in advance, making the
whole thing suspect. These days, no one apologizes to doctors for anything. Doctors have marvelous powers in some
respects, but socially and legally, we are serfs.

The logic of it exploded in my head. It must be *secret*,
so that it cannot be traced. It must be *legal*, so that we can
proceed without fear. It must be *right*, so that we can inte-
grate it into the impulse that led us into medicine in the first
place. It must be *us*, so that when it is inevitably found out,
the perfect scapegoats can be punished again.

Perhaps a few of the suicides of my colleagues were judicial silencings of outrage.

I stared at the screen, forcing myself to breathe slowly, relax. Well, why not, I thought. Misery loves company, and I can dish it out as well as take it. But I better not have that attitude, or I'd start to plan a few homicides, instead of Vector Eliminations.

The console demanded an answer immediately, and the implication was plain: it was too dangerous to have been asked without assenting. I don't want to die. I punched "Y" as ordered, punched it again for "Are You Sure?"

The gun is all plastic, air-powered, lightweight, silent, simplicity itself. It passes airplane inspection. CIA manufacture, I suppose. I was given two weeks to familiarize myself with it before my first vector was assigned.

Whoever was in charge of the VE program must have known I was straight, for they assigned me a male homosexual prostitute first. I had to go downtown to find him, which frightened me. No doctor can forget the beheadings, and I had had regular shifts down there. Some people were bound to recognize me.

I had hard copy from the console to guide me: addresses of hangouts, directions, and a picture, all shredoxed on a single sheet. The time-release saprophytes in the paper would digest it in about two hours.

It was hell on the train, trying to study all the information and praying that the sweat of my hands wouldn't turn it into viscid muck. Only government people ever receive shredox printouts, so all I'd need to announce my official presence would be for one to dissolve in my hands.

The bar was dim, noisy, and smoky, but I could have identified the vector at once even with a single reading of the instructions. The stench of the oil in his pompadour mixed with the sweet and sour stinks of greasy sweat and

cheap perfume to roil my stomach, but still I approached
him. He was six-four at least, no more than one hundred
and thirty pounds. Pulse pounded in my temples; my tongue
was as dry as sand. I couldn't talk. He knew what I sup-
posedly wanted, whispered "Thirty" in my ear, took my
elbow, and began to steer me toward the rest room.

"Fifty," I said, "and let's go outside."

There were lights in the alley, and four people in the
dark just beyond sharing a smoke. Blushing, I turned away
from their knowing, condescending eyes, following the vector around to the far side of a dumpster. Already I was checking escape routes like a pro. Only the certainty of legality
gave me any nerve at all, even though that had to be an
ephemeral fiction at best. What did I have, after all? A war-
rant from the National Security Council of the United States
of America printed on shredox?

In the dark he reached to me with a repulsive parody
of affection, and I couldn't wait any more. I brought my
right hand to his neck and fired. There was a very faint,
momentary hiss, and his eyes widened, his last volitional
movement. Then he was dead.

I caught him as he fell, and propped him sitting up
against the dumpster, his pale face immobilized in the
slightly startled look all dead people have. Then I was sneaking down the far end of the alley, walking briskly down the
street, running to get to the train, running as fast as I could
go, barely catching the northbound for home, shaking like
a leaf for no reason at all, for I had saved the lives of literally hundreds of men who would have been infected by that
walking petri dish of savage RNA. I didn't sleep for forty-
eight hours.

There's no need to report results. Whoever is behind
the console always knows. I must have been good at my job,

because about two months later, I received two assignments
for a single night. I had conquered passion and fear quickly;
I remember thinking that this was a nuisance, to have to
spend the whole night working.

Of course, I was still seeing patients all day at the Quiklinic. I'm a family practitioner, but we have a few specialists
in my building. Jefferson was a big, gregarious urologist
whose colloquial manner and superb neighborhood relation-
ships had saved him at the last minute, standing on a concrete planter next to a mall fashion shop with a rope around
his neck. Too much black history there. He talked his way
out of it, and became a much quieter fellow, but a few
months after I had accepted the Epidemiology assignment,
Jeff became silent, almost reclusive, tiptoeing everywhere,
his eyes shifting to every little ordinary noise as he scurried
from place to place.

There was no way to ask him without being instantane-
ously found out and executed, but I'm sure the console put
him on the spot. He was a very gentle man. I'm sure he
couldn't bring himself to actually kill anyone, and that's
why he was found dead at his desk one day. I pronounced
him, wrote off the cause of death as "massive M.I.," and
Govpath declined to perform an autopsy. That didn't surprise me. The government didn't want botulinus poisoning
to be detected.

I started to get assignments almost every night, which
meant no more time for the one solitary pleasure left to me:
my music collection. I have a fair number of audio tapes of
fifties and sixties jazz, music which gives me tremendous
peace. That didn't matter to the NSC or whoever it was that
supervised me. He, she, or it had decided that vector elimination was to be my hobby and that was that.

Almost all the vectors were the cheapest sort of whores,
of every sexual variety, but I had a few social and sports

celebrities as well. The console actually set me up with cash, clothes, a Lamborghini to sub for my old Iacocca, introductory letters, quite a bit of preparation for some of the classier vectors.

It came to mean nothing to me. The toys were always gone the morning after. I never knew why I was picked for these assignments, for I'm nothing special to look at, hair thinning, paunch thickening, my face so deeply lined I must have been born that way, gray, pale, always slightly sweaty.

My first intimacy with a vector was with a singer named Wildflower. The spec sheet from the console implied that she would couple with anything that moved; so, dressed fit to kill and spending what could only be ill-gotten gains, I bribed my way backstage at Vinnie's Club Fifty Two and met her rather intense gaze. I knew it must be true.

I followed her into the dressing room, locked the door, and when I turned back, she was on her knees, pulling my pants down.

This was too bizarre, but I couldn't stop her. "No teeth, baby," I said. "Yeah, slow and gentle." She heard me and did as I asked. Her mouth must have been a stew of virus, and I was terrified of her giving me an abrasion. I held my hands gently against her neck, but she distracted me with her phenomenal talent and sensitivity, until I could stand it no longer, firing the pellet into her neck as I came.

I felt vulgar for the first time since taking elimination assignments. Yet the distaste I felt for myself was more intellectual, more removed than I would have dreamt it could be. The whole sordid scene would have horrified me less than four months before. Now I just shrugged, and in the following weeks, if sex was required to get close to the vector, then I used sex—absolutely safely, of course—whatever worked. There was no titillation in it, no thrill. I was working about eighty hours a week, having doubled my hours without the hope of a raise.

* * *

Regardless of how the other members of the VE squad were doing, I knew I must be one of the more effective recruits. It wasn't paramilitary; *parajudicial* comes closer to describing the job. But regardless of terminology, I had eliminated about ninety AIDS vectors in a little over four months. I was exhausted. I could always send messages through the console, but I figured that pumping too much data into the system would brand me a troublemaker, and as I said, I try to keep a low profile. This workload was too much, though. I requested a vacation.

I sweated over an hour before the console lit up with the reply. I had expected to see my death sentence, but instead, I was offered three weeks, free credit, and a round trip to just about anywhere. There was only one more assignment before I could go.

The shredox machine hummed its two-toned note as the print head flew. As I read the too-familiar psychological profile, my heart began to pound so hard that I thought my ribs would break as Kathryn's face appeared in full color at the bottom of the sheet.

I can't believe that I'm a rat in a maze or that I'm so important to the whoevers above me that I should have been inflicted with this assignment. I have to have faith that this was pure chance, a random deal of the cards. To believe otherwise—that way paranoia lies. I'm not psychotic.

I took a cold shower, re-read the objective assessment, and settled down before the phone.

"Hello? —Oh. Hello." In an instant, her voice had gone through at least six changes.

"Hello, Kathryn."

"This is a surprise."

"Could you turn on the video, Kathryn? It's really impossible to talk to you without seeing you."

"Just a minute." A sound of motion, and then the screen lit up, revealing Kathryn pulling a robe on—just a flash of tan and pink before the thin cloth overlapped and molded against her perfect curves. How like her.

"You know," she said, "I had a thought you might be calling."

I answered as mildly as possible. "Really? Why, do you suppose?"

"To gloat."

I laughed easily. If I hadn't been working, she would have had no problem ripping off my disguise. How puzzled she would have been, if she had.

"Kathryn, if anyone has a right to gloat, it's you. You're rich, single, beautiful, healthy—and I'm a dead end government doc. The only reason I'm calling is that you're not the gloating type."

She appraised me, deciding that I knew nothing gloatable. She took charge, as always. "In all the fourteen years we were together—"

"Fifteen."

"—that's the nicest thing you've ever said to me."

A few of the other phrases I had whispered in her ear popped into my head: here's the keys to your new Mercedes, how wonderful to be in Paris with you, I love you.

"I could say others, but they sound better in person."

She smiled. "Let me check my book." She leaned forward to reach for something on the other side of the camera, and her robe bellied out like a sail in a breeze. The screen filled with her left breast. Absolute perfection of form. Of course, she only did it to tantalize me. She was so sought after as a model that she now stands twice life size in bronze next to the Guggenheim. I heard the voice in the back of my head repeating the mantra *she's riddled with a lethal disease,* for according to the console, she would be dead in less than twelve months.

She sat back in her chair, tucking her flimsy robe around the body I knew so well, contriving an unconsciously prim manner. "Seven-thirty tonight?" she asked.

"I can't wait."

She leaned forward to say three words I couldn't help hoping were true: "Neither can I."

In retrospect, I suppose I should have seen that she let me re-enter her life too easily. Why should she have bothered with me, unless she believed that I was something I was not? I'm everything she spurned: poor, aging, boring, and habitually despised, qualities frequently assumed to rub off on those who indulge in more than casual contact with the afflicted. Of course, I was indulging in the major theory of the broken-hearted: that all the love we had shared, despite evaporating in the heat of betrayal and recrimination, had left at least a residue of affection in the pretty, empty shell that was Kathryn.

I dressed, strapping the gun to my right wrist as usual, a habit that required no thought whatsoever. My imagination spun with a thousand reminiscences, good and bad. The impulse for the meeting, and its inevitable conclusion, were pushed out of my mind.

I paid for dinner with my Govcard. She made a point of not noticing, but her eyes dilated at the sight of the little rectangle of gray plastic. Free money seemed to be the magnetic key that switched us from our bantering pleasantries over the meal and Pouilly-Fuisse to promises and charm over Courvoisier Forty Year Reserve, a bottle of which I bought on the way to the car. I suggested that we repair to her penthouse, but she insisted on returning to my shabby, cramped flat. I drove—my own car; in her presence its collection of squeaks and rattles, which I always ignore, seemed magnified, intrusive: a soundtrack to my own decrepitude.

"Why this beater?" she asked. "Sounds like we might not make it home."

"There's no money in the doctoring business, in case you haven't heard. I'm even working extra shifts, with no bonus, and I haven't got the energy for another job."

"No need to snap at me. Anyway, you've got a Gov-card."

"I get to use it once a month, as long as I'm not too extravagant. Guy in the office went overboard, now he's driving a Jeep circuit in northeastern Nevada somewhere." The exile part is true. He had had a private clinic going for about three months.

Water stains wrote obscure graffiti in the faded stucco walls whose cracks had not merited even sloppy patching. A woman at the end of middle age slept loudly on an over-stuffed lobby sofa. Thus my domicile.

My front door is steel. Three locks later, we were inside.

"Why, this is charming!" she said, crossing the parlor in four steps, the kitchen in three, peeking into the silent console room, the grand tour. "Good-sized closets, too." I almost blurted that if her enthusiasm was authentic, she would be here, rather than the penthouse of the Parkview.

"Not too bad, if you're a monk," I said, "which I've become by default, I guess."

"No love life, hunh?"

"No one wants another doctor just trying to get by. Not to mention that you're a tough act to follow. No, I'm as lonely as if I had the Plague." She winced slightly. "Which I don't. I'm actually learning to like my new life."

She flung her shawl over the arm of my reading chair, a vinyl recliner much repaired with duct tape, and took my upper arms in her slender hands, her huge sea-green eyes totally focussed on me. "This is me," she said. "You don't have to pretend."

"I don't understand...."

She sighed, kissed me on the nose, and turned to look for the switch that let the bed out of the wall, and found it. "Pour me some brandy," she said, flopping down. I rinsed the toothpaste out of the glass by the sink, and filled it.

John Coltrane and Thelonious Monk serenaded us. Less than two ounces later, she began to pull her few clothes off.

For fifteen years we had never made love with our clothes on if it was at all reasonable for us to take them off. I stood paralyzed by ambivalence as she stretched her flushed, feline physique across my mattress, a glowing ember in the midst the gray-green gloom of my life.

I flashed an impossible dream: running away with Kathryn to some faraway secret place to enjoy a year of love before AIDS-related infections killed us, laughing and happy until the moment we were crushed. But it didn't convince for a moment. The console had explained a number of inexplicable news items, and it was clear that I wouldn't survive seventy-two hours after shirking my assignment. I don't want to die.

Kathryn would have to die tonight. The only question was whether I would share a last moment of passionate love with her, or not. We all have to die, after all, and there was nothing in my life worth living for any more anyway: treated as a distasteful body-technician during the day, hunter of the nidus of infection at night, always alone, alone forever. My conclusions were easy: so what if pneumonia finally takes me in a year? At least I will have had this one moment, this one last pure fiery moment to merge with all the goodness and love of my sweet beauty, one sparkling fountain to illuminate the dark corners until the end.

Trembling, I put off my clothes, hiding the gun, and lay down next to my beloved. My skin crawled at the thought of the virus churning out of her, but the virus was invisible, while Kathryn was warm and delicious. We teased each other playfully, then eagerly, until with no words at all I rolled over her and felt the embrace I had missed for so long. I had thought to love her with elegance and restraint, but only vigor and abandonment could drive away the fear of the plague. I wallowed in deadly kisses to forget the knowledge of my own death, until after the third or fourth pinnacle, I had expended all my hoarded ecstasies, driven off all dread and panic, and floated in sweet numbness, Kathryn flowing against my side like a spring breeze.

Something pushed against my psyche and I turned to see her looking at me, clear-eyed and intent.

"I thought I remembered," she murmured, "but I've forgotten so much."

"Me too, but I'll bet the things we each forgot are different."

She chuckled, then looked full of thought. "Maybe now you can trust me enough to tell me," she said.

"Trust you enough to tell you what?"

"Why you live like this."

"As if I had a choice."

"My little monk," she said, ruffling my hair, "in his little sports car."

"What?" Instantly, my drowsiness was gone.

She shook her finger in front of my face in a playful, I-caught-you manner. "I saw you chasing that little singer who OD'd. What was her name? Wildflower? At Vinnie's, about six weeks ago. Mighty good hunting, eh?"

I bolted upright. A pulse of fear clamped my guts, but instantly I realized that Kathryn thought my nightclub errand only sex, and not assassination. Denial was impossible.

Illustrated by Bob Eggleton

"No fancy car, no fancy clothes in the closet. Where do you really live?"

I started a dozen answers, but my mind raced ahead to clumsy stuttering dead ends. "This is it," I said. "There aren't any other places. All that was borrowed."

"From who?"

I ground my teeth together. There was no way even to begin to tell her.

"You know, I think I believe you. If you had the kind of money that buys Italian sports cars and backstage romance, you'd throw it in my face." Slowly she pulled herself out of bed, walked over to the little pile of her clothes. "I thought you'd finally gotten your act together somehow, that you had the bucks to meet me on an equal footing." She hoisted a little scrap of cloth to her hips. "But you're just another loser, Doc. Just another throwaway sawbones." She slipped a tube of gauze over her chest, and reached into her purse. "Very expensive mistake, Doc. Read this." She reached toward me without a hint of tremor, a Govlab red slip in her hand. I knew what it said, so I didn't bother to take it. My smile brought her up short in a pallor of curiosity.

There was a time when I might have been enraged at being used for my money, furious for allowing myself to be duped, when this final straw might have driven me berserk. But vengeance is mine, saith the Department of Epidemiology. I gathered my clothes, took them into the bathroom where I washed my face, dressed, and rechecked the weapon. All the questions had been answered.

"The knowledge of imminent death does strange things to people," I said. "Some hide. Some get religion. Quite a number just don't care. A few discover that misery loves company, and can't wait to give their infection away to everybody. You, Kathryn, belong to the last group."

"Please, no sermons. Let's just go." She sounded bored, tired. I did not turn out to be what she expected, so she dismissed me. She stood at the steel door with her hand on the knob.

"This is a special moment, Kathryn. I've never told the truth of my, ah, job, to anyone. You know, your social life is rather notorious. I just found out this afternoon."

"What's so special about finding out that your ex-wife likes to go out a lot? Look, this is getting tiresome. Let's go."

I spread my hands apologetically. "You're not going anywhere, ever again."

She marched to me, three steps, then swung her hand into my face as hard as she could. I was too numb to feel it.

"Kathryn, I couldn't care less about your sex life, much less about your health. But orders are orders. What did the sage say? 'People get the healers they deserve.' That red letter comes from the Govlab, I'm a Govdoc, there's a plague going on, and you're spreading it around. Did you know Wildflower? Then guess again: what was I doing there?"

I watched her face go through a series of calculations as she tried to discard the only explanation which fit the facts. There were no possible evasions. I think it was my casual attitude that unnerved her. She paled, her lower lip quivered, and she began to back toward the door, which I had locked. I know I'm going to die, her eyes said, but not today. Please, God, make it not today.

The vector saw me point to her neck, and instinctively batted my arm up as I fired. The pellet went straight into her left eye.

Botulinus works extremely quickly, but it has to absorb to do so. The blood supply to certain parts of the eye is very poor, so Kathryn had a number of minutes of clawing at her face, shrieking in agony, the vile jelly dripping down her cheek, until the paralysis took her. I propped her up in my

bed with a number of pillows, then sat in my reading chair,
watching her clear sea-green eye staring at me until at last
it had faded, and her lips had turned blue, and she was gone.

Medicine is fairly unpleasant, these days. After my generation has bought the farm, smart people will have to be
conscripted into it, because who would choose this? Of
course, I can't complain. If it hadn't been for the epidemiology squad, I would never have had the chance to regain
my self-respect. A lesser man would simply have beaten the
living hell out of that woman, but even though the last possible experience of love I might have had in this world
turned out to be a sham, I was able to distance myself from
a crime of passion, and let destiny, using my hand for its
tool, take its course.

There's really no use waiting around for pneumonia.
When I come up positive in the Govlab, in about three
weeks, they'll even take my work away. Eliminating this particular vector was the start of my permanent vacation. All
the precipitated botulinus toxin has dissolved quite readily in
a hundred milliliters of normal saline. A flip of the stopcock
and it will all flow straight into my vein, turning me off like
a light.

The grimace of pain has faded from the vector's face,
and sitting in front of me on the bed, she has an expression
of blank curiosity. My final hope is that when the Govpath
crew comes to take us to the morgue, it will be obvious that
I've merely brought some work home with me. For human
intentions are the sort of messages that can only be printed
on shredox, but professionalism should be as plain as the
serenity and peace on my face.

Old Times There

by
Dennis E. Minor

About the Author

Dennis E. Minor was born in Hannibal, Missouri, in 1940. In the 1950s, Minor's family moved to Texas. In due course, at Texas A&M University, he obtained a series of degrees culminating, in 1973, in his PhD in English and journalism, with a specialty in history. He is currently an Associate Professor of English at Louisiana Tech University.

Over the years, he has published a short story and poetry in academically oriented "little" magazines, as well as articles on writing and on technical writing. But he was also a runner-up in the second annual Bulwer-Lytton competition for satirically melodramatic fiction, and his story there is published in the Penguin anthology It Was a Dark and Stormy Night.

A boyhood fascination with SF has never left him; this Fall he will present a critical paper on Edgar Rice Burroughs' The Gods of Mars *to the Science Fiction Section of the South Central Modern Language Association, and a few Quarters ago he tested the waters of the W.O.T.F. Contest with an academic story. His next entry was deliberately written for the Contest, and you will find it here.*

We believe it will spark a specially enjoyable mood, shift your understanding of what is human, steer your mind toward a unique frame of reference, and thus advance your accelerated enjoyment.

"Look there. What you reckon that is?" Dipstick said, pausing with one mechanical hand in the brine.

"I expect I know," Flathead replied, glancing toward the flash in the sky that had now settled down behind the trees. "You know how mad that fussbudget was when he left last year after we told him little Tappet was gone. I bet they came to look for him."

"Hhm. Suppose little Tappet wants to go off for awhile? What's that hurt? I wouldn't mind a little time off myself. The stuff in this water is making my joints creak again. When they going to get enough of these crystals, anyway?"

"Don't know. We been planting them in this pond ever since I can remember. But we didn't have to work so hard in the old days. Then, we just made them for Earth. But since these new fellas took over, no telling who all we make them for now."

"I'm glad I missed that. Must have been bad to see all the folks took off after the Lull."

"Sure enough," Flathead replied, internally playing back a holographic portrait of the old crystal factory. The portrait had lost enough bits so that it was now brown-toned instead of being in color and was somewhat fuzzy around the edges, but it showed Flathead and Mr. Clyde standing in front of a low warehouse building with the sign *Clyde's Crystal Works* nailed to it. To the left and behind the warehouse lay the mile-long, flat-surfaced crystal pond.

By focusing on different parts of the old hologram, Flathead could see the surrounding landscape, which was generally orderly; but toward the rear he could see the towering junkyard which held the remains of both domestic junk, accumulated during a lifetime of collecting by Clyde, and extraterrestrial junk, from the War. If Flathead used his high-intensity enlargement on one little spot of the hologram, he could see the remains of the Air Force missile site and the nearby city that had been devastated in the battle. Both lay north of the crystal works, along the Red River, which meandered nearby.

Before turning off the Solid Data Review Module that transmitted the hologram to his memory, Flathead took another look at himself: big, skinny tires for wading through the chemical brine, the '47 Ford flathead V-8 engine sticking out on the rear—an engine that Clyde had lovingly reproduced using his computerized mill and patterned on old parts salvaged from the junkyard (when it was just domestic junk)—the mechanical hands on the front used for planting and harvesting the crystals and, on the top, the clear, quartz-like lump of the CRM—Clyde's Reality Module, version 1.14.

When he first turned on Flathead's CRM, Clyde had told him that it was the best part of a brain.

"This here stuff's harder than a teenager's head," Clyde had laughed, tapping his hand on the rounded top of the CRM. "You got eyes that will see most anything, inside and outside, real-time and memory. And with those crystals I found out back in the pond, I fixed you up one hell of a thinking pot. Don't know what those things exactly are, but they sure work good in AI circuits."

When Clyde got around to putting in vocabulary and speech modules (patterned on his own, Clyde had said, patting Flathead like a puppy), Flathead learned that AI meant making machines think like people, but with brains that were not made from fragile and unpredictable organic material.

Flathead had learned, as Clyde talked to him and his CRM developed, how the crystal works got started. Clyde had worked at the Freedom Enforcer missile base of the Strategic Space Command, but lived out in the country, on a little farm a few miles from the river. When the Palindrome fleet attacked the missile site in their PUP fighters, armed with Kapak missiles, Clyde was home and so escaped the attack that largely wiped out the base and its immediate vicinity, city included. However, one of the PUPs was damaged and crashed into the field behind Clyde's farmhouse, clipping several fertilizer tanks and an old pickup truck as it skimmed along the ground, finally pushing the whole assemblage into the farm pond filled with catfish.

Clyde had waited for an explosion, but instead the ship, half in and half out of the pond, simply leaked all sorts of liquids out of its fuel cells and life-support system into the water, which began to gurgle and smoke ominously. But, by the time the clean-up and intelligence crews arrived weeks later, during the temporary peace called the Lull, the water was calm again. However, Clyde never found what happened to the catfish; he never saw them any more.

The government hauled the ship away, stripped out everything that looked interesting, and dumped the rest on the now-growing junkyard that lay south of the base and north of the farm, updating the junk there so that it contained bits and pieces of motorized vehicles from the entire twentieth century and from more than one planet.

It was at the beginning of the Lull that Clyde, now out of a day-to-day job until the base was restocked with personnel, buildings, and the new Motherpie missiles, decided to go fishing. He took a cane pole, a bobber, and a wad of raw biscuit dough out to the pond one morning, to see how the catfish looked. He noticed that the water smelled odd,

odd, a little like the mandatory body washes at the government swimming pools. Clyde scratched in unconscious reaction and sat down to fish.

After sitting quite awhile without getting a ripple around the bobber and after moving all around the pond to try every possible hiding place of the fish, Clyde had a little luck: his line got hung on a chunk of the PUP. He reached into the water to try to free the line and noticed that his hand stung; when he pulled it out of the water, he saw what looked to be a mild chemical burn.

"That's where the fish've gone," he said, both in resignation and disgust. "The pond must've melted them."

Then, he gave the line a hard yank, dislodging the PUP part. He pulled it up into the shallow water and saw that it was simply a flat piece of shiny metal, like stainless steel or aluminum. But something about it caught his eye: there, glowing redly in the morning sun, were tiny crystals growing on the surface of the metal. They reminded him of rubies he had seen in old laser weapons systems.

Clyde carefully scraped off all the red crystals, put them in his shirt pocket, and took them back to the house. He put them in a dish on the shelf and watched them; nothing happened. So, a couple of days later, Clyde went back to the pond and filled up several big glass pickle jars with pond water and placed the crystals in them to see what would happen. Still nothing, as if they had reached full size.

So, the next week, Clyde took some into the base lab, which had by that time been rebuilt a further story underground. There, he subjected them to all sorts of mechanical and chemical analysis; what he found was that they had a before-unknown crystalline structure whose possible uses were also unknown.

Clyde experimented; he found that somehow or other, the crystals could store digital electrical signals and then release them when jogged by an electrical current above a

certain threshold level. He found that he could store a dig-
itized song in one; then, when it was subjected to a weak
incoming electrical signal or sufficient pressure to make the
crystal generate current, the music would be sent into his
amplifier: Clyde could literally squeeze a song out of one of
the crystals. He found that they could store all kinds of computer information, both data and programs; and, although
the capacity of each little crystal was limited, they could be
put in series to attain sufficient storage. The next two years,
those of the Lull, were spent in learning about the crystals.

Naturally, the military quickly found uses for them in
guidance and control of missiles; the red crystals became an
integral part of the Motherpie defense system. When the
military, in their haste to finish the new defenses, were
unable to duplicate the pond conditions that generated the
crystals, they turned back to Clyde: he became the
military's crystal farmer.

So, the great shallow crystal pond was formed out of the
old catfish pond and given over to crystal-growing; Clyde
did his further experimentation at home, in his collection
of workshop pickle jars. He did find one interesting new fact,
which he kept to himself: the crystals would continue to
grow, sending out connections, if they were part of an active
electronic circuit immersed in the pond water.

But Clyde's had little time for those experiments
because he also had to build a group of robot crystal
pickers—machines that could find and harvest the tiny
things without themselves being put out of commission by
the pond water.

His first product was Flathead, combining the best of
Clyde's love of antique machinery, his practicality, and his
knowledge of Artificial Intelligence. Flathead's motor was
modeled on the 1947 Ford flathead V-8 engine, fueled with
methane generated by a big trash burner at the side of the
junkyard; his working parts were formed from the latest

ceramic and carbon fiber and so largely oblivious to the corrosion of the pond, and his "thinking pot" was populated by thousands of Clyde's crystals—done on the sly because the crystals, being strategic items now, were to be grown for military use only.

Further robots had followed, with Dipstick being the second. But then the Lull turned into the Recent Unpleasantness, in which the Palindrome fleet unleashed their MOM and POP missiles on selected political targets, quickly leading to the Truce; then, the truce being one-sided in favor of the Palindrome politicians and warlords, came the Great Removal: all humans were hauled away, leaving the Earth as an outlying farm colony for Palindrome.

Clyde had been allowed to stay partway into the final stages of the Removal, the Overseers recognizing the importance of Clyde's crystals. But they wanted their own robots doing the work, so they sent down some sluggish and stupid Palindrome servant-class worker robots. They didn't work out, primarily because they were too clumsy and lacked self-direction, so Clyde talked the Overseers into letting him modify them with an additional intelligence module, one designed simply to facilitate efficient picking, Clyde assured the head officer—a spiky-looking military robot.

Finally Clyde was Removed also, leaving behind his own creations Flathead and Dipstick and a small crew of modified Palindrome workers, now with tiny gleaming red crystals in their new quartz-like intelligence centers. As he threw his transmission into low gear, Flathead thought of Clyde's parting instructions: "Remember now, Flathead, after those boys have been picking a year or so, give them a little water." And Clyde was off in the noise and flash of the Palindrome rocket.

Flathead and Dipstick now started for the incoming Palindrome rocket which, after the usual show of fire and smoke, had landed near the warehouse. As they opened the butterfly valves on their Stromberg 97s, they felt the cool rush of methane entering their intake manifolds, coursing through their engine blocks, and entering their cylinders through the side valves. That rush always made them feel relaxed and a little playful—even when faced with the rolling hand grenades that always came out of the company rockets.

When they got to the warehouse, their visitor was standing on the porch, looking around or at least examining everything with the gaggle of sensors that protruded from the upper third of his huge mechanical body. They noticed that the middle third was, as usual, heavily armed with an assortment of snares, toothed grippers, disintegrator rays, and a time clock. The bottom third, the motive section, was wheeled, Palindrome thinking evidently being to use the motive force of the indigenous inhabitants.

"My, look at that. He's a big one, isn't he, Flattie?" Dipstick said as they neared the building.

"Sure enough; and look at all that armament. He could probably vaporize all this and half the next parish. Hope he's not touchy."

By this time they had reached the porch and were facing their weighty visitor. Swiveling his sensors toward them, the Gogamagog, Model 696, reverberated out of one of his communication vents: "Which one of you is the worker/coordinator Flathead?"

"That's me, Mister Goggy," Flathead said.

"Oh, you're a stitch, Flattie. Goggy. Oh, my." Dipstick said, just too low for the company robot to hear.

"I have been sent to rectify a problem reported by the last production oversight team to visit this farm."

"You mean that little plastic calculator thing that went through our books last year?" Dipstick said, "Why, he didn't hardly. . . ."

"The problem of runaways," Gogamagog continued, as

if Dipstick hadn't spoken. "It was reported by the Oversight Manager that many of the company drones sent here and modified for harvesting crystals are no longer among the work force. Production has fallen."

"Here comes the speech," Flathead wrote on his backside communication board, out of sight of the visitor but plainly seen by Dipstick.

"You have been told by the Indoctrination teams innumerable times about the strategic importance of the work being done at this installation."

Gogamagog paused, as if taking a large breath. Dipstick and Flathead internally winced; it was the beginning of the standard worker pep talk and threat session.

"Since you are involved in an enterprise very important to the State in its efforts at solidifying its peaceful control of large sectors of this time/space region, you have been allowed the freedom to work for the State on this colony planet, as opposed to those who have been Removed and/or Dismantled."

At the word "Dismantled," Flathead blew a puff of methane out of all eight exhaust pipes, hoping it would corrode something important on the visitor; Dipstick lowered his head as if in obedience, all the while getting a good look at the robot's undercarriage and wheels.

"It is therefore necessary to find these missing workers, to correct their malfunctions, and to not only get the crystal production back to its former level but to increase it one hundred percent."

"Goodness. The orway's otnay oinggay elway, attyflay," Dipstick said.

"What was that?" Gogamagog boomed out of another vent.

"Just a temporary malfunction in communications, your Honor," Dipstick said. "The old pond's tough on parts."

"You are in charge. Where have these workers gone?"

"Well, Chancellor, I think they've gone to Frenchtown. Yep, I'm almost sure they went to Frenchtown." Then Flathead stood silent.

"Explain."

"Explain?"

"Explain. What is 'Frenchtown'? You are not cooperating." He swiveled one of the vaporizer nozzles toward Flathead.

"Sorry, your Worship. You need to remember that me and Dipstick here spend a lot of time in the pond. Stuff gets corroded up. And our memory modules are pre-war—I mean pre-liberation. They're pretty primitive compared to you."

Dipstick had restrained his urge to drop into Low gear and leave when he saw the nozzle began to glow plasma blue. Now he relaxed and began again to calculate the weight of the visitor.

"Frenchtown is an old village on the river. Humans lived there before the Removal; they farmed the water for biological specimens called catfish. You know what I mean?"

Flathead let in another rush of pure methane when he saw the time it took Gogamagog to look up the archaic words in his memory bank and then translate them into concepts.

"Yes. The missing workers are in this place called Frenchtown? What are they doing there? Their place is with the State."

"Beats me, your Maytagship. Maybe they're catching catfish, too."

All Flathead got in reply was a deep rumble and a twittering of sensors. Then,

"We must go there and bring them back; they must be dismantled and modified to prevent a repetition of this unprogrammed behavior."

"Actually, me and Dipstick are kind of tired; we been out in that pond for ten hours already today. And it's a ways to Frenchtown. Won't they keep for a while? Don't you have a couple of joints that need lubing or something?"

Gogamagog slapped his nozzles against his armored midsection and spoke in his thunderous Voice of Authority:

"Replenish your fuel supplies. My sensors can penetrate any conditions of light or weather. The State does not wait."

After filling up on compressed methane, Flathead and Dipstick found themselves at the border of the farm, where a paved road much the worse for wear led off into the distance toward the river.

"This is the road to Frenchtown?" Gogamagog asked. "How far is it?"

"Not quite sure. See, me and Dipstick never been down there. We didn't know what kind of condition the road or town would be in after the Recent Unpleasantness. And no telling what those crazy drones down there might have done. Heard some of them got blasters and such from somewhere."

"Blasters?" Dipstick began, and then silenced himself as he reviewed his memory module for bombed roads and guard drones with weapons and found no match.

"Course, there is the back road. It cuts through the swamp. But I think that a big armored guy like you, heavy and all, would be better off on the main road. We wouldn't want anything to happen to you. The company wouldn't like that."

"Oh, my, yes," Dipstick said. "You might just sink right down into the mud. And I don't think that old road even goes all the way to Frenchtown. We need to go on the good road."

"I expect you're right, Dip," Flathead said. "The old road hasn't been used since before the Lull. And those drones would go straight to Frenchtown. This dirt road probably winds around no telling how many extra miles. Drones aren't too smart, anyway. Not like Goggy, here. They'd go the shortest way. We might even find little Tappet on the way. He didn't have much fuel the day he left. Probably parked under a tree along the road. The more I think about it, I definitely think we should follow the main road.''

"I'm with you, Flattie. Shouldn't take that other road at all. It wouldn't surprise me if we didn't find most of those drones on the way. I don't believe there's a bunch of them at Frenchtown anyway. What would drones do in a town? They're just made to harvest crystals. We come in on the main road in plain sight, we'll just see them sniffing fumes to pass the time, even if they are there."

All this conversation, action, and reaction were slowly being filtered by the Truth Algorithm in Gogamagog's Military Intelligence Array. This Algorithm was based on two concepts the Palindromian military had found useful in the business of conquest: One, if an entity's actions contradicted that entity's statements, the statements were false; Two, if all statements made by an entity supported the same truth, those statements, because of their invariant agreement, were false. When the Algorithm found either of these patterns, the entity was subject to PVP—Preventive Vaporization Policy. PVP had greatly eased the task of post-conquest mop up.

The Truth Algorithm found Dipstick and Flathead to be lying; but in this case, PVP was held in abeyance by the overriding command to find the errant drones; consequently, there was only the slight twiddle of nozzles on Gogamagog's war chest. However, the company robot now took command, having filtered out the truth.

"We shall go to Frenchtown using the old road. Take me to that road."

"Oh, no, no, no," Dipstick began. "We can't do that. Too dangerous for you; much too dangerous."

Instantly, the central vaporizer nozzle centered on Dipstick and glowed blue. Even as it began to fire, the override command redirected the stream of destabilizing particles; Dipstick heard the air rush into the vacuum created in the beam path as it went by his head. An ancient rusty tractor sitting in the corner of the field disappeared.

"Right this way, your Powerhouse," Flathead said, after a moment of dead silence. "The turn-off's just around the next corner."

After they reached the dirt road and had traveled on it for a mile or so, gradually beginning to parallel the river, Dipstick, now bringing up the rear, noted that the ruts created by the wheels of Gogamagog were becoming deeper. He knew, of course, that to mention that negative factor might well result in a vaporizer blast, so he kept silent.

Finally, though, they reached a point where the growing difficulty of the road became a problem; they had reached a wooden bridge over a swampy area that eventually fed a bayou that in turn ran into the river. The bridge didn't look very strong; the swamp didn't appear to offer any substantial support. They all stopped; Dipstick and Flathead watched Gogamagog as he sensed all the available information and processed it. They knew better than to give advice.

"The organic material of this bridge does not appear strong enough to support my weight," the robot said. Then he again sensed and spoke.

"How deep is the liquid environment below the bridge?"

"Probably a couple of feet at least. Don't think you could get through it. We ought to take the bridge," Flathead said slowly.

The robot pondered.

"I'm not so sure, Flattie," Dipstick said, it being evident Gogamagog was in the midst of analysis. "These swampy areas sometimes are just a foot or so deep. They almost dry up in the summer. And that old bridge looks pretty strong to me. Some wood gets stronger when it gets old."

"Of course, it is pretty hard to tell what to do," Flathead replied. "The best thing might be to go back the way we came. I was afraid this road wouldn't get us there. I did say that. And look at it."

Gogamagog was looking, or sensing, and analyzing. A mosquito lit on his main vaporizer nozzle. A mud dauber was considering sticking a glop of newly mined swamp mud on the back of his intelligence module. Still Gogamagog pondered, now directed by the Reductionist Algorithm that brought decisions ever closer to chance when high-level analysis could not eliminate contradictory evidence. The mud dauber flew off when it felt the module begin to get hot.

Finally, Gogamagog reached the lowest level directive —the Either/Or/And formula. He spoke:

"001.1, you will go across the bridge to see if it will support my weight."

Flathead had not heard himself called by his number for years, so he was a little slow in replying.

"Yes sir, your Reoship. I'll get right over there."

"And you, 002.1, you get into the wet area beneath the bridge and see if the land there is passable."

Dipstick almost said, "Do what?" but reconsidered quickly and headed for the swamp, calling back, "Sounds like a good idea to me."

Then the two went to work. When Flathead got on the bridge, he paused and called back to Gogamagog:

"Don't know if it's going to hold or not; it's got some big cracks in it."

While Gogamagog was distracted by Flathead, Dipstick was down in the swamp, slowly spinning his wheels so as to sink further into the mud, which was deep but which he could negotiate because of his light weight and built-in buoyancy, necessary for his pond work.

Then Dipstick called out, "Not going to be able to make it here, your Honor. I'm mired down. Believe you're going to have to pull me out."

Gogamagog's internal data base then marked 002.1 as "Expendable—to be destroyed" and, without reply, trundled up onto the bridge which Flathead had just crossed. Flathead called back,

"It'll hold O.K."

At the same time, now under the bridge and so out of sight of Gogamagog's visual sensors, Dipstick was busily burning through the middle bridge support with his auxiliary cutting torch. And the bridge, which in fact would barely hold Flathead, quickly broke in two under the tonnage of Gogamagog; he slid down the broken planks and dropped five or six feet into the mud.

Gogamagog spun his wheels, causing him to sink more deeply. Flathead called out helpfully, "Give it the gas, big guy; you'll get out."

Then, when Gogamagog's armaments were far enough into the mud to make it difficult to aim them, Flathead said,

"Don't move any more; you might sink completely. Let me get a line on you. I'll pull you out."

Gogamagog was by this time confused and could find no algorithm that fit the situation. Escape was usually done on a ship or by blasting everything away; it was not done in mud and water, with one's motive power and vaporizers incapacitated.

Flathead looped out a long magnetic cable that wrapped itself around the head of the monitor robot. Flathead gave a mighty surge on the throttle and his winch and managed to topple the robot face first into the mud which, by this time, was very churned up and liquid. Gogamagog

went down with several gurgles and hisses and disappeared
into the quicksand. As he went under, the red mud dauber,
one of whose legs had become stuck to a piece of dried mud
on the robot's top, went down with him.

By this time Dipstick had made it to the far side of the
bridge and stood beside Flathead.

"Well, Flattie, we told him that mud was bad; and that
bridge too. But he had to see for himself."

"Yep," Flathead replied. "Now we're going to have to
go to Frenchtown by ourselves and look for little Tappet and
those other robots."

"Guess so," Dipstick agreed. "Well, we might as well
get going. It's about dark. What about him?"

"We'll have to send back a crane to get him out. But
we'll wait a while. Let him soak in that mud good. Nothing
much on him we want anyway. Maybe that blaster."

"That blaster scared me. Got to be careful with those
things. And Gogamagog wasn't careful at all."

"That's the trouble with all those Palindrome types.
Hope somebody gets rid of them," Flathead said.

"Me, too," Dipstick agreed.

They reached Frenchtown an hour or so later. The main
street was dirt, lined with old wooden buildings that were
falling down. To their left was the river; toward the end of
the street they came upon a wooden building with lights in
the windows; it had a wharf that jutted out over the water.

Flathead and Dipstick drove around to the side, which
had tall and wide doors, large farming machines having
been stored there in the past. A huge industrial construction
robot stood at the side of the door; it greeted them in a boom-
ing voice:

"How you doing, Flathead? How you, Dipstick? Never
seen you in Frenchtown before."

"We're O.K., Doubleclutch. We're supposed to be
down here looking for little Tappet. But the fellow who was

bringing us got stuck in the mud back by the bridge on the old river road,'' Flathead said.

"He sure did," Dipstick said. "I expect maybe in a week or so you ought to go and dig him out of the dirt. He'll be locked up solid by then. He's got a big vaporizer on his chest."

"One of them, huh?" said Doubleclutch. "Maybe we ought to just leave him there."

"We could use the metal in the pond. And he might have some of the fluid, too. We might as well look."

"I'll go get him out next Monday and bring him into the shop. We'll see what we can use. Tappet's over there at the other end. He built a special room, where things will be extra clean. We're putting out our first model now," Doubleclutch said, a touch of pride evident in his bass voice. "Go look at it."

They all went to the other end of the building. Dipstick knocked on the door, which was opened by a former inventory robot, looking like an intelligent grasshopper, with a bulbous CRM shining on top of his skinny body, obviously designed for inside work. His name was Zephyr.

"Flathead! And Dipstick! It's good to see you again. How are things up at the pond? Inventory still down?" Zephyr said. "But forget about that. Come and see what Tappet has done. His CRM is *so* imaginative."

Tappet was a small, ground-hugging, streamlined courier robot, one originally sent out for cargo and tool transportation between the pond and the warehouse and for special crystal deliveries on Earth. He had been the last robot to leave the pond for Frenchtown and so had the most complex electronic brain.

He was standing by an obviously new robot, one showing none of the wear of the older ones. He was also shaped differently from the others. Rather than the truck shape of

Dipstick and Flathead or the grasshopper shape of Zephyr
or the building crane structure of Doubleclutch, or the
upright armed tank appearance of Gogamagog, the new
robot was thin and upright, a humanoid shape like Clyde,
Flathead thought to himself.

"Where's his module?" Dipstick asked.

"It's built inside," Tappet said, "instead of being stuck
on like all ours were. And you see he doesn't have any combustion or electric motor sticking out like we do; all that's
covered up, too."

"What's it run on, Tappet?" Flathead asked.

"Energy conversion," Zephyr said proudly. "I learned
about it when I was doing inventory in one of the vaporizer
factories. Put something with a high energy content in
here," he said, opening a door on the back of the robot,
"and it's reduced to energy that is then converted into electricity."

Zephyr shut the door. "He's *very* strong. You wouldn't
think it by looking at him, would you?"

"Have you watered him yet, Tappet?" Flathead asked.

"No, we've been testing his circuits for a month. He
can do just about everything without water that we can do
with it. In fact, we're going to water him tonight. Why don't
you boys get a fresh charge from the tank outside, go
through the wash and silicone spray and come out on the
wharf about ten?"

A few hours later, an assemblage of ten or so robots
were standing on the wharf by the Red River, all in a circle
around Tappet and the new robot. It was quiet, with the only
sound being the hum of crickets and the gentle slap of water
on the pier posts.

"This is an important event," Tappet began. "This
robot is the first one to be made on Earth since the Removal.
We are through the testing phase; tonight, we pour the pond
water into his CRM and the crystals will send out their new

Illustrated by Jack Kirby

circuit paths everywhere. Then he will be like us." Tappet paused.

"But his Reality Module is much more advanced than ours; we have combined the best that we could see from all of us here at Frenchtown. When the crystal paths grow and combine, this robot will be the most intelligent one here. I hope he will be able to help us."

Then, slowly, Tappet removed the cover that went over the CRM and, using a suction cup, pulled a round plug out of the translucent material. He next inserted a funnel and poured a whole pickle jar of pond water into the CRM. When the CRM was full, Tappet took out the funnel, inserted the plug again and, using a light torch, welded the plug back into the CRM.

"He should be ready to go in a few hours," Tappet said. He flicked the switch at the base of the CRM to the "Standby" position.

For the next few hours, the robots talked and worked in the shop or took care of maintenance or simply went into their own "Standby" modes, recharging batteries or tuning up engines. By three in the morning they were all back on the wharf in a circle around the new robot. Tappet spoke to them:

"Since Clyde the human made us what we are and named us after machines, it seems fitting that we should name our first machine after a human. But it would not be right to give Mr. Clyde's name to one of us. In searching for another good human name, Zephyr remembered that before he came to Frenchtown a few years ago, he scanned the Palindrome Human Inventory Removal hologram for this area; he saw a picture there of Mr. Clyde and his brother, a young man called Georgie. We have named this robot "Georgie" to honor Mr. Clyde.

"I will now turn him on," Tappet said. He flipped the switch from "Standby" to "Activate" and replaced the cover over the CRM. For a while, Georgie did nothing. Then, he began a self-test, addressing each robot by name, lifting boxes and barrels on the wharf, and driving up and down the road through town. The other robots watched silently, evaluating what they saw.

Georgie drove back on the wharf and into the center of the circle. He took one of the empty silicone lubricant drums standing nearby and filled it with wood and paper. Then, he did something none of the other robots had ever done before or had even considered doing: he lit a fire in the drum. Then he sat silently and watched the fire.

As the robots all sat in the circle around the fire for a half hour or so, each began to power down a little. Finally, Dipstick asked Flathead,

"Why'd he do that?"

"I don't know, Dip; but I like it."

"You know, Flattie," Dipstick said, looking at all the robots gathered around the fire and at the river and at the darkened fields across the river and at the moonlit sky, "Earth *is* a beautiful place, isn't it? I don't think I ever noticed it before."

"Yes. And look at Georgie."

Georgie was adding more wood to the fire, making it send glowing red ashes into the sky. It reminded Flathead of when he was a boy and Clyde would make fires outside the warehouse in the winter.

Flathead let out a little puff of pure methane and settled lower onto the wharf.

"You know, Dip," he said, just before switching off all of his sensors except the visual and short acoustic ones for the first time since the Lull, "I think everything's going to be all right."

Dipstick just hummed beside him.

About the Illustrators
by
Frank Kelly Freas

The interior illustrators for *L. Ron Hubbard Presents WRITERS OF THE FUTURE, Volume IV* span the entire development of modern science fiction and fantasy, from the Golden Age onward. Among them are the artists who have been responsible for some of the best work done in the field. In addition, they have inspired each successive generation of SF illustrators. I'm delighted to see us all working together on this project to demonstrate what the best professionals know can be done. We hope to spark the emergence of fresh new creativity that in the next few years will go farther than any of us ever dreamed of doing.

Rather than attempt to write something that would describe the magnitude of our illustrators' achievement to date, I'll just call the roll:

Leo and Diane Dillon have been a team for over 30 years, producing award-winning illustration in many fields. (They hold two consecutive Caldecott Awards for the best childrens'-book illustrations of the year; a Hugo; the Hamilton King Award from the Society of Illustrators, two consecutive Hornbook awards from the Boston *Globe,* and the Lensman award, among many other tokens of recognition.) They were the first to successfully, repeatedly, introduce abstract art into SF illustration, where their book covers over the years make up an awesome gallery. They say (always together): "We love what we do. It's always exciting. Every job is new. It isn't easy; it's a challenge. And it's worth it."

Bob Eggleton won the 1987 Chesley Bonestell Award for Best SF Magazine Cover and the 1988 Jack Gaughan Memorial Award for Best Emerging Artist. Twenty-seven years old, he has been doing covers and interior illustrations for many major publishers over the past several years (and appears with some lovely artwork in *Vol. III* of the W.O.T.F. series).

One of the things I most like about Bob's work is that he thinks the story through; one of the things I most like about Bob is his readiness to help aspiring artists. He's a terrific speaker at conventions and a ready advisor to art-show entrants. Even while gathering "emerging" awards himself, he is already a solid contributor to the next generations.

Will Eisner prefers to work with words and pictures together, and in doing so since the 1940s he's become a legend. His *The Spirit* pioneered the cinematographic approaches used by nearly all comics artists today, in addition to captivating millions of readers with his characteristic interplay of high drama and whimsy in its stories.

He has consistently won major awards from the most prestigious judging bodies in the world. For the past fifteen years, he has been producing "graphic novels," writing the stories in interdependent words and drawings. He has little use for "illustrations" that merely duplicate what's already in the text. He likes the idea that we are now living in an age where the thoughts and ideas of illustrators are making important original contributions to the culture of our time. Certainly, Will Eisner has, and so have those artists he has been influencing for half a century.

Jack Kirby, like Eisner born in 1917, is perhaps most associated in the public mind with super-heroes and with developing the ideas that have since resulted in the richness and variety of that field of comics art today. Among many other honors, he was installed in the Comics Hall of Fame in 1987, received the 1974 Inkpot Award for work done in the comics art medium, and in 1976 was the first to receive the annual "Yellow Kid" award, in Lucca, Italy, as best cartoonist in the world.

Among illustrators, he is an "artist's artist," consistently exploring the possibilities of the media and extending them. His accessibility to young artists, and his helpfulness to them, are famous. He's a wonderful person, and it's because of this that there's special meaning to the fact that there are now Jack Kirby Awards.

Paul Lehr, like every artist I know, began drawing when he was so young he can barely remember beginning. Now in his fifties, with a professional track-record over thirty years long, he still approaches each new project with the enthusiasm that makes him say his entire experience is the highlight of his career; he loves using his imagination "to dream things up," and he's doing what he likes to do.

Doing it, he has produced some of the most fantastically beautiful book covers and interior illustrations seen in this field over that time, beginning with a painting for Bantam Books in 1957.

Honored with the Frank R. Paul Award for SF illustration, and twice Merit Award recipient from the Society of Illustrators, Lehr works quietly in Pennsylvania, modestly unaware of the full extent of the esteem in which we hold him.

Ron and Val Lakey Lindahn work together so closely that although they can point to "his" or "her" piece of art, most things they do are really a collaboration. Outstanding among young illustrators, the team formed when Ron, at that time a professional photographer, met Val, saw "how much fun she was having, and decided to try it." Val at that time was not only the professional illustrator but the SF reader from her youth; she was doing a great deal of black-and-white work for SF magazines and loving it.

Since then, they have done a high volume of work, shared many honors, and won individual awards as well. They tend to devote extensive time to preparation and research—the finding of props, etc.—before they actually get down to the drawing or painting. It gives them a feeling of confidence, and produces beautifully detailed art.

Moebius is the world-famous pen-name of a French artist who co-founded *Métal Hurlant,* the graphics periodical that became *Heavy Metal* in English; he is the creator of Arzach for that publication, and of Incal. He has also been responsible for conceptual design work on such films as *Alien, Tron,* and *Willow.* He has won just about all the existing comics art awards internationally, has had a painting adapted for issue as a French postage stamp, and holds France's highest award for achievement in the arts—he is a Chevalier des Artes et des Lettres; a knight of arts and letters. He's the only comics artist honored that way.

He deserves every bit of it. His concepts in illustration have transformed everyone's idea of what's possible in the field, and his creative ideas are backed by superb draftsmanship and compositional sense.

Alex Schomburg's four brothers had a studio in New York in the 1920s, doing window displays and advertising art. Deciding to go into business for himself, he got a job with one of the film companies then on the East Coast, working on "trailers"—Coming Attractions. Somewhere in there, he began doing magazine illustrations, but his film career didn't really reach its culmination until he worked on the art background for Stanley Kubrick's *2001*. He says he feels honored, but has never seen that work on the screen.

Schomburg black-and-whites were frequently seen in such magazines as *Thrilling Wonder Stories*, *Startling Stories*, and *Captain Future*, during the years of World War II, which began when he was 36. Also a prominent feature of those marvelous pulps were his eye-popping airbrush covers; miracles of patient frisket-cutting and detail that undoubtedly inspired the look of the spaceships and cities in such films as *2001* and *Star Wars* and of course their host of imitations.

Alex Schomburg is 82 years old at this writing. Take a look at the illustration he's done for us here. We all should live so long!

H.R. Van Dongen appeared as one of the premier illustrators for *Astounding* and then other magazines shortly after World War II and for some years thereafter. His body of work over the years is reasonably large and widespread, both in magazines and, later, in the form of book covers. It would be larger, however, if he hadn't interrupted his career preparations to serve in World War II, where he was made a prisoner of war and suffered permanent injuries as a result. When he came back, he simply went to work for the top media, and few are aware of that episode. Certainly he didn't allow damage to the mechanism to interfere with the expressiveness of his imagination.

Van is superb at being an illustrator. He has an uncommon gift for extracting the essence of what the author intended to say. Writer after writer from the 1950s onward has reported staring in awe at an apparently simple Van Dongen drawing that completely captured the spirit of the story and lent it drama. I particularly like his sense of locale; the

way in which every feature of a landscape, known or alien,
is exactly right, and working as an indispensible compositional element.

I wish there were more of Van's work. I'm very glad
he was able to add to it with the excellent example he has
done for us.

William R. Warren, Jr. drew his first picture in First
Grade—a drawing of his mother and a salamander. That
was in the late 1950s, and he says "As far as I know, I always
drew; I've always arted no matter what job I've had."

A cheerful, outgoing figure at SF conventions, a star of
art shows, (and an impressively talented guitarist and
singer), Bill moved into the professional ranks with small
drawings in 1984. Soon thereafter, *Analog*—the modern-day
title for *Astounding*—began sending him stories to illustrate,
on tight deadlines because he could meet them well. Soon
after that, he was doing book covers. After his first magazine cover, for the January, 1986 *Analog,* he began appearing regularly in that magazine at high volume.

He has been Artist Guest of Honor at many conventions, and holds many Best of Show and Best of Category
honors. He clearly deserves to be considered one of the most
promising new SF illustrators. His wife, Elizabeth, highly
respected in the SF community in her own right, is his manager, and that's good for his future, too.

So those are our interior illustrators; an example, and a
guide. For many of them, their appearance here is tanta-
mount to a labor of love. Time and again I heard from them
how much they appreciated the opportunity to associate
themselves with a program devoted to helping new talent.
And I know our cover artist, the incomparable Frank Frazetta, joins them in their enthusiasm.

When I was first setting out, many established pros

went out of their way to help me. The work I've done here is part of my own way of paying back for that, and I know I am not alone in looking at it that way. That was how L. Ron Hubbard looked at it.

It's a professional's way of paying back; with appropriate awards for work that deserves them, and sound, hard-won advice. Art, whether prose or in graphics, is a matter of arranging details under the artist's control, and its proper use then is communication. In pictures and in words, working together, I believe this book communicates that message.

CONTEST RULES

1. No entry fee is required, and all rights in the story remain the property of the author. All types of science fiction and fantasy are welcome; every entry is judged on its own merits only.

2. All entries must be original works of science fiction or fantasy in English. Plagiarism will result in disqualification. Submitted works may not have been previously published in professional media.

3. Eligible entries must be works of prose, either short stories (under 10,000 words) or novelets (under 17,000 words) in length. We regret we cannot consider poetry, or works intended for children.

4. The Contest is open only to those who have not had professionally published a novel or short novel, or more than three short stories, or more than one novelet.

5. Entries must be typewritten and double spaced with numbered pages (computer-printer output O.K.). Each entry must have a cover page with the title of the work, the author's name, address, and telephone number, and an approximate word-count. The manuscript itself should be titled and numbered on every page, but the author's name should be deleted to facilitate fair judging.

6. Manuscripts will be returned after judging. Entries must include a self-addressed return envelope. U.S. return envelopes must be stamped; others may enclose international postal reply coupons.

7. There shall be three cash prizes in each quarter: 1st Prize of $1000, 2nd Prize of $750, and 3rd Prize of $500, in U.S. dollars or the recipient's locally equivalent amount. In addition, there shall be a further cash prize of $4000 to the Grand Prize winner, who will be selected from among the 1st Prize winners for the period of October 1, 1987 through September 30, 1988. All winners will also receive trophies or certificates.

8. The Contest will continue through September 30, 1988, on the following quarterly basis:

    October 1 - December 31, 1987
    January 1 - March 31, 1988
    April 1 - June 30, 1988
    July 1 - September 30, 1988

Information regarding subsequent contests may be obtained by sending a self-addressed, stamped, business-size envelope to the above address.

To be eligible for the quarterly judging, an entry must be postmarked no later than Midnight on the last day of the Quarter.

9. Each entrant may submit only one manuscript per Quarter. Winners in a quarterly judging are ineligible to make further entries in the Contest.

10. All entrants, including winners, retain all rights to their stories.

11. Entries will be judged by a panel of professional authors. Each quarterly judging and the Grand Prize judging may have a different panel. The decisions of the judges are entirely their own, and are final.

12. Entrants in each Quarter will be individually notified of the results by mail, together with the names of those sitting on the panel of judges.

This contest is void where prohibited by law.